BRAVE **nu** WORLD

D1439814

Printed and bound in the United Kingdom by Cromwell Press, Trowbridge

Published by Sanctuary Publishing Limited, Sanctuary House, 45-53 Sinclair Road, London W14 0NS, United Kingdom

www.sanctuarypublishing.com

ISBN: 1-86074-415-X

BRAVE NU WORLD

TOMMY
UDO

Sanctuary

About The Author

Tommy Udo lives in London and has worked as a music journalist since 1981, his tirades, polemic and criticism appearing in *Sounds*, *City Limits*, *The Guardian*, *Vox*, *Uncut*, *Bizarre*, *Ammo City* and *Metal Hammer*. As News Editor of the *NME*, Tommy covered stories ranging from the suicide of Kurt Cobain to the rise of nu metal in the mid 1990s.

His other books have included a critique of the work of Japanese film director Beat Takeshi Kitano and a history of industrial music from The Futurists to Ministry. His first novel, *Vatican Bloodbath*, was published by Attack! Books in 1999 and his second, *When Hell Attacks*, is due to be published in autumn 2002.

Acknowledgements

The biggest debt I owe is to the bands themselves who have talked to me, on and off the record, over the past decade, most notably Limp Bizkit, Korn and Slipknot. To the long-suffering label and independent PRs who have been on the receiving end of belligerent phone calls – you know who you are – who have nevertheless been a valued source of solid information, contacts, gossip, hearsay and innuendo, though usually not about the bands they actually work with. To Chris Ingham and the editorial staff at *Metal Hammer* who have allowed me to get up close and personal with many of the nu breed, or filled me in on the details when I couldn't. To Andy Capper at the *NME*, GT at *Rolling Stone*, various high- and low-ranking folks at various labels and magazines who don't want names named, who have been an unparalleled source of old magazines and press releases, badly photocopied fanzines and interviews dredged up from the most obscure places. To Martina, who has to live with more CDs, back issues of *Kerrang!* and boxes of cuttings than one house can reasonably contain. And to Jeff Hudson, my old editor at Sanctuary, whose idea this was in the first place.

Contents

Introduction

Once again, it seems that reports of the death of rock and roll have been greatly exaggerated.

At the time of writing, in late 2001, the *Billboard* charts have been dominated by releases from Slipknot, Staind, Linkin Park and Limp Bizkit. Established bands such as Tool, Machine Head and Fear Factory have delivered their most accomplished and significant records to date, while a whole host of exciting, youthful newcomers such as Kittie, Vex Red, Ill Niño, Defenestration and Dry Kill Logic assault our ears with raw, parent-scaring sounds, brimming with an enthusiasm that suggests they have discovered the amplified and distorted guitar, 4/4 backbeat and pain-level bass, and sheer VOLUME for the first time ever.

The rest of the world seems to sit, poised and anxious, waiting for the latest communication from the States, like a new cultural Marshall Plan, the arsenal of democracy having become the arsenal of rock and roll. From Andrew WK, The White Stripes, The Strokes and The Black Rebel Motorcycle Club, the latest bands are debated and pored over in the pages of *Rolling Stone, Alternative Press* and *Spin,* but also in *Les Inrockuptibles* in France and *New Musical Express (NME)* in Britain, trying to discern if this is hype or the future. But one thing that *is* clear is that all of the bands with any importance at all are from the United States.

Towards the end of 2001, when the gold and platinum discs were totted up, this new wave of rock and roll seemed to be faring rather well: Linkin Park's *Hybrid Theory* was certified quadruple platinum; Disturbed's *The Sickness* double platinum; POD's *Satellite* platinum; Slipknot's *Iowa* platinum; System Of A Down's *Toxicity* platinum; Puddle Of Mudd's *Come Clean* gold. (Platinum discs are awarded for sales of 1,000,000 and gold for sales of 500,000.)

To the outsider, there seems little to separate the bands: the constant whine of critics, older bands and fans is that they are interchangeable, MTV-friendly record company puppets. Yet the range of music, of influences, is actually very diverse. What these bands do have in common is that they are young – many are teenagers though a rough average age would be around 22 – and hip, eschewing the look of traditional metal, punk, indie and alt.rock groups for a sharper image. Although it falls way short of the predicted 'revolution' that the tub-thumpers for digitally downloaded music told us was imminent, they have all used the Internet as a way to get their music heard and to build up fanbases that are served by tours, often with one of the major franchise travelling festivals such as Family Values, Tattoo The Planet, Ozzfest or the Warped Tour.

They do not behave in the way that rock and roll bands are expected to behave; there are few wrecked hotel rooms, drug overdoses, limos driven into swimming pools or spectacular suicides. As a reporter for British music weekly *NME* and then as a freelance writer for magazines such as *Metal Hammer*, I met most of these bands at various stages in their careers, usually at the start, and was always impressed by the sheer hard-headedness with which they approached their music. These bands had a particularly American 'can-do' attitude, a work ethic and a set of goals that most British and European bands sorely lacked. Watching Linkin Park on their first visit to Europe to promote *Hybrid Theory*, it was not so much like watching a rock and roll band as watching a military exercise. Their tour manager had the band's schedules down to the nearest minute and it looked as though fuck-ups – particularly fuck-ups by incompetent limey bastard no-marks putting on amateur-hour shows – were not going to be tolerated. The band members themselves trotted out interviews for over 48 hours, answering the same trite questions and managing to answer each one as though the journalist had been the first to ask it: 'How did you get your name?' 'How did you meet?' 'Is it true that you are a manufactured band?'

The values of Korn, Limp Bizkit, Staind, Slipknot or Kid Rock may seem a little artless and gauche to more 'sophisticated' European observers, but when it comes to the total economic and artistic domination of the music industry at the turn of the third millennium, they have obviously served them well. These bands trade on hard-and-heavy testosterone rock, which has struck a major chord with teenagers from Talahassee to Tehran (Iran's religious police were reported to have broken up gatherings of fans sporting Slipknot T-shirts in the nation's capital in 2001).

There's now a debate as to whether nu metal actually is heavy metal or some post-metal variant of alt.rock or pop. The term 'heavy music' – actually a revival of a term used in the early 1970s – is now more commonly used to describe such bands. But there seems little argument that whatever else it is or isn't, it's still rock and roll.

Although claims that 'rock and roll is dead' have been with us since 1956 (the year Elvis started to break through), there was an air of 'but this time we really mean it' in the mid-to-late 1990s. Throughout the late 1980s and early 1990s, informed pundits told us that guitar bands had at long last had their day and that anything from 'electronica' (an American catch-all term for post-house dance music) to new country was going to replace them. Mainstream newspaper columnists churned out fatuous copy proclaiming poetry, comedy or gardening to be 'the new rock and roll'.

The failure of the much-hyped wave of British bands, spearheaded by Oasis and Blur, to make a dent on America beyond a small cult of Anglophiles, coupled with the massive success enjoyed by pop, R&B, hip-hop and country artists in both the singles and albums charts, led many observers and analysts within the record industry to conclude that if it wasn't dead, rock and roll certainly smelled a bit funny.

There's an amusing scene in Cameron Crowe's *Almost Famous* (2000), a nostalgic hymn to the 'golden age' of touring rock and roll bands in the pre-punk mid 1970s. Legendary rock critic Lester Bangs (played by Phillip Seymour Hoffman) rants on to the film's protagonist William Miller (Patrick Fugit) about the death of rock: 'Rock music is dead because the musicians have become more corrupted by money and fame.' The scene is set in 1973, just as rock and roll was about to experience growth that was to be something of a global event.

But perhaps after the 1960s something *had* died: perhaps it was the belief that rock music would change the world. And while Lester Bangs wasn't the first to feel this sense of betrayal, that the music he felt a sense of ownership about had been taken from him, he wasn't the last. *Every* generation feels this; if *their* music hadn't been taken and commercialised, it would have the power to right all wrongs, to set people free and to make planet earth a better place. It repeats *ad nauseam*, proving Santayana's maxim that those who do not remember the past are condemned to repeat it. What is rock and roll but an eternal recurrence? Despite the phenomenal success of Nirvana, few of their contemporaries, such as Smashing Pumpkins, Stone Temple Pilots, Mudhoney, Alice In Chains or Pearl Jam, enjoyed quite the same combination of huge album sales, critical acclaim and mainstream public recognition. Nevertheless, Nirvana helped to reinvigorate rock and roll at a time when it seemed a creatively bankrupt form. More importantly, with British bands having dominated the music world since the advent of The Beatles and The Rolling Stones, Nirvana reclaimed rock and roll as a particularly American form, and almost made it seem that the music could barely exist outside of the American continent. Many thought that the party was over with the band's uncompromising and unapproachable third album *In Utero*. But in

1994, when Kurt Cobain stuck a shotgun in his mouth, it was like a big bloody full stop for grunge and for rock and roll generally.

Yet later that year, a four piece called Korn from Bakersfield, California, released their self-titled debut. It was an audacious and exciting release, from opening track 'Blind' onwards, but not even fanatical followers and informed observers – nor even the band themselves – guessed that it was to be the opening salvo from the Brave Nu World.

If the history of metal-derived rock and roll teaches us anything, it is that you write it off at your peril. The term 'heavy metal', like many band names of the late 1960s and early 1970s, was borrowed from the writings of William Burroughs. It was first used by legendary rock journalist and cultural critic Richard Meltzer to describe the guitar sound on The Byrds' 1967 psychedelic raga-rock classic 'Eight Miles High', though perhaps it was the phrase 'heavy metal thunder' in Canadian combo Steppenwolf's 'Born To Be Wild' that forged the association with the wave of post-acid Hendrix/Who-inspired bands in Britain and the United States, such as Black Sabbath, Blue Cheer and Iron Butterfly.

Heavy metal was always a 'people's music', a populist version of the turbulent acid-rock of the late 1960s. Patronised and sneered at by the critics, bands like Led Zeppelin grew into rock and roll superpowers during the 1970s. Heavy, blues-based, basic rock became the mainstay for mostly male, mostly working-class, mostly white teenagers throughout the 1970s, but in the wake of the onslaught of punk rock, from 1976, it seemed to be fighting a losing rearguard action. But, like a counter-revolution, bands on both sides of the Atlantic struck back. The so-called 'New Wave of British Heavy Metal' (NWOBHM) centred around bands like Def Leppard and Iron Maiden, along with a host of lesser names such as Samson, Angelwitch, Saxon and, a little later, Venom, who applied some of the punk DIY ethos to their own more traditional rock sound. In the early 1980s, bands like Metallica, Slayer and Megadeth incorporated chunks of punk's sound and attitude into a less compromising and less traditional variant of metal. Sub-genres proliferated – thrash metal, skate metal, speed metal, doom metal, dark metal, death metal, black metal, glam metal – cross-pollinating with each other and with other seemingly incongruous genres. In the 1970s, metal had a reputation as a reactionary and narrow-minded form of music; by the 1980s and 1990s, it was fertile ground where punk, hip-hop, funk, soul and even left-field jazz came together to create new music. Some of these collaborations were dead ends, but others, beginning with 1985's rap-meets-rock hit by Run-DMC featuring Aerosmith 'Walk This Way', spawned a monster.

Nu metal is first and foremost a marketing term, lumping together bands with a few surface similarities: they're young, depressed, angry, many of them have two nouns composited into one-word names (Mudvayne, Godsmack, Spineshank, Nonpoint, Nothingface etc), just as they fuse together two or more forms into metal (rap metal, funk metal etc). But the first step towards understanding something is to give it a name.

'Nu metal', like every term applied to bands or artists throughout the 50-odd year history of rock and roll – including, as it happens, the term 'rock and roll' itself – is meaningless, embarrassing and irrelevant. No band with a modicum of self-respect would actually describe themselves as a 'nu metal band', and in interviews they will – as bands have always done – deny vehemently that they have any connection with any movement, style or any other group of bands. 'A lot of the original bands doing stuff like us and Limp Bizkit and Orgy came up with [the sound] too. I don't think any of us were out to find a fucking sound. Then there are all these newer bands now – and I won't name names – that have kind of taken what we've done and sort of borrowed our style. That's flattering, but I kind of wish they would do something more original,' Korn's Jonathan Davis told *Guitar* magazine reporter Jon Wiederhorn in 1999. The term has been applied to a growing list of bands such as Korn, Limp Bizkit, Linkin Park, Crazy Town, Amen, (hed) pe, Ill Niño, Dry Kill Logic, Staind, Coal Chamber, Spineshank, The Deftones, Amen and Papa Roach, though what these bands actually have in common with each other is a moot point. It has also been applied, wrongly, to other major metal artists such as Marilyn Manson and Slipknot. Including Slipknot in the list can be excused, but Manson has very publicly attacked his contemporary Fred Durst and the whole nu metal movement, describing the Limp Bizkit singer as 'one of the illiterate apes who used to beat you up at school for being a fag'.

Nu metal is not the only current rock-based movement; at the time of writing, there is still a strong, extremely commercial variant of punk rock-derived music centred around bands like Green Day, Rancid, Pennywise, AFI, Earth Crisis, Jimmy Eat World and Blink-182. As we move towards the underground, so-called 'stoner rock' bands – whose music harks back to psychedelia and the classic heavy blues of early Sabbath – like Queens Of The Stone Age, Nebula, Unida and Spirit Caravan have all enjoyed some commercial success, though interest is still confined to a hard core of fans and critics.

So-called emo-core bands like At The Drive-In, The Icarus Line and Glassjaw excite the press though they are still playing club-level venues. And there are those like Marilyn Manson, Eminem and Kid Rock who aren't really part of anything, but whose controversy-courting tactics unearth hitherto unknown connections to nu metal: Britain's *Daily Mirror* has described all three as purveyors of nu metal. We will examine the rest of the scene in one of the later chapters and look at the ways in which nu metal both fits in with and stands apart from these contemporaries.

Nu metal most commonly describes a wave of bands, exclusively American, heavily influenced by late-'80s and early-'90s pioneers like Faith No More, Fear Factory, Rage Against The Machine and Biohazard, who fuse rap, metal and punk, lathered in furious teenage-angst rants and ultra-violent pronouncements delivered at high volume. Guitars are heavily distorted, the riffs are muted, and hip-hop influenced bass and percussion fills out the sound. Songs tend to be repetitious, built around cleaner low-key sections and pseudo-death-metal staccato riffing, generally short, structured along conventional pop lines, with typical verse/chorus vocal arrangements. The vocalist tends to snarl or shout the lyrics, with many bands making direct use of rap. The hip-hop groove and repetitive guitar lines are staples of the genre. Lyrics are usually aggressively angry and nihilistic, whether minimal or explosive. There's an element of woe-is-me introspection, songs from a first-person perspective that run through the author's personal angst and depression, which led one critic to describe the songs on Staind's third album, *Break The Cycle*, as 'musical suicide notes'.

Many of these bands employ an on-stage DJ, cutting up breakbeats, scratching records or playing samples. Sometimes the DJ role, as in hip-hop, is to supplement the rhythm section, to mix in selections from other songs, and sometimes it is purely decorative. Neither Amen nor The Deftones sit well in the nu metal camp by that definition – indeed, it can be argued that Amen are part of an ongoing project by nu metal's 'Dr Frankenstein' producer, Ross Robinson, to destroy the monster he created – and while there are an increasing number of bands who appear to have been stamped out of a factory mould like automobiles from Detroit, there are others who quickly distance themselves from the clichés and find their own voices.

Staind are a good example; their first release was standard angry shouting and screaming hardcore that sounded like a million other bands playing third-on-the-bill slots in 2,000-capacity clubs across America. Whatever the factors were that changed them – the involvement of Fred Durst as a mentor, a more vigorous approach to songwriting, better production – they managed to turn out an album of songs that is in the best tradition of American songwriting, as comparable to Bruce Springsteen as it is to any of their nu metal contemporaries. Nu metal has been called – mostly by its detractors – 'whinecore', 'mallcore', 'grunge for the zeros' and 'sports-rock'. The rage and aggression the bands articulate onstage is often compared to the theatrics of the World Wrestling Federation and, in many ways, these bands are acting out fantasies of anger and violence as much as commenting on anything that is actually happening around them.

Lorraine Ali in a defining 1998 article on The Deftones in *Spin* magazine wrote, 'New metal is a forward-looking hybrid that takes as many cues from alternative rock, hip-hop, and SoCal hardcore skate culture as it does it from Black Sabbath and Slayer. For instance, Limp Bizkit, with their rapped vocals and full-time DJ, are new metal. Creed and Days Of The New, both of whom use '70s hard rock (Bad Company, AC/DC) as a jumping off point, are not. Offering traditional metal ferocity minus the corny hail-Satanism, Tawny Kitaen videos, and big hair of the '80s, new metal delivers spandex-free hard-rock catharsis rhythmically attuned to the rap revolution. Like Beck and Cornershop, these bands have scavenged the remainder bins of hip-hop, hardcore, pop, industrial, and '90s rock revitalisers Nirvana and Nine Inch Nails for their sounds and lyrics. It only seems natural that kids weaned on the multi-genre programming of MTV would respond.'

This gets to the heart of what it is. It's white hip-hop, a suburban teen attempt to ally themselves with urban black culture. The phenomenon of the 'whigger' (that is, 'white nigger' – also known as wigga or whigga) was just the latest variation of the phenomenon of 'The White Negro', identified by Norman Mailer in his 1957 essay.

'One is Hip or one is Square (the alternative which each new generation coming into American life is beginning to feel), one is a rebel or one conforms, one is a frontiersman in the Wild West of American night life, else a Square cell, trapped in the totalitarian tissues of American society, doomed willy-nilly to conform if one is to succeed,' Mailer wrote, identifying jazz as the cultural catalyst, a product of black America born out of struggle, to which a few 'hip whites' also responded.

In many ways this is only a continuation of what rock and roll has been about in any of its recurring variants over the past half-century. The quote attributed to Sun Records owner Sam Phillips famously declares, 'Find me a white boy who can sing like a black man and you'll make a million dollars.' Elvis had always been steeped in black music, whether it was gospel, rhythm and blues or Memphis blues. He also used to shop where the black pimps and hustlers in Memphis bought their suits, and the young Elvis copied their walk, their style of speech and their mannerisms. Mick Jagger wanted to sing like a Chicago bluesman and thought he was doing a pretty good job, affecting an accent that was a small part Howlin' Wolf and a large part Home Counties public schoolboy. When a lot of the artists who inspired them actually heard The Rolling Stones, they certainly didn't recognise the sound; they thought it must be some weird English accent.

Jared, lead singer in brilliant up and coming band (hed) pe and one of the few black artists working in rock and roll told me, 'Look at Fred Durst and Jonathan Davis. Look at the dreadlocks and the chains and the low-slung jeans and the trainers. It's all from black culture, from gangsta culture. That's what these guys are. It's white gangsta rap.'

According to Chuck D of Public Enemy, in an interview with US website *Addicted to Noise*, 'The state artistically is better than ever. The co-opting and undermining of the art form by lawyers and accountants has twisted it and jaded the public's perception and the artist's perception of what it should be, instead of pushing the envelope. Limp Bizkit and Kid Rock are rappers rapping over rock tracks. Rap music is rap over music that's already been here. You might take a guy like Heavy D, who might choose to rap over an R&B track. You take Kid Rock, who might choose to rap over a rock track. The traditional structures might say, "All right, Limp Bizkit and Kid Rock, they're the new rock bands." Cool. But let's say a black group does it over a rock track? Let's say Run-DMC does another thing over a rock track. What are you gonna call them? A rap group or a rock group?

'There's a lot of racism still and stigmas going on in traditional areas that want to determine groups and artists under the old template. In the new template on the Internet, we're going into a whole new, different definition of terms and that's what's really making it interesting. What is Rage Against The Machine? What is [singer] Zack [de la Rocha]? Is Zack a rapper? He's rapping to me.

'In the next two years you won't be able to put a finger on an artist and say, "This is what he is," and Limp Bizkit and Kid Rock are examples of how you really can't put your finger on what they are. But I would say they're spawned out of hip-hop and rap. And to me, it should be no difference between Fred Durst and DMX; they're both rappers.'

Nu metal has helped to smash down the barriers between rock and rap, though perhaps mercifully a 1999 attempt by original white rapper Vanilla Ice to make a comeback in a lame Limp Bizkit-inspired vein on his Ross Robinson-produced album flopped miserably. The album was aptly entitled *Hard To Swallow*.

It seems as though all the bands that have formed or reinvented themselves as rap-metal groups have had to fight off major-label offers with sticks. But the key to their success is the willingness of these bands to get their hands dirty making singles, doing videos for MTV, allowing corporate sponsors to get involved – I remember one band being told by their manager to go and change into their sponsor's sportswear before they did an interview with me, despite the fact that I was not photographing or filming them – and 'playing the game'. Sponsorship does more than get them free stage gear and pay for swimming pools, it opens up other outlets for the music, in advertising, corporate events, and the underwriting of stage sets and pyrotechnics.

Sponsors from Coke, Pepsi, Budweiser and Microsoft to Nike and more exclusive sportswear brands like Dickies, Vans and Pony have all used popular music to promote their brands. Korn, famously, were originally sponsored by Adidas, even celebrating the company in a song from their second album; then, rival company Puma offered them more money and the band switched their endorsement overnight. But many bands have learned a thing or two from the big-logo companies.

It was, ironically, that most idealistic of hippy bands, The Grateful Dead, who first noticed that receipts from the merchandising stalls selling T-shirts and posters were outstripping the fees they actually received for playing the shows. The Dead had always had identifiable logos – the Mouse/Kelly-designed skull-and-roses icon, which they registered as a trademark, and the Rick Griffin-designed lettering and surf/hot rod-derived graphics – and they soon found their way on to licensed Zippo lighters, baseball caps and cigarette rolling papers. The band as brand was born. Until the late 1970s, few bands had seriously exploited the extra marketing push that kids sporting their merchandising gave them. Kiss, on the other hand, recognised immediately that fans wanted to identify with the band and with each other, and to sport their readily identifiable corporate ID on badges, T-shirts, jackets and caps. Kiss extended this further, selling everything from lunchboxes to a Kiss coffin, for the ultimate fan. Kiss tours became something akin to a show of strength for the brand, with the members arriving in a Kiss-liveried helicopter, their distinctive make-up copyright protected and a Kiss supermarket selling a dizzying array of product. The music almost became a secondary concern.

It was part of rock and roll's success that it was able to join the galaxy of corporate signifiers, that The Rolling Stones' lips logo became as well known as the McDonald's golden arches (or Christianity's crucifix for that matter!). To some extent the success of the nu metal school, particularly Korn and Limp Bizkit, has as many similarities with ever-growing franchise brands such as Starbucks or Gap as it does with any previous generation of rock and roll. But many bands regard success as a kind of failure, and limit their own progress by willfully displaying contempt for fans and record buyers believing that this demonstrates integrity. Other bands recognise that this aspect of their trade can be perceived as devaluing the music. Slipknot drummer and spokesman Joey Jordison (aka #1) told me just before the release of their second album *Iowa*, 'I think, with the last album, I don't know what happened. We had just changed merchandising companies or something. The next thing I knew you were seeing Slipknot on lunchboxes, which was the sort of crap you used to get with Kiss. I know we're a band for the kids, but all of that stuff in the stores made us look like some sort of kiddie-shit band. It misrepresents the band, so we're going to keep a tight rein on that shit from now on. Slipknot became more like a line of clothing and less like a band. But you live an' you learn.'

Slipknot – also protégés of Ross Robinson – were adamantly keeping their distance from their nu metal peers, partly because they are a stand-alone band, but also because they did not want to be associated with the 'bull market' hubris of the groups who licensed everything, who became, at best, brand managers of their own images and, at worst, in the parlance of rock and roll, 'corporate whores'.

Ever since Led Zeppelin refused to release a single and The Clash refused to appear on *Top Of The Pops*, bands have been drawing 'lines in the sand', releasing music only on poorly distributed independent labels, only releasing seven-inch vinyl singles in limited editions, refusing to do interviews, refusing to play certain venues, refusing to compromise on artwork so that chain stores refuse to stock their releases. Bands such as Radiohead, who are the undisputed darlings of the 'alternative' set, claim that their influences are more Olivier Messiaen than Elvis; they release singles that are almost intended to put casual listeners off the band. They made a big point of not allowing sponsorship of their Kid A tour in 2000. In many ways, this is a strain of elitism that has always run through pop culture; bands become embarrassed by their own popularity. Kurt Cobain, in his rambling suicide note, gave his own success as the reason that he couldn't go on. This elitism in rock and roll, this sneering cooler-than-thou attitude that pervades both performers and punters alike, is a trait that is absent from most of the nu metal bands; yet the fact that Fred Durst is wealthy, a workaholic and has many activities outside the band seems to draw the ire of the critics.

Writing in online magazine *Salon* in April 2001, Joey Sweeney said, 'In the absence of Nirvana – and just about every other good band that, for one reason or another, imploded and failed to produce decent singles during the latter half of the '90s – nu metal has done well with the seemingly always-fledgling modern rock radio format. This, in a lot of cases, might cause some of the bands mentioned here to be identified as the new sound of what was called alternative music.

'But make no mistake: there is nothing alternative about it. You can't swing a dead freshman these days without running into this sub-Bizkit band or that one. In fact, the influence of Limp Bizkit throughout just about all of modern rock these days is nothing short of epidemic; it's not even worth quibbling over what exactly lead singer Fred Durst and the boys are angry about. Take one listen to their last record, one look at *MTV News*, and it's obvious what's pissing off Durst: playa-hatas, charges of inciting riots, attorney bills and bitchy pop starlets. In so many ways, Durst is not a whit different from Puffy Combs.'

The writer is typical of many critics of nu metal who see the business acumen of Fred Durst as something to be suspicious of. The unspoken assumption of the writer – and of every band that makes a point of letting everyone know about its own 'integrity' – is that every previous generation of rock and roll has been populated by noble artists who toiled in poverty for the scant rewards of the appreciation of critics and a small circle of fans untouched by the grubby hand of commerce. And should said artist inadvertently make anything from his music other than a rudimentary subsistence, it would be donated to the cause of the downtrodden of the third world, or similar worthy causes.

In fact, looking at the record of many of the nu metal bands – and particularly Durst – their flaunt-it attitude to wealth and celebrity masks a willingness to lend support to up-and-coming bands. This may be self-serving altruism – he signed Puddle Of Mudd to his own label and hence shares in the band's profits – but it is an enlightened self-interest. Whether he realises that his time at the top will be brief or whether it is just good old-fashioned American know-how and driving ambition, Fred Durst's business acumen has made him rich, got him a seat on the board of his label's parent company Interscope and opened up the world of major motion pictures to him. But while Durst's involvement with Staind and Puddle Of Mudd is well documented, it never seems to attract quite the same amount of attention as his feuds with Creed frontman Scott Stapp, Slipknot (he is alleged to have called their fans 'fat ugly kids', something he denies), Eminem, Trent Reznor of Nine Inch Nails and his is-he-isn't-he? 'romance' with Christina Aguilera.

Nu metal bands crave success. They want to be stars. They will do anything to make their dreams come true. Sometimes this naked admission of a desire for celebrity will rankle with those who feel that somehow it is not a seemly ambition to have. Sometimes their willingness to compromise, to make their music or image in some way more palatable to their target audience, will be interpreted as a desire to 'sell out'. These criticisms, however, mean little to the bands themselves and less to the kids who follow them.

Of course, there are still self-defeating bands around who positively don't want success; At The Drive-In, a hotly tipped emo-core band – about which more later – released a staggering album in 2000 and after playing some astounding live shows seemed to be on the brink of Bizkit-like success. Yet rather than capitalise on their critical success and growing fanbase amongst the influential 'early adopter' kids who go out and find new bands, they decided to put all their activities on hold, and stop touring and recording.

And there's a certain amount of suspicion amongst fans about bands like Linkin Park who are felt to be 'manufactured', a sort of nu metal 'boy band'. Such qualms haven't stopped Linkin Park selling millions of albums worldwide, but the debate rages in magazines and on fan websites as to whether the band are 'authentic' and indeed whether 'authenticity' actually matters.

The debate is almost like some redundant hangover from punk or hippy days, when earnest male muso types debated such topics as 'Can white men sing the blues?' with all the convoluted sophistry and passion of a gang of monks arguing over the number of angels who can dance on the head of a pin.

Perhaps the most important thing about nu metal is that it represents a reclamation by the United States of rock and roll as an exclusively North American form. Nu metal is from America and the rest of the world consumes it. There are local versions, such as Apartment 26, lostprophets, Vex Red and Hundred Reasons in Britain, the anarchic Linea 77 from Italy, Rammstein – a borderline case – from Germany and any number of faceless Korn clones across the rest of the planet. But they are almost an irrelevance in comparison to the big dollars generated by the US acts.

Since The Beatles appeared on *The Ed Sullivan Show* in 1964, sparking off the so-called British invasion, rock and roll – and other variants of modern music, such as house – has travelled back and forth across the Atlantic, with the Old World seeming to dominate the scene for decades, if not always in sales then certainly in terms of creativity and style. What The Beatles, The Who, The Kinks, The Yardbirds and The Rolling Stones did was to take music that was particularly American – the blues, R&B, soul, rockabilly, doo-wop – produce a local version that managed to get some aspects of it wrong, and produce not a faithful re-creation but a completely new form. Many of the screaming teenagers who greeted The Beatles at Kennedy Airport in 1964 were unaware that the band were merely playing covers of songs like The Isley Brothers' 'Twist And Shout', along with other songs that were blatant rewrites of Motown, Sue and RedBird soul.

Again, though punk rock had existed in the USA for decades, it was when the Brits discovered it that they were able to sell it back to the Americans as something new. Britain, the workshop of the world, seemed to be able to take any American form, strip it down and sell it back, like car thieves. Yet somehow that changed. After years of dominance, it seemed that the British music scene had run out of steam. There were lots of interesting little art bands around, but nothing comparable to the relentless wave of major American rock bands starting in the late 1980s with Pixies then Nirvana and finally the nu metal bands. Perhaps, as has been suggested, this was because all the ambitious working-class and lower-middle-class boys who used to buy guitars and formed the backbone of a seemingly endless stream of great British rock bands, from Zeppelin, Sabbath and Deep Purple onwards, were now becoming DJs and getting involved in house, techno, garage and trip-hop. There was big money to be made and, as a mass youth culture, the 'rave' scene in Europe had supplanted rock as the major youth music. Yet despite the fact that it originated in the clubs of Chicago and Detroit, this scene barely existed in the USA and few of these British artists, such as Orbital, Leftfield or The Chemical Brothers, were able to 'break' America. Nor did American fans seem much interested in 'Britpop' bands like Blur, Oasis, The Bluetones, Shed 7, Echobelly or Sleeper (and, in truth, few Brits actually cared very much either). By the mid 1990s there were few, if any, British artists in the *Billboard* charts. The only major players on the American rock scene were Bush, an old-school band who were prepared to play the sort of exhaustive tours that snake through the American heartland, while Britpoppers would fly in and play to a handful of expats and Anglophiles in small clubs in New York, Chicago and LA, sneer condescendingly at a few reporters, and then throw all their toys out of the pram when America failed to recognise their genius and fall at their feet. And maybe, in comparison with the sheer energy and rage of Korn – a band driven by ruthless ambition, prepared to tour hard and make sure that the kids in Spokane, Champaign and Concord got as good a show as the kids in LA or New York – the Britpop bands were just too effete and drab to even compete. America dominated in pop, in hip-hop, in R&B, in country; the fact that it had taken back rock and roll, seemingly for keeps, left the Brits predominant in fields that only they cared about.

Perhaps it was this American dominance that also raised the hackles of Brit critics, resentful at having to fill their magazines with bands that they, personally, disliked in order to sell copies. It is often from this quarter that we hear that 'rock is dead', that 'nu metal is just the zombie brainless animated corpse of rock and roll, stumbling around smashing things, too brainless to realise that it is dead and should just lie down,' as one *Melody Maker* critic put it (shortly before that particular magazine lay down and died itself).

While the teenage years of the 'baby-boomer' generation are still an endless source of fascination for the baby-boomer generation, there's at best a lack of interest and a tendency to ridicule, and at worst a hostility to the music, dress, attitudes and culture of teenagers today. This, of course, includes music; as well as nu metal, there is hostility to hip-hop, to contemporary R&B, to house, to garage, from people steeped in the ethos of a previous generation. While bands such as Nirvana and Britpop acts such as Oasis were depressingly similar to bands from the 1960s and 1970s, nu metal is a clean break from the past; although it has a long history, it is assembled from contemporary elements. It addresses the concerns and the anger of contemporary teenagers, and hence re-opens the generation gap for business. After years and years of parents thinking that because they liked the latest Ocean Colour Scene album – and so did their kids – they were on the same wavelength, they 'understood' them, they were still hip; the first time they heard the virtually atonal screech of Korn's 'Blind' or Limp Bizkit's painfully dumb cover of George Michael's 'Faith', it provoked knee-jerk hostility.

Nu metal responds with white-hot anger. Unlike Rage Against

The Machine – undeniably one of the major influences of all of the nu metal bands – there are no politics attached to this anger. Limp Bizkit, Korn and Orgy are purveyors of what has been called disparagingly 'mom-and-pop anger'; it's white suburban kid blues. The blues is the very spine of rock and roll, the music of poor, dispossessed black sharecroppers from the Mississippi Delta in the early years of the 20th century, played on cheap guitars and out-of-tune pianos; moving upbeat and north, to the ghettos of Chicago, where the advent of electric amplifiers and recorded music brought their struggles with poverty, racism and no-good cheatin' women to the world, even to the world of the affluent white enthusiast. It was spiritually uplifting music created from despair.

Few, if any, of the nu metal bands, would even be aware of how the tradition of the blues has shaped their music. Like most generations, it is historically myopic, seeing only as far back as the artists and records it heard in childhood. The spiritual ancestor of nu metal isn't so much Robert Johnson, or Leadbelly or BB King, it's Eddie Cochrane's 'Summertime Blues' where he sings, 'Well my mama papa told me/"Son, you gotta make some money/If you wanna use the car/To go ridin' next Sunday"/Well, I didn't go to work/Told the boss I was sick/"You can't use the car/Cuz you didn't work a lick."' As a statement of the spiritual despair in which teenagers in the post-war affluent world find themselves, it is unsurpassed. This is echoed by Limp Bizkit in songs like 'Break Stuff' ('It's just one of those days/Where ya don't wanna wake up/Everything is fucked, everybody sucks/You don't really know why/But you wanna justify rippin' someone's head off/No human contact/And if you interact your life is on contract/Your best bet is to stay away motherfucker!/It's just one of those days!') or Korn in 'Falling Away From Me' ('Day, is here fading/That's when, I would say/I flirt with suicide/Sometimes kill the pain/I can't always say/"It's gonna be better tomorrow"/Falling away from me/Falling away from me'). Teen angst has always been the other side of the happy-clappy pop records that are assumed to be the soundtrack to adolescent life. Bands like New Order, The Smiths and The Cure honed this 'life-sickness' to a fine art in the 1980s; Nirvana, Pearl Jam and Soundgarden brought relentless negativity into the 1990s; but the nu metal bands go one better – they have neatly packaged bedroom misery and suicidal tendencies as a lifestyle choice for the young American male. The music, the clothes, the tattoos and the piercings – badges worn in the flesh, a profound and fundamental statement of rejection – bring this angst into the public arena, parading it around the shopping mall, the college campus and the skate park. What's more, they have the readily identifiable logos of bands that seem to be shorthand for 'discontented angry young white male' to bind them all together. These bands don't offer any solutions, but they do say, 'You're not alone.'

1 Old Skool, Nu Skool
The Roots Of Nu Metal

To trace the roots of nu metal, we must look at its antecedents in '80s hard rock, punk, new wave and hip-hop. The names most often cited by bands as influences are diverse, ranging from major '90s metal bands like Tool, Pantera, Jane's Addiction, Fear Factory and Machine Head, to others like Faith No More, The Red Hot Chili Peppers, Fishbone, 24-7 Spyz, Shootyz Groove and, particularly, Rage Against The Machine, who were among the first rock bands to bring hip-hop and funk elements into their music.

The very term 'nu metal' is a play on the hip-hop term 'nu skool', allegedly coined by Philadelphia DJ/producer/remixer Rennie Pilgrem, though the misspelling/alternate spelling can be traced back to Prince in the mid 1980s and further back to graffiti tags. Nu skool sounds nothing like nu metal, though in a sense the fact that nu skool was a way for hip-hop to reach out to the febrile techno, drum and bass and hard step scenes, so nu metal was a reinvigoration of hard rock through links with other genres of music. Although there are many genres feeding into nu metal – bands like Orgy, Spineshank and Static-X, for example, plunder techno, trance and industrial music – its most prominent adherents are making connections between rock and hip-hop. Nu metal was a perfect description for this fusion of rap and rock, though bands such as Limp Bizkit and Korn were only the latest in a long line of artists who had attempted to forge crossovers over divides between genres that may have seemed hitherto unbridgable.

Heavy metal and hip-hop are actually very similar in that they attract a predominantly young male audience, are suffused with equal parts nihilism and insight, in their most extreme forms cross the boundary between music and 'noise' (at least to the uninitiated) and have very distinct looks – both for performers and fans – that unite their adherents.

Both forms have recently been the target of a pro-censorship lobby in the USA, seeking to blame violence of many different kinds on the brutality and imagery of the lyrics. Both forms seem to upset the conservative 'family values' lobby every bit as much as the liberal 'politically correct' crowd, one objecting to the language and glorification of violence, the other to perceived sexism, homophobia and racism. And, most importantly, while both sets of fans and performers project an image of hardness and ruthlessness, whether of gun-totin' ghetto pimp or white trash macho redneck, the reality is that the real core audience is to be found in the affluent suburbs. Both, at heart, deal in fantasy.

Hip-hop, or rap, had its own roots in the heavy funk of James Brown, the politically motivated spoken-word raps of The Last Poets and the 'toaster'-style MCs of the Jamaican reggae scene. In the early 1970s DJ Kool Herc relocated from Kingston to New York, bringing the style with him, performing at house parties, teaming up with other DJs and MCs to form the first 'crew'. Early commercial manifestations included The Sugarhill Gang's 'Rapper's Delight' and Grandmaster Flash's 'Adventures On The Wheels Of Steel'. But, like heavy metal, these initial and crude forays into the genre bore little resemblance to the work of the myriad of artists who would be unleashed. Initially, rap seemed like just another novelty form, an underground reaction to the commercialised disco scene, a sort of African-American answer to punk, which was then revolutionising the rock and roll scene. Its crossover potential was limited to a few kitschy items like Blondie's 'Rapture' and The Sex Pistols' self-styled Svengali Malcolm McLaren's 'discovery' of the scene in the early '80s. But, like heavy metal, the hip-hop underground was a fecund scene, throwing up artists, DJs and producers who managed to find all kinds of creative possibilities in the form. Grandmaster Flash's international hit 'The Message' brought a new political militancy to the form, taking the raps beyond name-checking friends at parties to talk about the black American experience in the Reagan era. Afrika Bambaataa's 'Planet Rock' introduced psychedelia, electronics and African mysticism to hip-hop, this seminal track lifting wholesale the 'riff' from Kraftwerk's 'Trans Europe Express', making explicit the links between street culture and the European avant-garde. But the true rap roots of nu metal are to be found in the happy collaboration of four middle-class teenagers from Hollis in Queens, New York.

Russell Simmons, his brother Run (Joseph Simmons), DMC (Darryl McDaniels) and Jam Master Jay (Jason Mizell) were hardly stereotypical gangstas, though their style with Run-DMC brought a new toughness to hip-hop whose influence reverberates to this day. Russell Simmons established himself as a successful hip-hop concert promoter while still in college, graduating to management and taking Harlem-born Kurtis Blow into his stable in the early 1980s. Kurtis Blow struck up an acquaintance with the younger Simmons brother, who began DJing for him. Soon, Run struck out on his own, teaming up with schoolfriend DMC and Jam Master Jay, releasing a series of increasingly successful 12-inch singles – most notably 'It's Like That', whose B-side 'Sucker MCs' is widely regarded as the first hardcore rap track – which became local hits. Their eponymous 1984 debut album became the first rap album to achieve a gold record.

Brother Russell, meanwhile, formed Rush Management and a record label, Def Jam, with rock producer Rick Rubin. Their third album *Raising Hell*, released in 1986, saw rap evolve from high-energy disco and electro into something heavier and darker; muscular drum-machine beats, low-end bass riffs, rock power chords and hard-ass raps laid the foundations for gangsta rap. It also, notably, included 'Walk This Way', a remake of a track by Aerosmith, whose career at that time was in the drug-addled doldrums. The track was a wake-up call to anyone who had missed the rise of hip-hop; as well as being a massive international hit, the record propelled Run-DMC into the pop-star league as well as helping to revive Aerosmith's career.

Def Jam became a locus for this new cross-cultural phenomenon; The Beastie Boys – Mike Diamond (Mike D), Adam Yauch (MCA) and Adam Horovitz (King Ad-Rock) – three middle-class New York white kids formed as a punk band in 1981 and signed with Def Jam in 1985. Their debut album *Licensed To Ill*, also released in 1986, produced by Rick Rubin, blended rap with the cartoonish brattishness of New York punk. *Licensed To Ill* was as much the product of Simmons' partner in the label, Rick Rubin, as it was of the Beasties themselves. Rubin, originally working from his New York University dorm produced many of the company's mid-1980s hits. In many ways his was the 'white trash' aesthetic that laid much of the groundwork for nu metal. Certainly while Run-DMC won over the hip kids who are the first to discover any new style in music, the Beasties took rap to a mass audience.

'Back then it was a big deal to be hanging with kids, rapping, breakdancing, beat boxing,' Fred Durst recalled in a 1999 interview with *Rolling Stone*. 'My white friends loved A Flock Of Seagulls and Ratt. Then the Beasties came out and all my preppy white friends were like, "Oh, rap's cool."'

Rubin and Simmons parted acrimoniously in 1987, the latter taking Def Jam in a more soulful direction with artists like Oran 'Juice' Jones, the former being set free to indulge his suburban redneck tastes. Rubin launched his own label Def American, signing comedian Andrew 'Dice' Clay, soon to be death metal superstars Slayer and The Geto Boys, a proto-gangsta rap crew who made would-be hardmen Run-DMC sound positively sensitive in comparison. Fronted by Bushwick Bill – who originally joined as a dancing dwarf at live shows – the Texas trio were at that time the freakish extreme of rap. When Geffen – who distributed Def American – refused to handle The Geto Boys in any way, shape or form, Rubin took the label to rivals Warner Brothers. Def American – with a name change to American Recordings – moved out of the rap business very quickly, relying on a more traditional rock and roll roster of Slayer, Danzig, The Cult, early stoner rock band Masters Of Reality and a raft of grizzled Rubin favourites on their uppers ranging from Donovan to Johnny Cash.

But as a producer – particularly on The Red Hot Chili Peppers' 1991 album *BloodSugarSexMagik* – Rubin still had a strong influence.

The Red Hot Chili Peppers are a 'proper' rock and roll band, with a history littered by feuds, splits, drug deaths, overdoses, scandal, naked performances with only socks to cover their modesty, and insanity. They also made some of the most primal white funk of any band ever, creating a live spectacle second to none. It wasn't so much that they fused funk and rock as their conjoining of great intelligence with spectacular stupidity that seemed to make them such an incendiary band. The Red Hot Chili Peppers were formed in Los Angeles after three high-school students – Michael 'Flea' Balzary, Hillel Slovak and Jack Irons – formed a band called Anthym. Anthony Kiedis also attended their school, Fairfax High, and later joined the band, performing at LA clubs under the name Tony Flow And The Miraculously Majestic Masters, reputedly jamming their entire set while they were all tripping on LSD. Myth or not, the band signed to EMI and had ex-Gang Of Four guitarist Andy Gill produce their debut album. The Gang Of Four, a punk band from Sheffield, England, were a hard-left political band inspired by The Clash, albeit with a more developed (and less commercial) political perspective. Their debut album *Entertainment* is still regarded as a classic, though in may ways the follow up *Solid Gold*, with its politico-funk leanings, is the more interesting.

Gill, now an established and well-regarded producer (he has worked with everyone from the late Michael Hutchence to punk band Bis and UK Asian rap-metal band Sona Fariq) was a good choice, it seemed. The resulting eponymous album was a disappointment to all concerned and it was not until George Clinton – eccentric mastermind behind Parliament, Funkadelic and all their offshoots – produced second record *Freaky Styley* that the band found their feet. Although not a commercial success, the album showcased the band's hard funk-rock fusion, particularly on the single 'Hollywood Africa'.

Their breakthrough albums were 1989's *Mother's Milk* and its Rick Rubin-produced follow-up *BloodSugarSexMagik*, from which came the hit singles 'Breaking the Girl', 'Under the Bridge' and 'Give It Away'.

The RHCP sound was epitomised by Flea's 'rubber thumb' funk bass playing and Kiedis's atonal, whining singing style. They were never a rap-metal band, though their influence can be heard in virtually every band who has poked a toe into that particular pool. Also, despite the fact that they appealed to the straight metal crowd, the band weren't big-haired rockers in leather and spandex; Kiedis's tattoos and piercings pioneered a look that would also feed into nu metal.

Faith No More, contemporaneous with The Red Hot Chili Peppers, is the name that most often crops up as an influence on nu metal. 'I'm glad that people compare us to Faith No More and not to Limp Bizkit or Korn,' Papa Roach drummer David Buckner told me during a UK visit in 2001. 'They are still one of our favourite bands if not *the* favourite. I think we have more sides to us than just the rap-rock hybrid thing, and I think that's true if you listen to Faith No More.'

It was part of FNM's particular genius that they split up just as the rock-rap hybrid they pioneered and popularised was about to take off in a major way. Formed in the Bay Area of San Francisco, the band tried out a succession of singers, including Courtney Love (expelled in 1983 because she wanted to be a dictator while the band saw itself as a democracy, allegedly), before Mike Patton of local Frank Zappaesque band Mr Bungle was hired. Patton replaced Chuck Moseley who had already recorded an album with the band, but it was their 1989 album *The Real Thing*, and particularly the single 'Epic', that won the band massive accolades and their reputation as creators of rap metal.

As rock-rap crossovers go, 'Epic' was a relatively crude affair, with Patton rapping over the verses and singing the chorus over a heavy guitar riff and stacatto drums. It was really the sound of a band trying to get to grips with something they didn't fully understand and getting it slightly wrong but creating something else in the process. Such happy accidents include The Clash attempting to play reggae on 'Police And Thieves' and 'White Man In Hammersmith Palais', or The Beatles attempting to recreate The Isley Brothers' upbeat soul on 'Twist And Shout'.

Again, as well as the music, FNM's look was a shift away from traditional metal duds; they sported dreadlocks, trainers, track pants, hooded tops and reversed baseball caps, an early manifestation of 'white' hip-hop style, with only guitarist 'Big' Jim Martin left to fly the flag for leather bikers' jackets, long hair and bad beards. They looked every inch a modern rock and roll band, making contemporaries like Poison, Guns N'Roses and Mötley Crüe look faintly ridiculous and out of step. After 15 years the band split in 1998, never really able to top the success of *The Real Thing*, and with 'Epic' hanging like a 'Stairway To Heaven' albatross around their necks. Jim Martin was fired in 1993 after tensions during the recording of *Angel Dust*, the band's fourth album. The band hired a succession of replacements but never quite recaptured the magical formula of their classic line-up.

There are a few other key influences, such as San Francisco's Mordred, a band who brought funk and hip-hop influences to speed metal. Their second album *In This Life*, released in 1991, employed a DJ, Aaron Vaughn, scratching over the band's razor riffs. Primus, a surreal funk-metal band, also from San Francisco, have always stood out like a square peg in a round hole. The band have worked with Tom Waits, himself one of music's great originals, and have been described as 'funk metal if it had been invented by Captain Beefheart instead of The Red Hot Chili Peppers'.

Rather than cash in on a sound they were instrumental in helping to create, Primus seem to have snubbed their nu metal descendants. Primus frontman Les Claypool told me in 1998, 'We have always been in opposition to whatever is happening in the mainstream. When we started, the mainstream was Guns N'Roses, Mötley Crüe, Cinderella, Poison, all those bands we thought were ridiculous. In the '90s it seemed that there was a big change happening, there was this whole vibe and sense of camaraderie with the original Lollapaloozas, and touring with Jane's Addiction and Fishbone. Then there came all these bands that were definitely influenced by us, Korn and Limp Bizkit. We sort of became part of that scene. Funk metal. Everyone asked us about these bands in America. That scene, because it was such a huge money scene, it has somewhat turned into the same thing that we were running from in the old days...that big rock, excessive money and ego scene. That kind of disgusted me. I'm not into that type of thing. It is this whole angst scene, but angst with no point. I am not into that stuff at this point in my life.'

Suicidal Tendencies and singer Mike Muir's side project Infectious Groove, particularly their 1991 debut *The Plague That Makes Your Booty Move...It's The Infectious Groove*, also played a big part in creating a viable funk-metal hybrid. Suicidal Tendencies have been LA scene mainstays for over 20 years, appealing to the hardcore underground fans, particularly among the city's Mexican diaspora. Infectious Groove, the funk-metal offshoot, ironically became more successful than 'parent' band Suicidal Tendencies, though, oddly, the influence of the latter is stronger. Speaking to MTV, Fred Durst said, 'I listened to Suicidal Tendencies' debut album for so long when I was young. I felt like Mike Muir because I had parents telling me I was crazy for what I did. That song "Institutionalized" is a classic...'

The other band who are held responsible for the nu metal sound are Biohazard. Biohazard – comprising Evan Seinfeld (bass/vocals), Bill Graziadei (guitar/vocals), Danny Schuler (drums) and Leo Curley (guitar) – released their debut album in 1990, but their break came with *Urban Discipline*, the million-selling follow-up from which came the '90s metal classic 'Punishment'. The band collaborated with rappers Onyx, who recorded an alternate version of their song 'Slam', before signing to major label Warner Brothers for their third album, *State Of The World Address* in 1994. World domination seemed assured as more and more young upstarts started forming bands inspired by Biohazard; but disaster struck at the end of the 1990s when the band signed to a new label for the release of *New World Disorder*, a good album sabotaged by corporate machinations involving one label being swallowed by a bigger corporation. The band took a hiatus with Evan making his acting debut in TV series *Oz* and Billy writing a column for UK rock bible *Metal Hammer*. The band recorded their mighty new album *Uncivilization* in 2001 at their own studio with Phillip Anselmo of Pantera, Pete Steele of Type O Negative, Sen-Dog of Cypress Hill, and members of Slipknot, Agnostic Front, Sepultura, Hatebreed and Skarhead making guest appearances.

There is a long tradition of rock bands meddling in funk. John Lydon's Public Image Ltd, formed immediately after he quit The Sex Pistols, delved into the darker side of disco, heavy dub reggae and German avant-garde. The Pop Group, a radical Bristol-based band, even presaged the emergence of rock/rap crossovers and samples with their reworking of The Last Poets' 'One Out Of Many' on their second album, *For How Much Longer Do We Tolerate Mass Murder*. The Slits, 23 Skiddoo and mid-period New Order all tried to forge some sort of union with the emerging New York scene. Talking Heads offshoot The Tom Tom Club made an explicit link between the arty uptown scene of Warhol, loft parties and clubs like Area and the Peppermint Lounge and the scuzzier downtown scene. And, of course, The Clash in their dying days tried to rap on 'Magnificent Seven', from *Sandanista!*, and got it brilliantly wrong. There were other attempts in the 1980s to forge some kind of union between breakbeats, rap and hard rock. Arty Swiss goth/death metal band Celtic Frost on their *Into The Pandemonium* album (1987) had a stab at creating a dance crossover track with 'One In Their Pride'.

But where the rock/rap crossover sparked by Run-DMC differed was that it came from a street crew plundering rock and roll, not the other way around. And it was unselfconsciously populist rather than some anal retentive Brian Eno-spawned 'experimental' performance piece.

For a while, hip-hop DJs were using loops of Led Zeppelin drummer John Bonham to create breakbeats, and lifting guitar riffs from AC/DC records. Other rappers reworked metal classics in the manner of 'Walk This Way'; Seattle DJ/rapper Sir Mix A Lot unleashed a version of Black Sabbath's 'Iron Man'. Other collaborations – albeit sporadic – between rock bands and rap crews continued over the next decade, most notably Anthrax and Public Enemy on 'Bring The Noise'. Both groups were New Yorkers, Public Enemy having established themselves with their 1987 Def Jam album *Yo! Bum Rush The Show* as the most outspoken and militant rap group, Anthrax vying for a place atop the thrash-metal pile.

'We didn't know what sort of reaction we would get when me and Flav [Flava Flav – co-MC in Public Enemy] went out onstage at Madison Square Garden,' Public Enemy's Chuck D recalled in 1999. 'We thought they might boo us.'

Certainly, metal had a reputation – not altogether undeserved – as a 'reactionary' form. But the Anthrax/Public Enemy collaboration worked, and eventually both bands went on the road together in the co-headlining Live Noise tour. Public Enemy graced the covers of US and European metal mags such as *Kerrang!*, a situation that would have been unthinkable only a few years previously. The collaboration definitely had a long-term impact on many of the fans who saw those shows.

'The first concert I ever saw was either in 1990 or 1991,' Linkin Park's Mike Shinoda told US rock website *Shoutweb*. 'I saw Anthrax and Public Enemy play the Killer Bs tour. At the end of the show they did "Bring Da Noise" together. I saw them at Irvine Meadows [Hartford, Connecticut] and it was huge. Primus opened up. I saw a lot of shows after that but every time I saw a show I wanted to do something like that more and more.'

Chuck D eventually followed the lead of Ice-T in actually launching his own rock band. Ice-T launched Body Count and Chuck D formed Confrontation Camp. Although rock and roll was originally created by black artists coming out of the blues, swing and R&B traditions, the music was hijacked by the success of white artists like Elvis Presley, Jerry Lee Lewis and Carl Perkins in the 1950s, and by bands like The Beatles, The Rolling Stones and The Who in the 1960s. Black artists all but abandoned the form in the 1960s and 1970s.

According to the manifesto of the Black Rock Coalition (BRC), an organisation dedicated to furthering recognition of black artists in rock, 'As white faces were attached to the music, black artists were relegated to categories like rhythm & blues and soul. In subsequent years, rock 'n' roll took on many different styles and permutations, but remains the most popular form of music across the globe. Unfortunately, there is also still a great deal of segregation in the music industry. Despite the obvious rock underpinnings of artists like James Brown, Sly And The Family Stone, Jimi Hendrix, The Isley Brothers, Curtis Mayfield, Aretha Franklin, Otis Redding, Tina Turner, Parliament/Funkadelic, Stevie Wonder, Prince and countless others, Black artists still largely aren't widely recognized in the pantheon of rock music.'

Vernon Reid, one of the BRC's founders, launched his band Living Colour in the 1980s to promote the movement, to help reclaim rock and roll as black music.

One band affiliated with the movement was Fishbone, an energetic mid-1980s Los Angeles combo fronted by Angelo Moore, aka Fishbone, whose music was a fusion inspired by early '60s Jamaican ska (a regional variation on R&B that was the forerunner of reggae) as well as the late '70s post-punk British ska revival centred around the more political 2-Tone bands such as The Specials, The Beat and The Selecter. There was a heavy rock and punk input from influences such as George Clinton, Led Zeppelin, The Isley Brothers and The Dead Kennedys. Fishbone's 1988 album *Truth And Soul* is still one of the most influential records on the scene, helping to fan the creative spark of The Red Hot Chili Peppers as well as the countless American ska revival bands like The Mighty Mighty Bosstones, No Doubt and Goldfinger. But being an influential cult figure doesn't necessarily bring commercial rewards. Moore, although still playing live shows and receiving support from artists he has influenced, is relegated to club dates while his contemporaries sell out stadiums. 'I've opened up a lot of doors for other bands. I'm just tired of being a door-opener; I want to walk through that door!' Moore complained.

Despite the profound influence of black artists on white rock culture from Little Richard, Chuck Berry and Fats Domino right up to the input of rap into nu metal, there is still a demarcation in the music industry that keeps black and white artists separated.

There are landmark albums like the soundtrack to the 1993 film *Judgement Night*, which featured collaborations between hip-hop and rock artists including Slayer/Ice-T's 'Disorder', House Of Pain/Helmet's 'Just Another Victim' and Boo-Yaa TRIBE/Faith No More's 'Another Body Murdered'. But rap artists still found it hard to escape the ghetto, even if that ghetto was the category their music was consigned to.

Kyle 'Ice' Jason, singer in Confrontation Camp, summed this up in an interview with *Rolling Stone* at the time of the group's formation in 1999: 'When you listen to a KROK or any form of rock format, you can hear Method Man because he's down with Fred Durst who's Limp Bizkit who is also rapping, but they have a rock band. So in essence they're not doing anything that much different than what we're doing. But you won't hear Wu-Tang or Method Man by themselves on a rock format and I think it's ridiculous. But, whereas black radio will give Eminem credit because the kid can rap, bottom line, he can rap. So they respect his rapping ability and since he's doing rap it's in an urban format they'll play him. But they'll also play him on rock radio. We just want the explanation. It's cool if they want to do that, but if we deliver a record that's clearly a rock record, there's no question it should be played.'

Bad Brains, another reggae-influenced black band, enjoy a similar cult status to Fishbone without ever having been able to reap even a portion of the financial rewards that went to bands they influenced: The Beastie Boys cited them as their favourite band ever, yet the Beasties still enjoy international mega-stardom while Bad Brains are still an obscure cult.

It is still easier for white people to move into hip-hop than it is for black artists to move into rock and roll. It is still hard for black artists to cross over into a more lucrative 'white' market without the patronage of white bands. Public Enemy had a major influence on most of the earliest attempts at creating a viable crossover between rock and roll and hip-hop, infusing the music with a heavy political slant. Consolidated, for example, came from the 'industrial' underground. Their debut album *The Myth Of Rock* fused samples of noise, radio and TV broadcasts, breakbeats and raps such as 'Stop The War Against The Black Community', 'White American Male (The Truth Hurts)' and 'This Is A Collective', which proclaimed an anti-sexist, anti-racist, anti-corporate message similar to that of anarcho-punk bands like Crass. Their second album, *Friendly Fascism*, added militant veganism (pre-dating the likes of Moby by some years) to the mix.

At the same time in California, ex-skate/punk band The Beatnigs frontman Michael Franti unleashed his new project The Disposable Heroes Of Hiphoprisy. Their debut 1992 album *Hypocrisy Is The Greatest Luxury* included a stunning reworking of The Dead Kennedys' anti-hippy classic 'California Über Alles', updated as an attack on then governor Pete Wilson, who presided over the state at the time of the Rodney King beating and the attendant LA riots and who stamped brutal Reaganomics on the state, disenfranchising the black and Hispanic communities. The Boo-Yaa TRIBE, a collective of rappers of Samoan descent, not only pioneered a mix of hard rap and hard rock, but are now recognised as the forerunners of gangsta rap.

But as far as the influence on a new generation of nu metal bands goes, the unquestionable leaders of the pack were Rage Against The Machine. Formed in 1991 in Los Angeles, Rage Against The Machine's purpose, according to frontman Zack de la Rocha was to 'bridge the gap between entertainment and activism'. What marked them out from Consolidated and Disposable Heroes was the sheer commercial impact they had. Not since the heyday of The Clash had there been such a marriage between uncompromising radicalism and killer rock and roll. The curse of most 'political' bands is that they end up at best preaching to the converted and at worst dabbling in radical chic, with no substance to back it up.

Guitarist Tom Morello said of their deal with multinational Sony subsidiary Epic Records: 'When you live in a capitalistic society, the currency of the dissemination of information goes through capitalistic channels. Would Noam Chomsky object to his works being sold at Barnes & Noble? No, because that's where people buy their books. We're not interested in preaching to just the converted. It's great to play abandoned squats run by anarchists, but it's also great to be able to reach people with a revolutionary message, people from Granada Hills to Stuttgart.'

Rage Against The Machine toured with The Wu-Tang Clan and The Beastie Boys, worked with Snoop Dogg and are close to Chuck D of Public Enemy; they involved themselves in protests against the execution of Black Panther activist Mummia Abu Jamal, for the release of imprisoned Native American campaigner Leonard Peltier and for Tibetan Freedom; Tom Morello actually got arrested taking part in a protest against the employment practices of

Guess? Jeans. In 2000, police fired rubber bullets, pepper spray and smoke bombs at fans at a Rage Against The Machine show held opposite the venue in Los Angeles where the Democratic Party National Convention was taking place. The gig was part of a protest that addressed a broad range of issues including calls for nuclear disarmament, for an end to the death penalty and for Vice-President Al Gore to end his investment in Occidental Petroleum. Rage, like The Clash before them, seemed to articulate the political anger of a new generation. This was not a 'movement' in the sense of the anti-war movement in the 1960s, more a loose coalition of activists involved in everything from direct action against 'globalization' to 'culture jamming', such as the creative defacing of advertising to subvert corporate messages. This was the crowd on the streets of Seattle, London and Genoa, the tear-gassed transvestites and the ski-masked anarchists throwing bins through the window of the nearest McDonald's. It was a movement whose catch-all description came from the title of a bestselling book by Canadian journalist Naomi Klein: No Logo.

But the music of Rage Against The Machine in many ways was even more radical than the message; it seemed to be the perfect synthesis of metal and rap, almost laying down the blueprint that Korn and Limp Bizkit would later follow. The guitar-as-percussion instrument, distorted riffs, sloganeering over breakbeats, Rage Against The Machine created something that sounded 'natural' rather than forced, a failing of many rap/metal fusions. Sadly, few of the bands inspired by Rage Against The Machine seemed to take onboard any of the politics, the awareness or the intelligence of the words. This, though, is nothing new; from Bob Dylan onwards, artists have discovered that it's as easy to shift records without all the cumbersome protest and consciousness getting in the way.

Inevitably, Rage Against The Machine's protest extended to what they saw as a 'sell out' by Limp Bizkit; at the 2000 MTV Music Video Awards, while Fred Durst made a speech about how Bizkit were the 'most hated' band in the world, Rage Against The

Machine bassist Tim C was led away in handcuffs after climbing up a 15-foot-high piece of stage scenery, which almost toppled down on the singer on live TV.

Rage's promo for 'Sleep Now In The Fire' was up against Limp Bizkit in the running for Best Rock Video. After being released from jail, Tim C blamed hearing Britney Spears' version of '(I Can't Get No) Satisfaction' for sending him over the edge.

The departure of Zack de la Rocha in 2001 was a watershed for the band in the wake of their monumental album *The Battle Of Los Angeles*. Whether Rage can survive as a successful band with a different frontman remains to be seen.

As well as rap, the nu metal sound is rooted in '80s thrash and punk. Although, on the surface, nu metal is a reaction against everything that mid-1980s metal was about – it was narrow-minded, homophobic, crass, sexist and, occasionally, racist – it was often the first music that young nu metallers came across.

'I only switched on to music when I got into high school. During the seventh and eighth grade, new wave. In the '70s and '80s new wave, metal, hair bands were cool, it all co-existed. It was fun and exciting. With the grunge scene everything got fucked. I think history repeats itself and it will be rock 'n' roll again,' said Jonathan Davis of Korn.

'When older people hear about heavy metal music, they think about the lousy period it went through in the '80s when it was really bad,' Deftones bassist Chi Cheng said in an interview with *The Washington Post*. 'Now when people talk about heavy music, they're talking about bands like us, or some of our contemporaries, bands that have grown up listening to different things. Heavy music has changed a lot. The influences now...you'll get bands that are mixing up rap, reggae grooves or anything they feel like putting into the music. It's still called heavy music because there's the loud electric guitar, whatever the style.'

By the late '70s, the first wave of metal superstars – Led

Zeppelin, Deep Purple, Queen – had become something of a joke, slipping into self-parody (usually unwittingly), becoming increasingly remote from their fans. It's something of a cliché to say that punk *had* to happen, but for a generation of fans and performers, sickened by the increasingly bland corporate easy listening of The Eagles, Fleetwood Mac and Peter Frampton, and left cold by the clichéd bombast of the old warhorses, something had to give. Punk bands like The Sex Pistols may have set out to destroy rock and roll but they ended up breathing new life into it. And, as when all revolutions go sour, the new boss began, increasingly, to resemble the old boss.

To extend the revolution metaphor even further, this revolution gave birth to its own White Guard in the form of the clumsily monickered 'New Wave Of British Heavy Metal' (NWOBHM), bands such as Iron Maiden, Def Leppard and Saxon, who took a defiantly traditional stance against punk. Despite the fact that New York, Detroit and Los Angeles were the epicentres of their own regional underground scenes, America was largely unaffected by punk, at least in the short term. Although the bands who were at the roots of the whole phenomenon – from The Velvet Underground, Iggy And The Stooges and The MC5 to The New York Dolls, The Ramones, Pere Ubu, Suicide, Richard Hell And The Void-Oids, Johnny Thunders' Heartbreakers, The Dead Boys, The Flamin' Groovies and The Dictators – were American, rock dinosaurs like Ted Nugent, Kiss and Ratt continued to fill stadiums and sell millions of records, appealing to the same teenage kids who had always been the scene's mainstays. Only a hardened cult following knew or cared about punk.

The stadium rock acts were all about good times and concerned themselves with the traditional rock and roll subjects of cars, girls and partying on down. Yet times were changing and the hedonism and optimism of the '60s gave way to the more cynical '80s, an era of a renewed Cold War, economic downturn and the influx of massive amounts of hard drugs into the American mainstream. By the early 1980s, the small cult of punks was actually a growing army of discontented kids with mohawks who sneered at the residual hippy idealism and dumb beer-swilling party ethic of the metal bands. Bands like San Francisco's The Dead Kennedys, The Dils, The Nuns, X, Crime and The Avengers – all heavily influenced by British punk – and a whole host of new, regional American punk groups such as Black Flag, Minor Threat and Bad Brains gave voice to an angrier, angst-ridden generation. This second wave of American punk laid the foundations for much of the heavy moodiness, the negativity, the introspection and the unformed protest that we hear in bands like Korn and Limp Bizkit. Whether there is any actual causal link – in an interview Fred Durst said that he was unaware of these bands – is a moot point, but these bands were instrumental in creating hard, brutal rock and roll songs that incorporated protest – hitherto the preserve of earnest folkies with acoustic guitars – autobiographical navel-gazing, expressions of depression and barely articulated rage.

'We are tired of your abuse/Try to stop us it's no use' sing Black Flag in 'Rise Above'. And as an antidote to the fast cars, cocaine and cash concerns of the metal acts, Minor Threat's anti-drug puritanism in 'Straight Edge' was like a manifesto: 'I'm a person just like you/But I've got better things to do/Than sit around and fuck my head/Hang out with the living dead/Snort white shit up my nose/Pass out at the shows/I don't even think about speed/That's something I just don't need/I've got the straight edge.'

Just as rap was giving a voice to discontented young black men who were suffering the sharp end of Reaganomics and the hard-drug tsunami sweeping America's inner cities, punk – though often inarticulate – gave a similar kind of expression to a population of largely suburban white males.

Of course, it wasn't the only expression for the angst-ridden adolescent; movies like John Hughes' teen comedies *The Breakfast Club*, *Pretty In Pink* and *Ferris Beuller's Day Off*, new wave bands like The Cure, The Smiths and The Psychedelic Furs, and books like SE Hinton's tales of small-town gang life, *The Outsiders* and *Rumblefish*, all mined the same strata. There's an argument as to whether teenagers were any more angst-ridden in the 1980s than at any other time – the outpourings of the 'beat' generation in the 1950s and the sensitive singer-songwriters of the 1960s would suggest that they weren't unique – but socio-economic factors such as the increased divorce rate, the lack of entry-level job opportunities and the rise of the minimum wage 'McJob', as well as an impending sense of nuclear or environmental global catastrophe, must all have been contributing factors. If previous generations had escaped from the 'misery' of teenage life through relentlessly upbeat and positive music, whether it was the high-energy shock rock of Little Richard, the joyous life-affirming soul of Tamla Motown or the sexually charged potentate bluster of Led Zeppelin, the post-punk kids wallowed in their sadness or bristled with ill-directed anger.

This was common to almost all music with the exception of mainstream pop, R&B and the then emergent house scene in Chicago, which was to provide the soundtrack to a hedonistic, drug-fuelled counter-blast to rock and hip-hop's angst and anger. Although at the time punk, new wave, hip-hop and metal seemed like irreconcilable forces – almost like hostile armed camps waging a cold war, seen from the perspective of the 21st century – they had much more in common than they had differences. In the 1980s it would have been unthinkable to see, for example, Mötley Crüe, Boogie Down Productions, REM and Bad Religion sharing a bill. It hardly seems worth remarking that a band like Orgy – protégés, to some extent, of Korn and producer Josh Abrahams – could quite comfortably go out on the road on The Family Values tour with Limp Bizkit, Rammstein and Ice Cube, claim that they were influenced by death metal bands like Obituary and Slayer and also do a straight-faced cover of New Order's 'Blue Monday' and support Depeche Mode on their American shows.

But in the 1980s, metal was hardly a monolithic edifice; while 'big hair' bands in spandex pants and cap-sleeved T-shirts from Skid Row to Bon Jovi dominated the scene, a pared-down, much harder version was starting to emerge from the Bay Area of San Francisco, from the slums of São Paulo in Brazil and from the scuzzy streets of New York. While the British NWOBHM bands had responded to punk by adopting a sort of rock version of fundamentalism, the new breed of thrash bands, such as Metallica, Slayer, Sepultura and Anthrax, took their inspiration from it, making the drums harder and faster, and the riffs heavier. A decade before nu metal we had 'new metal'. If Rob Reiner's 1984 film *This Is Spiñal Tap* had made it virtually impossible for a metal band to be anything other than a laughing-stock, Metallica were about to wipe the smiles off their faces. Although audiences remained partisan right up until the 1990s, there was little to choose between thrash and punk, and sometimes it seemed that the clothes and the hair were the only ways you could tell what a band were about. Heavy metal had become, albeit briefly in the late '70s and early '80s, a vast monoculture, a reassuringly conservative form of rock and roll that appealed to less 'cosmopolitan' elements than punk. Now the consensus had fallen apart; thrash began the modernisation of metal and led to the proliferation of increasingly diverse subgenres within metal. Metal no longer existed as a besieged fundamentalist regime seeking to shut out change – it actively embraced it. The idea of metal being in any way avant-garde would have seemed ridiculous at the start of the '80s. By the end of the decade, comparisons between Metallica and Miles Davis, Celtic Frost and Shostakovich, were not out of place.

These thrash bands reflected teen pessimism and angst in a

less straightforward way than the punk bands. Metallica and Slayer's lyrical concerns were serial killers, HP Lovecraftian horror, apocalyptic sci-fi, black magic and Nazi torturers. An even more extreme variant of thrash – death metal – played faster, to the point where you could barely hear actual music amidst the accelerated cacophony, the vocals reduced to a low subhuman growl, the lyrics taking negativity to levels that would have made hardened misanthropes like Louis Ferdinand Celine and William Burroughs balk. Obituary once allegedly made a record that was just 'too heavy' to be released. Deicide all claimed to have sold their souls to the devil, branded inverted crucifixes on their foreheads and claimed that they would all die aged 33.

By the early 1990s it was difficult to keep tabs on the bewildering array of metal subcultures and as one lapsed into clichéd formalism, another radical variation sprang up to shout and scream the rest down. We had industrial metal, centred around bands like Ministry and Skinny Puppy, who allied furious riffing with pulverising electronic beats and cyberpunk imagery. We had speed metal – the best example of which would be Nuclear Assault – which, as the name suggests, was accelerated to a musical blur. We had grind or grindcore, an atonal and brutal variation on speed/death metal, based mostly around a cabal of bands like Bolt Thrower, Carcass and Godflesh, mostly signed to Nottingham, England, independent label Earache. There was black metal, doom metal, funk metal, goth metal and just about any fusion conceivable. The mainstream of metal, the bands who appeared on magazine covers and sold out the major stadium tours were still the fairly straight meat-and-potatoes traditional bands like Poison, Bryan Adams and Bon Jovi – who could all have walked straight out of *Spinal Tap* – who churned out the cock rock, sugary ballads and overblown anthems that got the children of suburban white America waving their lighters in the air to show approval. But the underground was growing like a virus. Like Ebola.

There were still divisions – the metal kids were still a scene unto themselves – but by the early 1990s this had began to change. 'I think you have to thank Kurt Cobain for a lot of that,' Metallica's Lars Ulrich said in a 1995 interview with UK magazine *Metal Hammer*. 'If you go back five years or so, we had the punks and the metal kids and the modern Hüsker Dü crowd, if you will. Cobain came along and somehow fused it together.

'The aggression and attitude of Nirvana appealed to a lot of the metal kids. There were definite hints of Black Sabbath riffs in the music. At the same time, Nirvana wasn't about being a great guitar player. It was about emotion and purity and opening up, which is what a lot of the alternative crowd loved about Nirvana.'

Nirvana, grunge, the impact of Kurt Cobain's brief superstardom and death has been exhaustively documented elsewhere. Suffice to say that their second album, *Nevermind*, and single 'Smells Like Teen Spirit' represented a major sea-change in rock and roll; it was the event that finally shattered any remaining divisions between 'alternative rock' and metal. For a while, anything seemed possible. The basic format of rock and roll – guitar, bass, drums, a 4/4 beat, three chords and a singer – has been around since the 1950s. Suddenly it seemed renewed and reborn, and a new generation heard it for the first time. Then Kurt Cobain, for whatever reasons – disgust at his own success, chronic heroin addiction, depression – blew his brains out. It seemed for a while that he had quite literally blown the head off the movement that he had been instrumental in creating. Bands like Pearl Jam, who also mined the depths of personal disaffection and misery, inherited Nirvana's crown of thorns but hardly cared to capitalise on it. Many other bands, from contemporaries like Alice In Chains, Smashing Pumpkins and Stone Temple Pilots to established artists like Neil Young, were sufficiently shaken by the suicide to question their own authenticity and many wondered aloud if they were not merely some karaoke of despair, milking teenage angst for their own ends. In a deliciously post-modern moment, Smashing Pumpkins appeared in an episode of *The Simpsons* to proclaim that selling angst to teenagers was like shooting fish in a barrel. Yet the barriers were down and without a 'leader' like Cobain, all bets were off. It was from this rich and fertile ground that nu metal sprang.

2 Feel My Pain
Korn

Nu metal has three superstar-level bands (four if we include Slipknot, but we'll discuss that in a later chapter): Limp Bizkit, The Deftones and Korn. Korn were the first to emerge – though The Deftones had been together longer, having played around Sacramento in northern California since the 1980s – and while Fred Durst's willingness to play the celeb game gives him the edge in terms of public recognition, Korn are the most important of the three. Korn never thought small: when asked by *Launch.com* what the band's goal was, singer Jonathan Davis replied, 'To be the best rock band in the world. Like Led Zeppelin.'

Whether they *are* the best is a matter for debate, but what is beyond question is that they have established themselves as a great brand as well as a great band; their readily identifiable logo is as recognisable as the Nike swoosh or the McDonald's golden arches. Their annual Family Values tour has become one of the most important live rock franchises. Most bands want to be as big as The Beatles; Korn want to be as big as Coca-Cola. The story of Korn and Jonathan Davis is a bit like the comic strip that used to run in the ads for Charles Atlas's 'Dynamic Tension' body-building method, which appeared on the inside back pages of American comics. Beside a picture of Atlas – an avuncular pomaded strongman, flexing his muscles – was a crudely drawn strip called 'The insult that made a MAN out of Mac'. It's a simple story of revenge, maybe a story as old as stories go, about a skinny nerd, presumably Mac, who takes his girlfriend to the beach. While they enjoy a picnic, a more robust, muscular alpha male comes by and kicks sand in the face of pigeon-chested Mac and his girl. Mac complains to this tough. The macho man responds by grabbing him and telling him that he could hit him, but he's afraid that Mac would crumple up and blow away. Everyone laughs. Mac's humiliation is compounded when his girlfriend says in a sarcastic voice, 'Don't let it BOTHER you LITTLE man.' We next see Mac at home, impotently lashing out at a chair, deciding that he is prepared to gamble a 10¢ stamp to see if Charles Atlas can make good on his promise to make him a REAL man. Mac gets the book and works out. Mac is then miraculously transformed into the Athenian ideal of manhood, and stomps off to the beach where the bully is performing more sand-kicking tricks for his girlfriend (the subtext is, of course, not that the brute has stolen Mac's woman but that she has gone to him willingly). BAM! Mac knocks the other alpha male cold with a punch. 'Here's something I owe you!' says Mac. The tale ends with Mac's girl, her love renewed, feeling his flexed bicep and proclaiming, 'Oh Mac, you are a REAL man after all.' Overhead, the waving caption 'HERO OF THE BEACH' annoints Mac like a laurel wreath or a heavenly halo. Other men look at him with envy. Women look at him with lust. Can it be long before his faithless woman is cast off for another?

Jonathan Davis is Mac, the Everyman figure transformed from nerdish, bookish loser into Hero Of The Beach. This transformation is not one of brawn, but of cool, a cool that shows up his teenage tormentors as the fools they are, turning the tables on them, laughing as he watches them dance to his tune.

Korn's hometown of Bakersfield, California, is one of the many unlovely unsung cities across America where they don't set movies, where they don't write songs about it, where people don't want to run to in order to 'make it' and, when they leave, don't get too sentimental about it. Just go into any diner or bar and you will find a plethora of locals eager to describe to you in detail what a dull, mind-numbing hellhole the city is.

'There is NOTHING to do,' complain the kids. 'What isn't compulsory is illegal.' Adults complain that Bakersfield is a cultural desert as well as an actual one. Walking around, it looks like some David Lynchian town – conformist and resolutely mainstream on the surface, but festering with despair, darkness, sexual tension and occult forces just beneath.

Although the city changed a lot in the 1990s, with oil companies relocating many of their white-collar workers there from Texas, revitalising the downtown area around Western California Avenue, it still has a legacy of redneck ignorance, a reputation for police brutality and job opportunities for many that begin and end with a shift at the local Dairy Queen. New York it ain't.

As you drive in through the dun-coloured desert (the area is hit by periodic droughts, which often last for decades), passing the oil derricks, many of them rusting, you seem to leave the cultural vibrancy of Californian cities like San Diego, San Francisco and Los Angeles for a poorer, plainer America that seems to stretch all the way back to West Virginia. You can still recognise the country from John Steinbeck's *The Grapes Of Wrath*, the dustbowl America of the 1930s: Kern County was the gateway to California for the poor, dispossessed 'Oakies' fleeing ruin and depression in the heartland for the 'promised land'. For many of them, the promised land turned out to be a labour camp where they worked for slave wages. But the exodus from Oklahoma, Texas and Arkansas boosted the citizenship of Bakersfield, growing the city into a blue-collar metropolis, its labourers finding work in the oilfields, or on the farms of surrounding Kern County, an area larger than the entire states of Massachusetts, New Jersey or Hawaii.

The musical heritage of Bakersfield, and the surrounding towns and villages, is the hard-bitten cowboy romanticism of Buck Owens and the slicker '60s country of Merle Haggard, as well as the modern-traditionalism of 'New Country' superstar Dwight Yoakam.

'Bakersfield, it's the other home of country music,' Jonathan Davis of Korn tells me. 'It's called Nashville West. I did some of my tracks in Buck Owens' studio. I don't know, we got a weird upbringing. We're inbred Oakie guys.'

Bakersfield, also disparagingly referred to as 'the armpit of California', is an unlikely starting point for a contemporary American rock and roll phenomenon. Nirvana, who hailed from Aberdeen, Washington, helped to put the city of Seattle (where the band relocated) on the world's cultural map. The rise of regional American scenes, centred around college towns and 'third cities' has been one of the most interesting legacies of punk. It is safe to say, however, that the success of Korn will do nothing to make Bakersfield cool. Tourists will only come here by accident. There is no Starbucks waiting to spread a taste of Bakersfield around the world, unless the world develops a sudden taste for deep-fried meat.

Korn was formed in 1993 from members of two bands: SexArt and LAPD. Jonathan Davis sang in SexArt. LAPD included Fieldy, aka Reggie Arvizu, on bass, Brian 'Head' Welch (guitar), James 'Munky' Shaffer (guitar), and David Silveria, known only as David (drums). The bands crossed paths one night in Bakersfield when Munky and Brian were in a club where SexArt were performing. According to Munky, 'We were getting ready to leave, and just as we're walking out the door... Jon was the singer in that band, and we heard him sing, and me and Brian turned to each other and our jaws just...oh my God. And so we turned around and went back in and watched the whole set.' Later they asked him to join the band. Davis was unsure. He knew Brian from junior high and, although flattered by the offer to join their band, he weighed up whether he wanted to leave the band he was already in, if it would be disloyal to his SexArt bandmates. Then, as he told Jaan Uhelszki, a reporter for US music website *Addicted To Noise*, 'I went to my astrologer, my aunt's teacher, in Bakersfield. She told me about this band and told me I'd be dumb if I didn't get in; she totally predicted the whole thing. I have the tapes to prove it.'

Whether or not their success really was foretold in the stars, Korn were set to revolutionise and redefine hard rock in the aftermath of Kurt Cobain's suicide. Shaffer and Welch had spent years perfecting their twin-guitar attack, playing seven-stringed instruments for greater range, using their own unique tunings, giving Korn a unique, occasionally atonal, sound – perhaps the closest metal has come to the '12-tone' serialism of Arnold Schönberg. Fieldy adopted a hammer-thumb bass technique, which resembled a beefed-up version of the technique pioneered by progressive jazz musicians like Stanley Clarke in the 1970s, funk pioneer Bootsy Collins and metal-funk crossover bands like The Red Hot Chili Peppers in the 1990s. David's drumming was brutal and precise.

'We're presenting the new genre of heavy music,' Fieldy told an interviewer after their stint on the 1996 Lollapalooza tour. 'Old school metal is gone. I'm tired of all the sissy stuff on the radio. It's not rock and roll anymore. Nothing grabs you.'

But it was the raw, emotional voice of Korn's newfound singer that was their highly marketable unique selling point. Davis, a bagpipe-playing former coroner, has one of the most astonishing voices in rock and roll, a voice that goes from agonising suffering to ultra-violent threat and pleading in the space of a few bars. LAPD, as they were even after Davis joined, might have continued to eke out their career in the clubs and bars around southern California's semi-professional circuit were it not for a fortuitous connection with a then relatively unknown former guitarist and fledgling producer called Ross Robinson. Robinson had played in a band with Dave McClain, now of Machine Head fame, and at the time the nascent Korn were coming together, was struggling to work on the recording of songs by another emergent band: Fear Factory. Fear Factory signed on the strength of the demo he produced, but Robinson found himself cut out of any further involvement with the band, a situation that still angers him almost a decade later. At the time, Robinson started to work out in a gym so that if he ever met Fear Factory again he would be capable of beating them senseless!

Robinson and McClain's band Murdercar played with LAPD at some indeterminate point in the early '90s; he knew Munky – they had bonded – and was surprised to run into him again while the reshaped band with new singer Davis were playing at a club called the Coconut Teaser.

Robinson recalled in a Radio 1 interview, 'In the early '90s all the kids wanted to be Eddie Vedder or Alice In Chains. Korn were just way out there on their own. The first time I saw them I was, like, in tears. They came out and started playing...then when Jonathan came on wearing all this Robert Smith from The Cure make-up...'

Robinson stayed close to the band until they signed with Immortal (a division of Epic) after interest from a lot of major labels, including RCA and Atlantic. Immortal won the band over with their enthusiasm. Korn and Robinson set about recording the album at Indigo Ranch Studios, located outside Los Angeles in the Malibu Hills.

Korn was released in October 1994. 'It was done on my knees, I didn't know how to produce shit,' Robinson told UK website *Metal-Is*. 'It was a time in my life when I woke up; I stepped away from the anger, and directed it into music and art. That album gave me an outlet, it saved my life and it moved millions of people. That record was very important for me. And those guys stuck by me when all the big producers were coming and going, "Yeah, we're gonna do your band. Use that producer or that producer." They stuck by me and gave me a career. They're my fucking brothers, man. I'll never forget what they did for me.'

Robinson now feels that his part in creating the Korn sound has helped spawn a monster that he now wants no part of.

'We created a genre of music which today I think totally sucks,' said Robinson. 'I'd hate to do this now. I don't hate Korn, but I really dislike all the bands copying them. It's time for a change. At the time it was OK, but now it's not cool for me. I don't think it's good any more at all. Anything I can do to destroy that genre today I will, 'cause any band that copies it is pure garbage. Total garbage.'

Nevertheless, Korn's debut became a growing success, gradually propelling the band into the vacuum at the top of rock and roll's first division, selling 500,000 in its first year and nearly 2,000,000 to date. The band's debut was virtually ignored by the critics, by the increasingly powerful rock radio and by MTV, apart from 'Blind', the opening track, which was a minor hit. Korn toured incessantly, headlining smaller club venues and supporting 311, the then-emerging Marilyn Manson and Ozzy Osbourne on their tours, building up a hardcore following of skaters, punks, disaffected grunge fans and just kids who knew a good thing when they heard it.

Korn's high-energy 'detuned' sound struck a chord with this new generation of post-grunge teenagers, still disparagingly referred to as 'Generation X' by the mainstream media. They liked the aggression of the music and identified with what Davis talked about in the songs.

The skateboard subculture has been as important to punk and hard rock in America as surfers were to a previous generation. Just as the feelgood melodies, singalong harmonies and sunshine sentiments of The Beach Boys, Jan And Dean and The Surfaris suited a more laid-back, hedonistic Californian beach-based culture, so thrash metal, speed metal, hardcore rap and nu metal suited the more urban pursuit of skateboarding. Skate culture inhabited the borderline between sport and criminal activity; skaters were, and are, banned from many public spaces and harassed by law enforcement officials who prefer to corall them in designated skate parks. For the dedicated skater, however, only the streets and slopes of the urban jungle are a fitting playground. As with other semi-criminal subcultures, skaters had their own look, their own slang and their own graphic style inspired by graffiti and comic books. The look – fob chains, incredibly baggy jeans, baseball caps, training shoes, dreadlocks, body and facial piercings – dovetailed neatly with that of most of the nu metal bands. Look at early pictures of Limp Bizkit, The Deftones or Korn and it looks like they've come straight from the skate park.

Davis started in music young. His father, Rick, worked in a music store, he also worked in Buck Owens' recording studio. Jonathan says that he recorded there as 'revenge' against his father who was against his son following him into the music business. But it was almost a foregone conclusion for Jonathan. At the age of five, he was playing drums, learning piano and bagpipes (his Scottish grandmother also played the pipes and he was inspired to learn after hearing 'Amazing Grace' by The Royal Scots Dragoon Guards, an unlikely hit record in both the UK and the USA in 1972) while in high school. Success, they say, is the best revenge, but Jonathan is taking his revenge in other ways too. Nicknamed 'HIV' – 'My nickname. When I first got in the band, I was so skinny they said I had AIDS. So I got "HIV" tattooed on my arm' – the young Davis was a classic outsider: skinny, bookish and nerdy, not part of the high-school aristocracy of 'jocks' who played sports and made life miserable for those further down the pecking order. 'Faget', from Korn's self-titled debut album has occasionally been misconstrued as a homophobic statement, and in fact has become so for the bonehead element who rarely look beyond titles.

Further fuel was added to this rumour when it was explained that the name Korn was inspired by Jonathan overhearing two gay men at a party talking about 'rimming' (oral sex performed on the anus of another). One of them said that he had diarrhoea and excreted on his partner's face; when the partner opened his mouth, he found a corn kernel on his tongue. From then on, whenever he said the word *corn* to anyone, he would get close to puking. Hence the altered spelling, Korn with the reversed capital letter R in the middle, the way a child might spell it. (It's worth noting that there are a number of other versions of the origins of the band's name: one, that it is short for 'Kid Porn', strenuously denied by the band; two, that it is a play on Kern County; three, that it is an abbreviation of coroner, Jonathan's day job.)

Drummer David also changed the spelling of sponsor Jagermeister to 'Fagermeister' for one track, though Jonathan strenuously denies any accusations of homophobia, explaining the song thus: 'I wasn't in the cool crowd with all the jocks. I got called "faggot" a lot. If you're not in the "cool crowd", you get picked on, so that song is my revenge song – 'cos now all those jocks who used to call me a faggot come to our shows and jump up and down to "Faget" and I just laugh at them,' Davis told UK metal weekly *Kerrang!* in 1996.

'Faget' is more a statement of Jonathan's own alienation: 'Here I am different in this normal world/Why did you tease me? Made me feel upset/Fucking stereotypes feeding their heads/I am ugly/Please just go away.'

The bitterness and resentment in Korn's lyrics is almost entirely drawn from the ongoing autobiography of Davis, from his own personal experiences and from the darker side of life that he witnessed while working as a coroner. While charges against nu metal bands that they are wallowing in 'mom-and-pop anger' have also been levelled at Korn, such accusations are unfair. While Korn created the blueprint for many of these bands, the sentiments and the subjects of their songs are drawn from very real experience. There have been a few rock stars who had stints as gravediggers – Joe Strummer of The Clash, Ian Dury – and while a few death metallers would like to pretend that they are necrophiliacs, Davis is one of the few frontmen to have spent any time with his arms buried in human intestines.

And his 'mom-and-pop anger' is every bit as genuine and painful as that expressed by Kurt Cobain. Like many of his fans and many people of the baby-boomer generation, he is a product of divorce. His mother and father separated when he was three years old, his father remarrying when he was 12. He makes no bones about the fact that he hated his stepmother and feels he was abused by her.

'Daddy', the harrowing closing track on the first album, about the rape of a child, was mistakenly assumed to be about abuse that Jonathan had suffered. 'People think "Daddy" was written because my dad fucked me up the ass, but that's not what the song is about. It wasn't about my dad or my mom. When I was a kid I was being abused by someone else and I went to my parents and told them about it. They thought I was lying and joking around, so they never did shit about it. They didn't believe it was happening to their son,' Davis said in a *Kerrang!* interview.

But 'Kill You', on second album *Life Is Peachy*, was directed against his stepmother. 'I fucking hate that bitch. She's the most evil, fucked-up person I've met in my whole life. She hated my guts. She did everything she could to make my life hell. Like, when I was sick she'd feed me tea with tabasco, which is really hot pepper oil. She'd make me drink it by saying, "You have to burn that cold out, boy." Fucked-up shit like that. So every night when I'd go to sleep, I'd dream of killing that bitch. In some sick way I had a sexual fantasy about her, and I don't know what that stems from or why, but I always dreamt about fucking her and killing her,' he said.

Korn's second album showed a more diverse side to the band without sacrificing any of the aggression and anger of the first. It included a cover version of War's seminal early '70s street-funk hit 'Low Rider' on which Jonathan played bagpipes. The increasingly explicit connections with hip-hop were compounded by their cover version of Ice Cube's 'Wicked' (with Deftones frontman Chino on vocals): 'Hip-hop is heavy and full of emotion. I've never heard a wimpy hip-hop song.'

The album received mixed reviews ('Life is patchy,' sneered one critic) but went straight to Number Three in the *Billboard* album charts in its first week of release in 1996, and was eventually certified platinum by the RIAA.

Also produced by Ross Robinson, *Life Is Peachy* lacked some of the brutal impact of Korn's debut, though lyrically songs like 'Swallow' (about drug abuse) and the uncompromising naked misogyny of 'Kunt' showed that Davis and the band were still capable of courting controversy. Songs like 'ADIDAS', an acronym for 'All Day I Dream About Sex' as well as a nod to the Old Skool three-stripe footwear favoured by Run-DMC in the '80s (they paid similar homage on 'My Adidas'), also showed a band capable of taking themselves less seriously. Adidas, the sportswear company, sponsored Davis, providing him with stagewear in return for his endorsement.

Sponsorship had been creeping into rock and roll since the late 1980s, with brewers and soft drinks companies eager to reach that all-important teenage demographic. While many mainstream pop stars like Michael Jackson were happy to endorse Pepsi, to sing songs about it, to have their logo displayed prominently at shows and on tickets, and to appear in TV and cinema commercials for it, the punk and hippy legacy of metal and alternative rock made these artists less enthusiastic about such things. It smacked of sell-out and 'sucking corporate cock'. Bands may do deals with the companies who produce their instruments, like Zildjan drums, Fender guitars or Marshall amps (often credited on album covers), but are uncomfortable with other endorsements.

Yet Korn not only embraced Adidas, they mercilessly dumped them a few months later for a more advantageous deal with rival sportswear company Puma. A new attitude to sponsorship was emerging. Korn never compromised on their lyrics – their albums still proudly bore the Parental Advisory sticker. They saw nothing at all wrong with being associated with brands and, despite the growing anti-corporate movement in the 1990s, neither did the fans.

Korn's biggest year was to be 1998. Their third album *Follow The Leader* was their breakthrough release. The hit song 'Freak On A Leash' – a rant about the position of entertainers in the music business, equating them with prostitutes – won the MTV Music Video Award for the best music video of 1998. They also enjoyed two other hit singles that year with 'Got The Life' and 'All In The Family', a duet between Jonathan and Fred Durst of Limp Bizkit, the two trading insults back and forth ('You look like one of those dancers from the Hanson video'/'You little fairy/Smelling all your flowers/Nappy hairy chest, look it's Austin Powers!'/'Throwing rhymes at me like Vanilla Ice'/'You call yourself a singer/You're more like Jerry Springer/Your favorite band is Winger') the title a nod to the '70s sitcom about a reactionary father and his liberal hippy family. This third release held few surprises, but managed to consolidate the achievements of the first two, throwing out more accomplished songs that managed to be commercial without undermining the band's hardness and abrasiveness. Production was credited to Steve Thompson, Toby Wright and Korn, Ross Robinson having left the band's orbit for better things. Guest appearances other than that of Durst included Ice Cube, Tre Hardson from The Pharcyde and Cheech Marin (of '70s stoner comedians Cheech And Chong fame) on the 'hidden' track at the end. Again, despite generally disparaging reviews in the mainstream press, respected critics like *Rolling Stone*'s David Fricke were wheeled out to pronounce on the record. Fricke was enthusiastic: '*Follow The Leader* is...true to an older, vital hard-rock tradition of cleansing brutality and transcendent guitar choler – Blue Cheer's 1968 speed freak's delight, *Vincebus Eruptum*; early Metallica and very early Black Sabbath; the molten heave 'n' thump of Funkadelic's *Cosmic Slop*; the claustrophobic fury of Steve Albini's mid-'80s band Big Black. It may be the fact that Shaffer and Welch both play seven-string guitars, but there is an extra, weighty abrasion to their riffing that, at full throttle, seems to cleave the music in half, pressing everything else in the mix toward the margins. Silveria's *bona fide* disco beat is the sucker bait in "Got The Life" but it's the crisp crush of bass-and-dual-guitar menace that makes the track fat with tension. When the band abruptly switches from the cold, clipped chorus of "It's On" to the bright, Big Chord bridge, it's as if Korn have suddenly stepped out of their angst bunker into A-Bomb-white daylight.'

The album topped the US album charts. Also that year, a student who wore a Korn shirt to school in the Midwestern town of Zeeland, Michigan, was suspended because his principal said that Korn's lyrics were 'obscene'. The band responded by giving away free T-shirts outside the school, got the principal to overturn his position and got a lot of publicity for themselves.

The band capitalised on their fame by launching their own tour: Family Values. In the summer of 1998 they played with Limp Bizkit, Orgy and Ice Cube, a nu metal package show that rivalled the more traditional Ozzfest – launched by Black Sabbath frontman Ozzy Osbourne – and replacing the more broadly based Lollapalooza.

Korn also got involved in the fledgling Internet, launching *Korn TV* on their own website to give fans updates on their new album, live shows and sneak previews of new music, and to help knit together the solid community they were building. Davis certainly recognised the potential held by the Internet as a medium, telling me at the time, 'I am online every night, talking to fans, posting replies on message boards. They want to know about us and they want me to help them with their problems. That's good, that's flattering and I do what I can. It shows that they relate to what I'm singing about. But it's important to us that we can reach out to them and know what they're thinking. We can get our music out to them. One day it might be the way we do our new albums.'

In 1999 Davis collected the first 'Silicon CD' award for *Follow The Leader* after it was certified as an album among the most frequently played on fans' computers worldwide. (Internet database company CDDB provides information about CD titles for more than 200 different software applications for playing sound files, including RealJukebox and Winamp. The disc-recognition technology CDDB invented 'spies' on users while they are online and its database compiles charts representing those albums being played most often.)

Having achieved 'rock and roll superpower' status, Korn consolidated that success in 1999 with their biggest-selling album yet. The title, *Issues*, bordered on self-parody and, despite occasional manifestations, Korn's failing is that they were, at times, found to be lacking a sense of humour.

Critics had never supported the band, so the reviews that *Issues* received could hardly be called a backlash. *Rolling Stone*'s Jon Pareles said, '...there's a sense, subtle but unmistakable, that the band has started to seek a formula. The lyrics revisit thrice-plowed ground: father–son warfare, borderline psychosis, begging, falling, rape, beatings, pain. Davis used to blurt private details alongside general complaints, but *Issues* stays with non-revelations like, "There's so much shit around me" and "We crumble under pressure". Korn's new subject – and it's not promising – is fame. Davis flip-flops between moaning about the hollowness of it all and kissing up to fans.' It was, as English music weekly *NME* said, '...high on low self-esteem and heavy on rage'.

Opening with the melancholy skirl of the pipes and the wistful refrain 'All I want in life is to be happy', *Issues* is a far more accomplished record than its predecessor and, despite the rock/rap cliché now firmly established as *the* major cliché of the late 1990s, it is actually the Korn album that employs this the least. Employing an orchestra – the curse of the '90s; slap a string section on something to make it sound 'sophisticated' – as well as some very tight harmonies on tracks like 'Falling Away' (a technique imitated immediately by Korn's follower bands), the album is generally felt, even by fans, to represent a bit of a hiatus.

Ensconced in the studio working on their fifth record with producer Michael Beinhorn (whose previous credits include Marilyn Manson and Hole), Korn are under pressure – not least from themselves – to deliver something as astonishing as their debut or as populist as *Follow The Leader*. The pressure is on not least because of the sheer number of identikit Korn bands who have sprung up in their wake, bands who have listened closely and lifted the formula for their own. All the major labels have their token nu metal acts and in 2001 a band called Adema was at the centre of a fierce bidding war before signing with Arista. Adema's lead singer Mark Chavez is the half-brother of Jonathan Davis.

Korn opened a lot of doors for a lot of bands; indeed, the story of nu metal is the story of bands passing a baton like relay runners and, despite all the bitching, there is a lot of co-operation along with the ruthless competition. In 1994, while still on the way up, Korn played in Jacksonville, Florida. The lead singer of another band on the bill was working there as a tattooist. After the show Fieldy and Head stopped by for some skin art at the singer's parlour. The three bonded and became friends. The next time Korn played there, the tattooist gave them a demo of his band, which Korn promised to pass on to Ross Robinson. Robinson loved the demo. The tattooist was Fred Durst and the band was Limp Bizkit.

3 Whiggers With Attitude
Limp Bizkit

In July 1999, an attempt to re-stage the legendary Woodstock Festival 30 years on was held in upstate New York. The original festival – billed as 'three days of love, peace and good music' – featured Jimi Hendrix, Jefferson Airplane, Country Joe And The Fish and a veritable who's who of late-'60s rock, folk and jazz. It was the culmination of the idealism of the '60s, the anti-war movement, the idea that the young generation could all get together and build a better world. It was a dream that would be brutally shattered a few weeks later on the west coast at Altamount when Hell's Angels stabbed a young black man to death during The Rolling Stones' set at a similar festival. There was little sense of idealism about Woodstock '99; the organisers made gestures to the usual causes – including, ironically as it turned out, the Rape Crisis Helpline – but the bottom line was that Woodstock '99 was about turning a buck. It seemed to be a celebration of corporate sponsorship, with company logos replacing peace symbols. The poisonous atmosphere at the festival was exacerbated by the availability of drugs and booze, coupled with a sporadic security presence. While the first Woodstock had been enjoyed through a haze of marijuana smoke with only the notorious 'brown acid' to mar the hippies' mellow vibe, Woodstock '99 was awash with beer, ecstacy, amphetamines, crack and cocaine. When the first bloodied casualties were dragged out of the mosh pit in front of the stage, it was clear that this was about anything but 'love and peace'.

The festival ended with a riot; fans turned over cars, looted and burned concession stands, and destroyed ATM machines. They eventually had to be dispersed by riot police. After the festival ended there came reports that a woman had been horribly gang-raped in front of the stage. The band who were playing at the time were Limp Bizkit and there are still those who accuse them of virtually sparking off the whole ugly incident. Durst was criticised for encouraging the volatile crowd, inciting them to 'break stuff', though in fact their set took place almost 24 hours before the closing riot. The burgeoning chaos – there were numerous injuries in addition to the rape – forced festival organisers to pull the plug in the middle of their set. Durst later told music website *Dotmusic*, 'We looked out in front of us and there's 100,000 people going off, looking like they're having a blast. The sun is setting, you can't believe what's happening, there's cameras in your face... People are surfing on plywood and you're like, "Wow! That's amazing!" You get off stage and you're like, "Holy shit that was amazing! See all those people having a blast?" The next thing you know, "You guys ruined Woodstock!" We were performing, we weren't inciting riots. But, it's easy to point the finger at us and we kinda like that, we like that it's your easiest way out. I'll be your scapegoat.'

In 1994, following an ill-advised stint in the Navy and a 30-day jail sentence for assaulting his ex-wife's lover, Fred Durst decided to form a band. Whether intentional or not, the group he formed with guitarist Wes Borland, drummer John Otto, bassist Sam Rivers and – eventually – ex-House Of Pain turntablist DJ Lethal was about more than just the music. The intense blend of hip-hop, metal and punk it created was almost secondary to the lifestyle it advocated: celebrity parties, high-profile arrests, public feuds with other bands and an aggressively don't-give-a-fuck attitude to anyone who wanted to put them down. They revelled in it.

There has always been a strain of this brat behaviour in American rock, and some have pointed out that their story is almost like a re-run of the early Beastie Boys story from the mid 1980s. And occasionally this is a welcome antidote to the pomposity, the inflated self-importance and the furrow-browed seriousness of rock and roll. Even their mentors, Korn, seemed to have had a bit of a humour bypass. The music may have been fresh, but they were still not so far removed from the hand-wringing college rock set, the Pearl Jams and Smashing Pumpkins who worried about saving rainforests and Tibetans and other worthy causes. Not that they didn't think that life sucked; they just dealt with it in lines like 'I did it all for the nookie.../So you can take that cookie/And stick it up your...yeah!' ('Nookie' from second album *Significant Other*). They have been singled out as the cause of everything from teenage suicides and killings – in the wake of the Columbine shootings in 1999, there were reporters desperate to establish a link between the band and the deranged high-school gun-rampage killers – to the decline of standards in rock and roll. They are everybody's scapegoat. If Limp Bizkit did not exist, it would be necessary to invent them.

'I've sinned so many ways it's unbelievable. I've robbed stores. I've had plenty of sex. I've lied terribly. I've cheated. I've been greedy. I've lusted. Everything. I've done it all. I need some support and help from above now. I grew up as a rebellious kid who was always locked up in his room. When I got out, I wasn't bad, I just didn't know what was right or wrong. My dad was an adoptive dad – we didn't get along that killer. I have another brother that's his son. My mom and I were always confronting. It was real easy for me to snap on my mom and for her to snap on me. It was just a weird thing,' confessed Fred Durst, eager to nail his broken-home credentials to the mast. Limp Bizkit may not have been his redemption – despite his professed Christianity, Durst remains a high-profile hellraiser of the old school – but they were his salvation. His life could have been that of millions of other blue-collar white American males, trapped in unemployment and dead-end jobs in nowhere towns and cities, growing bitter without a clue as to what to do about it. Instead, Durst transformed himself in into America's greatest modern 'white trash' superstar, a lowbrow renaissance man, a spokesman for a generation, a brat icon, like a real-life Bart Simpson who has reached his 30s relatively unaffected by adulthood. With his red baseball cap worn back to front – allegedly to hide his unfortunate male pattern baldness – his low-slung baggy jeans with fob chain and big trainers, Fred looks like a grown man pretending to be a white suburban teenager pretending to be a bad-ass ghetto pimp from some fantasy blaxploitation world. He's as likely to be photographed for the celebrity gossip columns of *Hello*, *USA Today* or *Playboy* as he is for features in *Rolling Stone*, *Alternative Press* or *Spin*.

Limp Bizkit are, by their own admission, the band that everyone loves to hate. And they have plenty of 'haters' out there prepared to oblige them. 'There is so much Hatorade being drunk out there,' Durst wrote in a message on the band's official website in 2001. 'Every magazine, paper, band, etc is on a Limp-hating rampage and it is really giving us the fire. We have so much built up inside and we wanna let it all out on the new album.'

For every fan site you find on the Internet dedicated to the band, there is almost an equal number dedicated to the proposition that 'Limp Bizkit Sucks'.

One rant seems to sum up what it is that riles people about Bizkit, and particularly about Durst: 'Limp Bizkit and Fred Durst make up one terrible band. Fred durst is just a loser who thinks he's a black 'gansta' from the inner city (or Eminem – same difference). I don't understand how you can take anything this pathedic man says seriously. He trys to act so extremely tough and whatnot by swearing 5–6 times in one line and screaming of violence and how he "...packs a chainsaw..." GIVE ME A BREAK. This guy's a wuss. First off, what does he accomplish by dropping the "F-bomb" constantly in almost every line more than once. It gets sad after a while. Have of the time he just throws the word in to make himself seem tough even though the word makes no sense whatsoever in what he's trying to say. Hey Fred... IT'S

NOT WORKING. Also, what's the deal with him doing it all for a "nookie". The only way I can see him doing this is that if a nookie symbolizes money. The sellout is only on MTV every other day promoting another one of his poor quality product that were made for "the nookie" (or money because he knows his fans will purchase and love any of the trash he puts out)' (quoted verbatim from *AntiBizkit* at http://www.angelfire.com/rock/Static7/limpbad.html).

It was hard to find critics with anything positive to say about the band's first three albums; even the good reviews seemed to be shot through with distaste. 'They badly want to be credible but desperately want to repeat the 1.5 million-selling success of their debut album and the result is a muddle of hardcore hip-hop and limp radio-friendly choruses. The guys at MTV may be impressed. But we aren't,' sneered the *NME* in its review of second album *Significant Other*.

'*Significant Other* may be a problem for Limp Bizkit, who bill themselves as the band you love to hate. It could also be a problem for their conditioned audience – not to mention the rest of us, who might find the idea of liking this obnoxious band unpleasant. But at this point, hating them seems a little disingenuous. They're actually (gulp) good,' wrote Lorraine Ali – as if through gritted teeth – in *Rolling Stone*.

'The jury's still out,' concluded Britain's 'dadrock' bible *Q* magazine, the same week that the album rocketed into the charts at Number One. With 25,000,000 record sales worldwide and growing, Durst's slightly retarded ageing skater persona and his band's volume-OD thrash obviously strike a chord with at least a few members of the public.

A fan of Kiss, Blondie, Eric B And Rakim, Suicidal Tendencies, Smashing Pumpkins and Tool, Fred became a punk and got into rap at the same time in the early 1980s, DJing occasionally, never really thinking much about making music himself. Durst, who was born and raised in Gastonia, North Carolina, moved to Jacksonville,

Florida, in his late teens. The state of Florida has a mixed rock and roll heritage; death metal bands like Obituary and Deicide were based here around Miami's Morrisound studio in the 1990s, but Jacksonville's other famous sons were redneck rockers Lynyrd Skynyrd, whose performances took place under the Confederate stars and bars flag, and whose 'Sweet Home Alabama' was an anthem of southern pride, coming while memories of Klan attacks on black churches, and Dixieland cops attacking civil rights marchers with firehoses, batons and dogs were still fresh in people's minds, forging a new kind of rock and roll. If the '60s radicalised rock music, Skynyrd helped make it reactionary.

Like Jonathan Davis, Durst's childhood was troubled, though Fred was less of a sensitive soul: school, he confesses, 'was like a social event for me. It was a place to skateboard and rap and beatbox and breakdance.'

Putting together a band with a jazz-trained drummer, a funk-sussed bass player and a guitarist who commanded a great deal of respect among Florida's punk/metal cognoscenti, 'I wanted the perfect balance between hip-hop, alternative rock, everything I was into,' he said.

If Fred is the public face of Limp Bizkit, with an unrivalled talent for self-promotion and soundbite philosophy, then Wes Borland has been the musical talent, the man responsible for the real meat of the Limp Bizkit sound. Whether the band will be able to survive the departure of Borland – who quit the group in October of 2001 after a few months of speculation – remains to be seen. The band played their first gig in Jacksonville in 1995, a show with Korn who, as previously noted, struck up a relationship with the band when Fieldy and Head went back to Fred's place to get tattooed. Ross Robinson was immediately enthusiastic about the demo, passed on by Korn, and the buzz around the band started to grow. Durst, famously, spent hours on the phone every day, calling up record companies.

'I was acting like I was my own manager on the phone,' Durst said in 1997. 'I'd change my voice and I'd change my name and I was talking shit to all these record companies. Everybody. Just bull. Crap. Not knowing a thing about the industry, but they were believing me because I'm a good bullshitter. Some lapped it up. I thought God they MUST see through this. Then I really needed management because people were flying out to see us and there was no one here to talk to.' Finally Jordan Schur, CEO and A&R man at independent label Flip records, signed the band.

It was a foregone conclusion that Ross Robinson would produce the record that eventually became *Three Dollar Bill, Yall$*, though the group was still not in its final shape. Towards the end of 1995 they went on tour with House Of Pain, a white Irish-American hip-hop band.

House Of Pain were one of the pioneering groups that tried to cross over into the hip-hop market, rather than being a 'novelty act'. In many ways they are the band who cleared the way for Eminem and Kid Rock, establishing the idea that white rappers were anything other than Vanilla Ice-style 'fake-hop' pop acts. Produced by Cypress Hill's DJ Muggs, they enjoyed a hit debut album but were unable to capitalise on this success. By the time they went out with Limp Bizkit, House Of Pain were saddled with an album called *Truth Crushed To Earth Shall Rise Again*, which was virtually ignored by their record company and a rapidly dwindling fanbase. Frontman Everlast went on to a relatively successful solo career while DJ Lethal (aka Leor DiMant) struck up a relationship with Limp Bizkit and joined the band.

With a line-up that now included a DJ cutting up and scratching records and breakbeats onstage, Limp Bizkit looked like few other American heavy rock bands. Although many other bands – most notably Linkin Park – would soon adopt this blueprint, the addition of the DJ added a whole new dimension to the guitar, bass, drums and vocals line-up of rock and roll bands from Elvis Presley onwards.

The sound on *Three Dollar Bill, Yall$* was more Ross Robinson's trademarked raw noise, detuned and cranked up high than the more listener-friendly mosh of follow-up *Significant Other* or 2000's *Chocolate Starfish And The Hotdog Flavored Water*. The lyrics were a combination of beer-addled frat-boy humour, aggression aimed at the world (and possibly some ex-girlfriend) in general and an expression of gratitude to other bands like Fear Factory, The Deftones, Korn on 'Field Dog' and House Of Pain on 'Indigo Flow' ('Yo what up/got Christian and Dino in the house/Fear Factory action kick off this new joint/here for all my homies/separating the true breeds my friends and my family/had the vision when the bounds now it's blowing up/props to the Field Dog/with/the funk through the campaign gold records and Champaign/Everlast for the tour on St Paddy's/Chino, man we had a blast with ya/Deftones rock that microphones/daily props to the maestro Ross you're an angel'). It was picked up by the metal press and rock radio, and became a slow if steady seller. Tours with Faith No More and Primus – both pioneers of the sound Limp Bizkit were building on – helped to nudge them further into the consciousness of the rock and roll public. But it was their slightly cheesy cover of George Michael's 'Faith' that won them their first hit. This was compounded by their Stakhanovite approach to touring in the wake of the record; Ozzfest and Family Values, two juggernauts on the US live scene followed. They stole Ozzfest with their stage set, a gigantic filthy toilet, and the Family Values show was equally over the top, like a live-action *Star Wars*. Limp Bizkit were also, it seemed, prepared to do anything to get on MTV, from playing on their spring break special to doing their New Year's Eve show. They or their videos were seldom off the screen in 1998.

A storm erupted over the fact that the band's label, Interscope (which had absorbed indie label Flip), was paying radio stations to play its records. A Portland, Oregon, station was paid US$5000 for five weeks' guaranteed play of Limp Bizkit's single 'Counterfeit'. This 'pay for play' scandal made the front page of the *New York Times* and brought back memories of the payola scandals of the

1960s when DJs such as Alan Freed (the man who actually coined the term 'rock and roll', and promoted it tirelessly throughout the 1950s) were indicted and disgraced. The practice was not actually illegal, however, because before the song was played it was preceded by the taped announcement, 'The song you are about to hear is sponsored by Flip/Interscope.' Only one radio station and a minuscule amount of money was involved, and the overall contribution to Limp Bizkit's national and international success was negligible, though it seemed to indicate that the band were prepared to play dirty to break their music.

One-time mentor Ross Robinson, who fell out with the band after turning down the opportunity to produce their second album, berated Fred in an interview with *NME* in December 2000, comparing him to pop queen Britney Spears: 'Fred's willing to put his face in front of every camera and that's pretty rare for bands because they get tired of it. He's always out there. He's willing to do whatever it takes and so is she. I don't know, maybe it's a race to sell more records. Y'know, that's their game. It can't last too much longer, but if it does, good for them.'

The band started work on second album *Significant Other* with producer Terry Date, who had previously worked with metal giants Pantera and White Zombie. While their debut album was hardly a sweetness-and-light release, their second was shot through with bitterness against a former girlfriend. 'It's a record about betrayal,' Fred told MTV. 'I guess I ask for it sometimes. The way I get treated by back-stabbing friends and girls, it's probably due to my own actions.'

On 'Nookie', Fred sings 'I came into the world as a reject/Look into these eyes/Then you'll see the size of the flames/That are pullin' on my past/Burnin' on my brain/Everyone that burns has to learn from the pain/Hey, I think about the day/My girlie ran away with my pay/When fellas came to play/Now she's stuck with my homies that she fucked/And I'm just a sucker with a lump in my throat.' 'Trust', one of the album's strongest tracks, starts with a howl of 'Backstabber! Two-faced low-life! It's time to step up to the plate! One-two-one-two – what the fuck ya gonna do?', berating a friend who has betrayed him, finishing up with 'I don't trust anybody cuz nobody trust me/Never gonna trust anybody And that's the way it's gonna be.'

In the months after Woodstock '99, Limp Bizkit were held up as an example of a new misogynous strain in rock, with journalists citing everything from the lyrics on *Significant Other* to the band's decidedly pre-feminist attitude to women. Longtime gay activist and music industry executive Jim Fouratt published a scathing editorial in *Billboard* magazine attacking the band along with Eminem, claiming that their music 'propels their anger at women, gays, each other, and the people perceived to have power. Eminem fits right into the stupid, hateful rhetoric of Limp Bizkit, who choose to rip off Rage Against The Machine and substitute adolescent male angst for a potent political message'.

Writing in the January 2000 issue of *Spin*, Charles Aaron cited Eminem, Korn and Limp Bizkit as being culpable in the Woodstock '99 rape/riot: 'What made Woodstock the year's watershed event was its thunderous desire to establish rock, angry-white-rap-style, as the voice of defiant youth. Tragically, that came at the expense of anyone, particularly women, who got in the way.'

Aaron also suggested that Bizkit represented a reaction against the 'feminisation' of rock in the early 1990s, a period dominated by artists like Alanis Morissette, Hole and 'sensitive' males like Kurt Cobain.

This was echoed by Corin Tucker of all-woman band Sleater Kinney in an interview with US website *Snowball*: '1999 saw a lot of ugly changes in rock, particularly a backlash against the success that women have had in mainstream rock. For example: the rapes and sexual assault that happened at Woodstock, along with signs from the audience like "Show me your tits" or the popularity of bands like Insane Clown Posse or Limp Bizkit that have misogynist lyrics. In a way, I see it as a more blatant power struggle for recognition within the capitalist corporate world. With the massive success of Lilith Fair, Alanis Morissette and The Spice Girls, no one can dispute the selling power of female rock acts, but some people are not happy about it.'

Certainly Limp Bizkit were part of a wider movement that was a definite reaction to 'sensitivity' and the 'new man', and which was uncomfortable with women calling the shots. It was apparent in the success of men's magazines like *Maxim* and *Loaded*, the films of Adam Sandler and the 'ironic' rediscovery of 'swinger' culture, the Rat Pack, Las Vegas, and nostalgia for old-school pornography in films like *Boogie Nights* and *The People vs Larry Flynt*.

But Fred Durst modelled himself on rappers like Snoop Dogg, Tupac Shakur, Ice-T, Ice Cube, Method Man and Puff Daddy, who employed the image of pimps, drug dealers and gangsters as an empowering one. Women were 'hos', 'bitches' and 'sluts', and took part in live rap shows as go-go dancers in cages. White liberals have always had a problem with attacking the 'macho' myths in black culture; as white males, however, Eminem and Fred Durst were softer targets. Not that Limp Bizkit didn't set themselves up for liberal brickbats. Their Ladies' Night In Cambodia tour admitted the first 200 women to turn up free.

Courtney Love, who briefly dated Fred Durst, said at a feminist music conference, 'Fred is always calling me up and saying that he wants to respect women but he doesn't know how to go about it. I tell him "Fred, for starters you don't hold your birthday party at the Playboy Mansion."'

Despite this, or even because of this, *Significant Other* was a *Zeitgeist*-defining record. It sold a remarkable half-million copies in its first week of release and for a time at the end of 1999 it seemed to be impossible to avoid. Limp Bizkit took a stand in favour of Napster, the file-sharing protocol fans used to exchange MP3 files all over the world. Metallica and Dr Dre were two of the high-profile artists who had joined a Recording Industry Association of America (RIAA) action attacking the service,

Metallica actually serving injunctions taking their own fans – most of them teenagers – to court. Limp Bizkit went out on the road on a Napster-sponsored free tour.

'A lot of labels like to have, like, a dictatorship going on, controlling everything, and it's just not where we're at with our label, fortunately,' Durst told *MTV News*. 'They're not taking either side, because they're in limbo, going, "I wonder, what is the outcome of this?" Everyone's having to conform with the future. It's just happening in every single way all the time. It's just becoming this thing that's unstoppable. Things are just insane, like the technology, the cars, the phones, the homes, the computers, Internet, watches, everything, the pagers... It's all just going there, and they're all trying to figure out ways to make it more convenient, and to make it new. There's just people not stopping it. Our fans on the Internet and doing their thing, they're still our fans and coming to the shows. They're supporting us. They're getting our record.'

Durst was of the opinion that Napster was a great way for fans to sample an album before buying it. 'I would think the only people worried about that are people that are really worried about their bank accounts. The Internet is here, and anybody trying to fight that, which would be people who are living by certain standards and practices of the record industry – those are the only people who are scared and threatened,' Durst said at a press conference to launch the tour.

The tour, though controversial (disgruntled fans hurled bottles at police and security in Illinois after the first-come-first-served free tickets ran out), won the band a few friends among fans and in the media, though Napster succumbed to an injunction passed by a California court and, though it still survives, is now a drastically reduced service. Yet if any of their detractors believed that Limp Bizkit were another passing fad who would be back flipping burgers before anyone missed them, their third album would prove them so wrong.

Limp Bizkit and Fred Durst seemed to bestride the globe like a colossus in baggy pants. Durst was offered the chance to direct a major motion picture, *Nature's Cure*, with help from David Fincher (*Se7en*, *Alien III*, *The Game*) while 'Take A Look Around', Bizkit's contribution to the soundtrack of *Mission Impossible II*, had fans wet with anticipation for the new album.

Chocolate Starfish And The Hotdog Flavored Water echoes David Bowie's *The Rise And Fall Of Ziggy Stardust And The Spiders From Mars* and Eminem's *The Real Slim Shady* in that Chocolate Starfish (a slang term for anus, as it happens) was an alter-ego that Fred Durst created for himself. Whether this was insecurity on Durst's part – a way to distance himself from the more obnoxious sentiments that had him lambasted on the previous two albums – or an unsuccessful gimmick is unclear. Certainly he never really made a great deal of it and the 1,054,511 punters who bought their copies in the first week didn't seem to care either. The album featured guest appearances from troubled Stone Temple Pilots singer Scott Weiland, the Wu-Tang Clan's Method Man, Red Man, DMX, Xibit and pop-star-turned-movie-star Mark 'Markey Mark' Wahlberg, and pulled out all stops in terms of creating hook-laden pop songs tailor-made for radio, MTV videos and rabble-rousing live performances. Songs like 'My Generation' were more focused and even more articulate expressions of discontent: 'Generation X/Generation Strange/Sun don't even shine through our window pain/So go ahead and talk shit/Talk shit about me/Go ahead and talk shit/About my g-g-generation.'

Fred also made a meal of his tedious slanging match with Nine Inch Nails frontman Trent Reznor. Reznor attacked Durst in the pages of UK weekly *Kerrang!* magazine: 'It's one thing if you know your place but it's another thing when you think you're David Bowie after you've stayed up all night to write a song called "Break Stuff". I mean, Fred Durst probably spelt the word "break" wrong the first couple of times.' Durst retaliated, 'Trent Reznor must think of me every day. I must take up 80 per cent of his life. It sucks for somebody to hate someone they don't even know for no reason.'

Ironically, Durst – taken on to the board of Interscope in 2000 – was now Reznor's boss, since Nine Inch Nails' label TVT was now a subsidiary of Interscope. Durst got the last word on 'Hotdog', the opening track of his new album, parodying the dark lord of negativity's own words over a Nine Inch Nails sample from 'Closer'. 'You want to fuck me like an animal, you want to burn me from the inside, you like to think I'm a perfect drug, just know that nothing you do will bring you closer to me,' Fred sneers.

Durst was now one of the scene's major players; as an executive at Interscope and as owner of his own label, Flawless, the much-reviled Durst proved himself to be an adept A&R scout, a mover and shaker on behalf of others, which belied his image as some pig-ignorant money-grubbing redneck. He was instrumental in getting fellow Jacksonville band Cold signed to Flip records and also, as we shall see in the next chapter, in shaping and guiding the career of a young New England band called Staind, who are now a major band in their own right. Flawless released the *Family Values* live album as well as the debut by Limp guitarist Wes Borland's side project Big Dumb Band, and signed a band called Puddle Of Mudd who have already sold half a million copies of their debut album *Come Clean*. He also signed a young rapper from Las Vegas called Swish and another band called Sinisstar. None of these bands has much of a resemblance to Limp Bizkit yet all have enormous commercial potential in their own right.

Again, the really successful movers and shakers in hip-hop, from Dr Dre to Sean 'Puffy' Combs, have all built their own empires with other artists, taking protégés and moulding them, putting something back into the community that spawned them. Fred Durst and Limp Bizkit may be the scapegoat for a lot of people, but ultimately this brand of enlightened self-interest, helping others up the ladder, may be their greatest legacy – like a co-operation virus. It has to be good for music. Actor Ben Stiller – Fred Durst's showbiz bud – rambles over the outro to *Chocolate Starfish And The Hotdog*

Flavored Water, 'Who else could take rap, hip-hop, thrash, punk, metal, take it, throw it in a can, and come out with something that wasn't fertiliser?'

Who indeed?

4 Generation Next
Staind

Staind are part of nu metal's second generation. Protégés of Fred Durst, they have wisely avoided the Korn-derived formula that made Limp Bizkit massive. There's no rap, no onstage DJ, no dreads and no 'white gangsta' stylings. *Break The Cycle* shot to Number One on the US album charts and everyone from *Rolling Stone* magazine – which put the band on its cover – to the countless critics on local newspapers and magazines across America was standing in line looking for insights into the band, as if they were being handed out in a goody bag along with a free T-shirt and a complementary copy of the CD. Staind were blessed and cursed around July 2001 with being flavour of the month. But as Fred Durst kept on pointing out to the band, just when you think you have the rock and roll game figured out, and you think you're big and tough enough to play for keeps, 'they' are likely to change the rules on you, suddenly and without warning.

Staind's live performance has been honed by almost seven years of relentless gigging around the New England club scene and touring on packages with other bands. They formed as a covers band in 1995 after a chance meeting between Mike Mushok and Aaron Lewis at a Christmas party. They built up a reputation around New England as a solid live outfit. It's possible the band would have progressed if left to their own devices – Mushok and Lewis are driven and ambitious individuals – but the intervention of Fred Durst certainly helped them on their way. In October 1997 Staind supported Limp Bizkit in Hartford. Just before Staind were set to take the stage, Fred Durst stormed up to the band holding a copy of their self-produced debut CD *Tormented*. The cover art – which the band now admit was naïve – featured a crucified (upside-down) Barbie doll with a knife through her. Durst accused Staind of worshipping Satan and tried to have them removed from the bill. 'I just explained the way it was,' Mike Mushok said in an interview years later. 'He [Durst] said, "You guys are whack!" and just yelled at us. I tried to get him to calm down and explained that it was supposed to depict this person who seemed normal going through a difficult time, but he had this place where he went where he did all this whacked-out stuff. That was supposed to be his room. It's where he went to get away from everybody. It was just someone who had lost belief in everything. It was not supposed to be this big religious thing, but it came out that way because the Bible was the most shocking image. We had to move back the CD release party because four different places would not print the CD cover.'

Staind played that night anyway and Durst wound up being so impressed that he invited them to do some recording with him and fellow Bizkit, DJ Lethal, at their Jacksonville studio. A few months later, Durst got Staind signed to Flip and an appearance at the party to celebrate Limp Bizkit's debut album *Three Dollar Bill, Yall$* being awarded a gold record in 1998.

Staind's Flip/Elektra debut, *Dysfunction*, was released in 1999; they played the Family Values tour with Method Man and Red Man, Run-DMC, Mobb Deep, Primus, Korn and Limp Bizkit. Staind broadened their audience and built lasting relationships with Korn and Limp Bizkit. Korn took Staind on the road with them for their Sick And Twisted tour in 2000. Fred Durst directed the video for third single 'Home' and they landed a headlining slot on MTV's Return Of The Rock tour. Staind are managed by The Firm, the same company that handles Limp Bizkit (as well as Backstreet

Boys, Korn, Orgy and Michael Jackson). Terry Date, who produced Limp Bizkit's breakthrough second album *Significant Other*, also produced *Break the Cycle*.

But perhaps it was Lewis and Durst's duet on 'Outside' during the 1999 Family Values tour that contributed most to Staind's leg-up to popular acclaim. An acoustic version of the song, it became the highlight of the Family Values tour and was included at the last minute as a bonus track on the live album released by Durst's record company, Flawless. Rock radio stations picked up on the track almost as soon as the album was released. Limp Bizkit were, by this time, superstars and Staind were seen as the 'anointed ones' who would follow them. The song topped the *Billboard* charts as well as rock charts, and paved the way for *Break The Cycle*.

Despite their massive overnight popularity, Staind are another band who have fallen foul of the critics. The *NME* dismissed *Break The Cycle* with a derisory score of two out of ten. 'For those who grew up to the sound of Nirvana, there's been nothing quite as spirit-crushingly miserable as the grunge hangover – a refugee line of tousle-haired slackers shivering along the corporate gangplank, clutching at dimes, all the while praying their "alternative" cover doesn't slip.' In his review, Louis Pattison wrote, 'We owe it to nu metal for hammering the final nail into grunge's coffin. But it hasn't been enough. On *Break The Cycle*, the Ghost Of Corporate Grunge shrugs off the old plaid shirt, pulls on the box-fresh hoodie, and rebrands itself as the Angst Of A New Generation... *Break The Cycle* is nu metal as envisaged by Tipper Gore – 14 tracks of parent-friendly grunge-flavoured soft rock that make Creed sound like GG Allin.' Even the normally more enthusiastic metal magazines have been slightly disparaging about Staind; happy for them to grace their covers while dismissing the music as 'secondhand Deftones'. Inevitably, there are others who unfavourably compare the Terry Date-produced *Break The Cycle* to the rawer, less commercial early work.

It is a common theme with all the 'Nu' generation of bands that there is a huge gulf between the opinions of the critics and the opinions of the fans. This, to a certain extent, has always been the case: Black Sabbath, Led Zeppelin and Deep Purple were all lambasted during their heyday. And it's not just rock and roll – any form of popular entertainment creates a vast tide of critical hostility. As one commentator wrote of the reaction to the films of Laurel And Hardy in the 1920s and 1930s, 'Nobody loved them except the public.'

Perhaps this is because music journalists see the music business up close; they see how the 'industry' works. Any illusions that a band can come out of nowhere armed only with great songs and win over the whole world with the power of that music are blown away after only a cursory glimpse into the deal-making world of entertainment. Music is made, marketed, sold and bought in much the same way as soap powder. It isn't that there was some kind of golden age in the past when this wasn't the case; it's just that they do it better today. (We'll look more at the clash between perceived authenticity and phoniness when we discuss Linkin Park in a later chapter.)

Staind followed a traditional rock and roll route of playing gigs wherever and whenever they could set up their gear, and winning over fans who would spread the news by word of mouth, bringing along a couple of friends the next time the band played. It worked for Elvis, The Beatles and Black Sabbath – it's just that today they call that sort of thing 'viral marketing'.

Jordan Schur, president of Flip records, who signed Staind on Fred Durst's recommendation in 1998 said, 'We see this band spreading their music on a street level and letting people discover it before radio and MTV.' To some extent that is exactly what happened. When I flew out to see the band in May 2001, however, it was clear that there was a ground-level fanbase that had been built up by incessant touring. Many of the kids who had come to see the band had caught them several times over the past couple of years (not hard in the New England area). But it was also clear that there was a hyperactive industry working around them that was literally ramming the band to the top. The band's management company, The Firm, is one of the biggest entertainment companies in the world and doesn't, as a matter of course, have too many failures on its books.

Staind, fresh from the Wake The Fuck Up tour with Godsmack in mid 2001, were still a phenomenon waiting to happen, though nobody seemed to be in any doubt that the album and singles would sell by the shedload, that they were destined for the A-list.

Whether the sheer love that showered the band when they stepped onstage is typical of the rest of their US shows is hard to say, but some of the devotion in Hartford was fanatical, maybe worryingly so. Fans hung around the lobby of the Meadows Concert Hall in Hartford discussing lyrics from forthcoming album *Break The Cycle* that they had read on an unofficial fan website. When Staind finally hit the stage, the kids sung, shouted or spoke quietly along to old favourites like 'Mudshovel' or 'Just Go' from second album *Dysfunction*, or newer material like 'It's Been A While', the first US single from *Break The Cycle*, which was getting heavy play on local rock and college stations. One could sense that what Aaron Lewis sings in his angry, melancholy and occasionally uplifting songs actually matters to them.

The night before the gig, Staind had appeared on *The David Letterman Show* and already their name had spread out of the fan ghettos into the 'real' world of pseudo-celebrity. The cab driver who took me to the gig knew who they were because he had seen them on TV and had thought they were pretty good. He was in his late 50s and a fan of country singer Jimmy Buffett. A bad sign perhaps?

Staind still have a whiff of cool underground band about them; any resentment felt towards them, that they are 'favoured sons', that they haven't 'paid their dues' – the saddest complaint of any failure begrudging another artist's success – is founded on ignorance. Staind are artists first and businessmen second. But they have some pretty scary people handling business for them.

They are surrounded by an assortment of American rock and roll hustlers, the 'can-do' foot soldiers from the band's record company, management company and tour promoters, who make shows – like the one I have just described – happen with apparent ease. All of them try to convey the impression that they are just hanging out, having a good time, but you can tell that they're working and sweating. Seemingly armed with two cellphones each, like latter-day gunfighters, they line the walls, telling some people to go to hell and inviting others to come along and meet the band. Local radio, TV and journalists are herded through to the band's dressing room to get their soundbites of wisdom. Others – the chancers, the over-enthusiastic fans and would-be groupies – are courteously, but firmly, steered away. If they worked for the Mafia, these people would smile as they shot you, and leave you bleeding to death feeling that they had done you a favour.

After the show, Staind are rounded up to pose for photos, dressed from head to foot in Dickies sweatshirts and jeans; Aaron Lewis actually changes out of his top and puts on one with a Pony logo on it because, apparently, some deal has been struck. The band are unsmiling but you can tell they are still really amused at the whole circus taking place around them. They swap stories about the increasingly weird things that are said to them by fans and questions asked by journalists, and look forward to meeting MTV comedian Pauly Shore who has dropped by to show the band some out-takes from his movies.

They are, as guitarist Mike Mushok tells me, business partners rather than some gang of rock and roll outlaws who grew up together and worked in their garage to hone their skills to take on the world. But there's no doubt they are having fun. There's a carefully cultivated enigmatic quality about the band that still sits a little uncomfortably with their status as relative newcomers. Singer Aaron Lewis, laconic, looking as though he's been awake for a week, doesn't really like talking about the songs much, though he's in a good mood and glad to be on home turf. They're really pleased with their new record and steeling themselves for some hardcore touring on the back of it. On stage or on record, Aaron will open himself up, revealing himself in a way that few other artists have the guts to do, a blast of pure communication that bypasses any barrier between audience and performer. But he won't be drawn too much on any inner meanings to the songs or the process whereby they came about. 'We didn't *try* to do anything necessarily,' says Aaron. 'We just kept writing songs and they sort of got better.'

Break The Cycle sounds like a more positive record than its predecessors, which are like shrieks of rage, a violent temper-tantrum with guitars. What inspired this, I asked them. 'Growth and life. Growth of all of us in the band. As far as breaking the cycle goes, it's about opening my eyes wide enough to see the vicious cycles in my life,' says Aaron.

'It's the melodies, the structures of the songs that are more mature as a whole,' says guitarist Mike Mushok. The anodyne answers give you no hint of the power of the music.

Right now, as you read this book, there are hundreds of thousands of spotty teenagers across the globe in garages trying to make a sound like Korn. There are a few thousand other established bands who are debating whether they should change their sound, to go in a more rap-metal direction. Like The Deftones, when you look even a micron beneath the surface, Staind are actually a very conventional rock and roll band who could have been contemporaries of Nirvana in the early 1990s or Smiths/REM wannabes in the 1980s. Like The Deftones, they make their personal anger about everyday life into grand tragedy on an almost cosmic scale. And like The Deftones they have struck a chord with disaffected teens who may be too cool for Limp Bizkit and for whom 'complaint rock' bands like Smashing Pumpkins are just a name that their older brothers and sisters were into earlier in the day.

When Aaron Lewis sings 'You can feel my anger, you can feel my pain...' during 'Mudshovel', huge sections of the affluent, well-dressed middle American teen crowd join in. Unlike the grand guignol theatrics of Disturbed who preceded them on this bill, there's a terrifying sincerity from both band and crowd, and that's where Staind's strength lies: they tap into the very real anger and pain of discontented teenage middle-class America in the way that Nirvana and Pearl Jam did a decade ago. Unlike Korn and Limp Bizkit, who appeal predominantly to the jump-around beer drinkers, the frat boys and the 'whiggers', Staind go for the inhabitants of that more introspective heartland who in the past have dedicated their lives to the comforting misery of artists like The Cure, The Smiths, Leonard Cohen, Joni Mitchell or Nick Cave.

Aaron Lewis, slowly prowling around the stage belting out his dissatisfaction, his rage, his don't-know-the-answers pissed-offness in a rich, warm tenor voice that manages to sound rough but still soars to hit notes you think are impossible, is more like a conduit for everyone's frustrations and doubts than someone revelling in his own emotional scars for our entertainment. You can tell that Staind have honed themselves to be this major-league band and suffered just to get the details right.

To go back now and listen to Staind's 1996 debut, *Tormented*, back to back with *Break The Cycle* is like listening to another band; *Tormented* is one long rush of hardcore brat-rage, a 900mph scream of a man smashing his head against a wall with frustration. There's very little about the album that makes Staind stand out from the countless other regional punk-rock bands who plug away in the underground like background noise. However, 1999's *Dysfunction* is the sound of a band trying to get to grips with all the anger and shape something else that will reach beyond the hard core of devotees; not 'selling out' or 'going commercial', just making it bearable. But *Break The Cycle* is a breakthrough record that takes the band to the heart of classic American songwriting.

There are inevitable comparisons to be made with Nirvana, Soundgarden, Alice In Chains, Pearl Jam and Stone Temple Pilots, but also with vintage grizzled American dadrock icons like Neil Young And Crazy Horse, Bruce Springsteen and even the harder-edged country singers like Steve Earle. Surprisingly, the names that are trotted out as influences aren't the usual Sabbath/ Zeppelin/Nirvana axis. Crosby, Stills, Nash And Young, Jim Croce, Gordon Lightfoot and Cat Stevens were all mentioned as formative influences. 'I've always really appreciated singer-songwriters,' confesses Aaron.

Certainly some of the confessional qualities in Aaron Lewis's songs – whose lyrics sometimes sound like they were lifted straight from the pages of his diary – have much in common with another troubled New Englander: James Taylor. But while James went through years of drug abuse and withdrawal, and finally found some peace with himself as a modern-day troubadour, Aaron is still struggling with the anger and disgust he feels at the world around him.

On 'Outside', the opening track on *Break The Cycle*, he sings, 'A boy just 13 on the corner for sale/Swallows his pride for another hit/Overpopulation there's no room in jail/But most of you don't give a shit/That your daughters are porno stars/And your sons sell death to kids/You're so lost in your little worlds/Your little worlds you'll never fix.'

On 'It's Been A While' – a love song, a redemption song – he writes, 'It's been a while/Since I could say that I wasn't addicted/ Since I could say I love myself as well/Since I've gone and fucked things up just like I always do/But all that shit seems to disappear when I'm with you.'

'If you look from the first to the second to this album, it definitely follows where I was at lyrically, and I think you can definitely see maturity and growth in terms of our musical writing capabilities. I'm still angry, there's still lots of anger in the record...there's just a little glimmer of hope,' says Aaron. 'I think there's a certain time in your life, in your teenage years, that you're very angry about everything, whether you need to be or not. I think as you get older you're angry for a reason.' Are we talking about teenagers all over the world or only those in the USA or maybe Europe? 'I dunno,' shrugs Aaron. 'I've only been to America.'

Staind aren't a feelgood band, then. But neither are they a band who wallow in misery and negativity; a lot of Aaron's songwriting is more searching, it asks questions. 'Epiphany', a gorgeous ballad that could almost be a mournful country and western song or some bleak post-punk Joy Division track, deals in a genuinely moving way with Aaron's own doubts and discomfort about wearing any spokesman-for-a-generation hats: 'I speak to you in riddles because/My words get in my way/I smoke the whole thing to my head and feel it wash away.' 'I feel like sometimes I'm talking to the kids as though they're children when I don't know how I feel,' he says. 'The reason it's called "Epiphany" is that it just came to me all at once. I could hear the whole song, the drums, everything in my head, and I went into the studio and did it until it was the way I first heard it.'

Inevitably, any artist who writes anything deeper than 'awopbopaloobopawopbamboom!' will attract the obsessive fans, the ones whose devotion goes beyond merely appreciating the music and the meaning for what they are. Staind are one of the few proper rock bands since Pearl Jam turned lame and Kurt Cobain shot himself to dip a toe into this territory. The passion and the honesty in Staind's songs, as well as addressing the angst common to most teenagers across the USA and indeed the world, are like a homing beacon to more damaged souls.

'Waste', on the latest album, deals with Aaron's feelings about a fan who committed suicide. 'His mom came to us and stood outside the bus crying and wanted me to come out and talk to her, and the song is just about how I felt about it all. It covers how I felt about him killing himself, and what could have brought him to that point and about her coming to the bus.'

Did she blame you? 'No. No it wasn't like that, she just wanted answers. She just wanted to talk to me and get answers that she should have been the one to know. I didn't know him.'

How did you deal with it?

'I didn't. I didn't get off the bus.'

The laconic response is at odds with the words of the song, which are shot with pure rage: 'Did Daddy not love you?/Or did he love you just too much?/Did he control you?/Did he live through you at your cost?/Did he leave no questions for you to answer on your own?/WELL FUCK THEM!/AND FUCK HER!/AND FUCK HIM!/AND FUCK YOU!/For not having/The strength in your heart/To pull through.'

I ask if he feels any responsibility to these fans whose interest becomes unhealthy. 'It's hard not to,' he says. 'It's another fucked-up dichotomy of it all. It's hard not to feel responsible, but you don't wanna preach, you don't want to take yourself too seriously. We're just playing music and having fun. But it's hard not to feel responsible, reaching so many individuals that obviously can relate to how I'm feeling at the time... It's tough.'

Do you never feel like just going off and playing surf music or R&B or instrumentals or something? He laughs. 'Nah, I gotta say what wants to come out.' Is it how you deal with life? 'Absolutely. It's how I purge, and I get to do it every night.'

Is it the writing or performing that's most cathartic? 'Both. In different ways. I like to feel the energy in the room...' Do you crave adulation onstage? 'No.' But do you enjoy it when it's there? Do you get off on it? 'Maybe not like you think I would. I feed off it. It's good to feel that we're successful. I'm a very private person when I'm offstage. I don't go out much and I know that Mike's the same deal. I'm either at home on my couch or I'm out fishing.' Yet you work in a medium that destroys privacy and, like it or not, makes your life public property. 'When I'm on tour, that's when I'm on the job!'

Do you never worry about the public side spilling into your private life? 'Oh we've made provisions for that. A big piece of property that will be my private sanctuary... I got into this to write music and be a musician, not to be a rock star, not to score all the chicks. I'm married and I'm a recluse!'

Right now, as a middle-ranking American rock band on the way up to the bigger leagues, Staind are still amused by the small details of celebrity that have crept into their lives. 'I've started noticing that people in Springfield whisper behind our backs,' says Mike. 'You'll be standing in a store and you'll notice somebody whispering "That's the guy from that band" or something. It's in a good way, though.'

'For me it goes two ways,' says Aaron. 'They're either too intimidated to approach me or I can be in the middle of dinner with my wife and they'll come right up to me and say "I don't want to be a bother and interrupt you while you're eating..." and I'm like, well, you just did!'

There's a lot of debate now as to whether Staind are a nu metal band; they have little in common with the sound of contemporaries Korn, Papa Roach or Godsmack. They certainly have little in common with the amped-up rabble-rousing rap anthems of their mentors, Limp Bizkit. They *look* like their contemporaries – sportswear, skate-pants, hooded tops – and they address the same adolescent dilemmas in their songs. Is that enough? Given that all such labels are fairly arbitrary and meaningless, that is enough, given that all Nirvana had in common with Soundgarden was a penchant for plaid shirts, a geographical common denominator and woe-is-me lyrics. Yet we know what we mean when we call them grunge bands and don't really question that they were part of a movement.

Staind are, however, the band most likely to be left standing when the term nu metal is a half-remembered term from the past and many of their contemporaries are eagerly standing in line for jobs at Burger King. Although they are friends with bands like Godsmack, they are reluctant to be drawn on any similarities other than age and the fact that they come from New England. It seems that, at the moment, there are still a lot of politics involved in touring, the two major US live franchises being the bands associated with the nu skool Family Values Korn/Limp Bizkit axis and the slightly more traditional Ozzfest. It's an idealistic philosophy of touring: putting together bands at different levels of success with different experiences, and the more established bands can be mentors to the newcomers. Staind won't be drawn into a debate about any rivalry between the two camps. 'A friend of mine put it best when he said that we could go out on the road and open for The Foo Fighters or for Pantera,' says Mike. 'I mean, not that we're actually planning to go out and open for Pantera...'

'We could definitely put together a set to open for Pantera,' says Aaron. But there is no doubt where Staind's loyalties currently lie. 'I will be grateful to the day I die for the Family Values 1999 tour. We will always be grateful to Fred Durst, not only for getting us on the tour and the record and...everything, but we learned a lot from them on tour. They taught us stuff.'

The constant questions about Durst are, however, beginning to rankle. 'I don't think Limp Bizkit's connection to Korn held on as long as ours has to them,' said Mike Mushok in the August 2001 issue of US rock magazine *Circus*. 'Fred did, and still does, so much for us. He directed the new video ("It's Been A While") and I think he did an amazing job. He definitely has advice for us and, the thing is, look at what him and they've done for themselves – it'd be almost stupid not to listen to advice from a person like that. If you surround yourself with people who are successful and know what's going on, hopefully a little will rub off on you. They've been great to us and Fred's been great to us, but we went and did this record on our own.'

The encouragement that Limp Bizkit gave to Staind was one of their more inspired moments, not only their input into their breakthrough album and taking them on tour, but most of all for encouraging the band to go in a direction that showcased Aaron's remarkable soaring voice to its best advantage. Again, the difference between the 'Nu' generation and the old school is this: bands always lend their support to other bands. It's just that the nu metal bands lend support to other bands that are likely to sell records and win fans. In the past, bands would form their own labels and help bands they saw as being no threat to them, creating an underclass of mediocre support acts.

During grunge, Kurt Cobain revived the careers of some of his own personal favourites, such as an obscure Scottish punk band called The Vaselines (he recorded two of their songs 'Molly's Lips' and 'Son Of A Gun') and defunct left-field feminist band The Raincoats (who reformed to support Nirvana). But these were bands who, despite the patronage of Cobain, were simply incapable of capitalising upon it and moving beyond the confines of the tiny cult followings they already had. Staind, on the other hand, could possibly outstrip the sales of Limp Bizkit – with doubt over Bizkit's future following the departure of guitarist Wes Borland, it is not out of the question. Staind also appeal to a much wider audience. It's often said that nobody over the age of 24 could possibly like Limp Bizkit or Korn, but Staind are a more mainstream band and their songs are likely to appeal to a much bigger fanbase.

And just as Fred Durst gave Staind the boost they needed, so they will one day become mentors to another band. 'That was part of the whole package,' says Aaron. 'We just finished working on a video for 'It's Been A While' with Fred and he took us aside and said, "You know, when the time comes, all I ask is that you find a band and do for them what we did for you."'

How will you find them? I ask. 'No idea,' shrugs Aaron. 'But we will.'

5 Real Phonies Or Fake Authenticity?
Linkin Park

Linkin Park's *Hybrid Theory*, since its release in 2000, has been certified quadruple platinum – that's four million copies sold – and has neatly placed the band at the forefront of nu metal and smack in the centre of a debate about the authenticity of rock and roll.

Frontman Chester Bennington has looks that are pure boy-band pin-up. He's quiet and thoughtful offstage, respectful and slow to anger. Yet, like all frontmen, Chester is driven by a burning ambition. 'I want to be a rock star,' he tells me. 'I've always wanted to be a rock star as long as I can remember.'

When he arrived from his home in Arizona, met the other members of Linkin Park and heard the band, he thought, as he told *Kerrang!* in January 2001, 'This is the one. This was the golden ticket to get inside Willy Wonka's chocolate factory.'

The rest of the band don't necessarily want to be rock stars in the way that Chester does, but they have their own ambitions within the band, whether these are just to make their music better for more people, to make a living at it or to make a lot of money at it.

All bands make a Faustian pact to achieve this end, though these days they don't go down to the crossroads at midnight and sell their souls to the devil, they do it in the air-conditioned Los Angeles offices of major-player record companies. In that respect, Linkin Park are no different to any other band with ambitions beyond pressing up a few seven-inch vinyl singles and winning their local battle of the bands contest. Linkin Park are a band doing what has to be done in the third millennium: once, bands made records, played gigs and spent the rest of the time befuddled on drugs surrounded by groupies or working their way towards their fatal swimming pool overdose. But that changed: a lot of bands cry about their lot, but they never last particularly long in the game. It's an easy life compared to, say, that of an aid worker in Afghanistan. But for a naïve small-town kid in his or her early 20s, who got into rock and roll to avoid doing any work whatsoever, it can be an arduous shock to the system.

Today, a band's routine will include posing for photographs at any time and appearing to be happy to do so, glad-handing retailers, DJs, media people, record company employees, journalists asking asinine questions and an army of foot soldiers who get their records on the radio, their posters displayed around town, their album prominently displayed in local record shops. It involves making videos, doing endless interviews, making appearances in countless record shops to sign albums and meet fans. It involves performing no matter how exhausted the band is. Linkin Park don't mind; it's part of why they signed up to the quest for mainstream rock success. They are a band using every tool of the modern age at their disposal, from marketing techniques to coming offstage tired and cranky, and sitting with a laptop answering questions in an Internet chatroom for a handful of fans thousands of miles away.

Yet, there has been a persistent, knowing rumour amongst people in the music business or just 'in the know' that Linkin Park are a manufactured band, a bunch of malleable puppets assembled in the same way as pop bands like The Spice Girls, N'SYNC or 5ive. There's a great deal of suspicion – though not from the kids who go to see them and buy their records – that there's something not right about them, like a Taiwanese Rolex.

Nobody can give you any real hard evidence of this; it's all friends of friends and whispers behind hands. It could be 'black propaganda' from rival record companies eager to sabotage their career; it may be that Linkin Park just got unlucky; nevertheless, it persists. And given the history of the music business – even the recent history – it's a rumour that is, sadly, easy to believe.

Ever since the late 1960s, when Screen Gems productions assembled a cast of young hopefuls to play the part of a zany Beatles-style rock and roll band, complete with English lead singer, for the TV series *The Monkees*, there have been disdainful noises from the hipper elements in the rock and roll subculture, looking down their noses at 'plastic' pop bands. Don Kirshner, the man behind The Monkees, assembled a team of top songwriters, including Neil Diamond and the Carole King/Gerry Goffin team to churn out pop hits, blurring the distinction between the fictional band on TV and the 'real' world of the Top 40. The Monkees toured and attracted crowds of screaming girls, who made no distinction between the 'artificiality' of The Monkees and the 'authenticity' of The Beatles, The Byrds or The Beach Boys.

The truth is that great pop records had always been 'manufactured', whether it was the stable of acts centred around 'Tycoon Of Teen' Phil Spector or Detroit's Tamla Motown, where label boss Berry Gordy approached pop music the way General Motors approached making cars. Neither Spector nor Gordy saw anything amiss in assembling a group of good-looking boys or girls, sticking them in the studio with a great pop song, churned out by a Brill Building songwriter-to-order like Neil Sedaka, Ellie Greenwich or the Motown in-house team of Holland/Dozier/Holland, and creating a hit record. It didn't matter to them or the public that none of the people 'fronting' the record necessarily knew each other before they went into the studio. The Monkees just made the process a little bit more transparent.

The blueprint has been applied ruthlessly and successfully ever since, from genuinely manufactured groups like The Smurfs to bands like Britain's Hear'Say, assembled from auditions of a cast of wannabes on a 'reality' TV series. But there has always been a smug and knowing superiority about the fans, critics and bands involved in 'authentic' rock and roll. They, it is felt, have integrity. They write their own songs – since The Beatles, this has been the great rock and roll sacred cow – they do not mime onstage nor do session men play their parts in the studio. Groups form from a shared high-minded desire to make great art rather than merely to make money.

The 1960s saw the sharpest division between pop and rock; and when rock bands became pop bands – as did Alice Cooper and T Rex in 1972 – they were deemed to have sold out.

The transition from pop band to rock band after the 1960s was a much harder one to make; after the TV series was over, The Monkees attempted to knowingly subvert their 'manufactured' image in the film *Head*, a psychedelic mess that had appearances from Frank Zappa, Jack Nicholson and a gigantic Victor Mature. They even went on tour, showcasing songs written by Mike Nesmith, who was actually a talented songwriter in his own right. But pop is ephemeral and rock is what lasts.

In the early 1990s, the sad case of Milli Vanilli showed that fakes can prosper...as long as they aren't found out. Fabrice Morvan and Rob Pilatus were two male models hired in by German producer Frank Farian, who had previously unleashed Boney M on the world, to front recordings he had made with session singers. Milli Vanilli had a string of European hits and four American number ones. They won a Grammy Award for best new artists, but the award was withdrawn when the man who had actually sung on the record suggested that it might be more fitting if instead the award went to him.

Their record company, Arista, dropped the band, claiming to be shocked that they had been hoaxed and that they were unaware of any fraud when they signed the band. They were then forced to issue vouchers to disgruntled Milli Vanilli fans who felt that they had been had. This was ammunition to the rock faction; proof that pop was dishonest, that the kids were being conned.

Even for those fans, critics and bands who actively disliked everything Limp Bizkit, Korn and The Deftones stood for, there was no doubting their authenticity. They were real bands playing real music. When Linkin Park arrived, however, they smelled a rat. Again, it goes back to the hard-slogging musicians' complaint about paying dues; Linkin Park never spent years flogging their act around the circuit. Unlike Staind, for example, who nobody could accuse of lacking a work ethic, Linkin Park just seemed to spring from nowhere.

The band – Chester Bennington (vocals), Shinoda (MC/vocals), Brad Delson (guitar), Phoenix (bass), Joe Hahn (DJ) and Rob Bourdon (drums) – all knew each other through school or college and had formed two years previously as Xero, then as Hybrid Theory (also the title of Linkin Park's debut album). They played a series of showcase gigs for major labels, most notably at the Whiskey A Go Go, before signing with Warner Brothers in November 1999. The name change was forced on them by another band using the same moniker. They decided that because every city in America has a Lincoln Park, that would be their name; the spelling complete with Cyrillic-style Ns was so that they could buy the Internet domain name and not, they claim, to in any way suggest connections with Korn or Limp Bizkit. The Internet is important to them both as a marketing tool and as a way to communicate with their fans.

'Our album went out on Napster months before it was actually released,' drummer Rob Bourdon told me. 'We also spent ages sending out MP3s of our tracks before that, going into chatrooms and leaving messages on other bands' sites to get people to come and download our track. Every night after our gigs I go online, talking to fans back in the States about the show. Fans can email us through our site. We'll also start doing a tour diary soon which will be updated on the site every day.'

More cynical observers point out that the name Linkin Park looks a bit like Limp Bizkit; they will usually be listed after Limp Bizkit anywhere from Internet search engines to mail-order lists; and the Cyrillic-type reversed Ns are a bit like Korn's reversed K.

Speaking to *Metal Hammer* writer Neil Kulkarni in early 2001, Linkin Park singer Chester Bennington hit out angrily at the stories that preceded the band on their first European visit. He said, 'What one question pisses me off the most? It's when people say we're contrived, or we were put together artificially. That's the most deeply offensive thing that anyone can say about this band, to everyone in it, to everyone who's ever helped us, and I think it's enormously patronising to the fans. I don't have to repeat the history of this band to prove that's bullshit. I don't have to explain the way we work, how hard we've battled every step of the way to get heard, how much the actual success of this band is down to what we've done with our fans and the relationship we've built up with people into our music. I just think we've come at a time when we're being linked in with shit that has nothing to do with us – fads that bear a real superficial resemblance with what we do – but dig just a tiny bit deeper and you realise they bear no relation to our music whatsoever.

'I guess some people hate the simplicity of a band who work hard, do what they do and people like it; they need the angle, the hook, they need to try to decode a secret that isn't even there. In the end they can think what they like but, fuck, if they say that shit to me they're gonna have a whole world of hurt to deal with.'

Oddly, Linkin Park seem evasive, reluctant to actually discuss the songs on *Hybrid Theory*: songs like 'One Step Closer', for example, are written from a first-person perspective. The song, like many a good metal lyric, deals with somebody who is 'on the edge': 'Everything you say to me/Takes me one step closer to the edge/And I'm about to break/I need a little room to breathe/Cause I'm one step closer to the edge/And I'm about to break.' Emotive stuff. Yet in an interview about songwriting in *CD Now*, Mike Shinoda said, 'We were in the studio working on lyrics for a very long time and some days got to be really long and frustrating, and that song was written during one of those periods of time, where we were extremely frustrated with writing; we were extremely frustrated with a lot of things going on in our personal lives, so we just let it all out.'

This reluctance arises from the fact that they write collectively and, since there are two frontmen, they are careful to avoid attributing a single viewpoint to the songs, even though, since only one of them may be singing at a particular time, the words have to be in the first person.

'We had to figure out a way of talking about things that we both could relate to, and then be able to write about them. 'Cos I can't tell somebody something that happened to me and then expect them to be able to write about it and have the same feelings. So we'll listen to the music and go "OK, what are you thinkin' when you hear this?" and we'll go from there. Then we'll create a story and try to adapt expressions to capture what we're feeling,' Chester told Australian magazine *Time Off*.

Interestingly, there are no swear words at all on the album, something of a first in the current 'Nu' climate.

In the March 2001 issue of *Rolling Stone*, Chester told reporter Rob Sheffield, 'When Mike and I sat down and wrote the lyrics we wanted to be as honest and open as we could. We wanted something people could connect with, not just vulgarity and violence. We didn't want to make a big point of not cussing, but we don't have to hide behind anything to show how tough we can be.'

'It was scary in the beginning, when we started writing about what we felt,' Shinoda said. 'But once we realised we weren't the only ones who felt that way, once we saw the audience was coming along with us on that, it freed us up. We wanted to be a little more descriptive, instead of just going "fuck" all the time. We wanted to go into detail.' Although there is no formal censorship beyond stickering of product with the infamous Parental Advisory tag, some major chain stores refuse to carry material they deem to be obscene. Many bands now issue two versions of their albums: a 'clean' version, where swearing is bleeped or edited, or songs are actually re-recorded, and an 'explicit' version in all its effing-and-blinding glory. Yet rather than see this as compromise, or kowtowing to the censorship lobby, many bands see this simply as a way of getting their music to the fans. When Wal-Mart refused to stock Nirvana's *In Utero* because of the track 'Rape Me' and because it deemed the artwork to be obscene, the band issued a new version, reasoning that, when they were growing up in Aberdeen, the only place that Kurt and Krist Novoselic could actually buy records was the local Wal-Mart. Making a stand hurts sales but, ultimately, in provincial cities where there are few record shops, it hurts fans. An alternative 'conspiracy theory' around Linkin Park was that they were a 'Christian Rock Trojan Horse', trying to sneak clean lyrics and wholesome values into the dirty drug-addled world of nu metal. Certainly Chester thanked 'God' on the album credits and can occasionally be seen sporting a crucifix around his neck; the band also played with out-and-out Christian bands such as POD and Project 86. It is an irony of the times that people are suspicious because a band doesn't swear enough on record.

It's also a sign of the times that supposedly 'credible' bands like Linkin Park are being accused of 'fakeness'. They aren't the first 'credible' rock band in recent times that such accusations have been levelled at. Hole, the band formed by Courtney Love, enjoyed a massive hit with their second album *Live Through This*. Courtney was, at the time the album was written and recorded, married to Kurt Cobain. There were a lot of knowing innuendos that Kurt, in fact, wrote most of the songs on the album. The evidence is plentiful but circumstantial, and the parties concerned are either dead or have something to lose by talking about it. Yet at the heart of this accusation is that sacred cow of 'proper' rock bands writing their own songs; *Live Through This* is a classic album, regardless of whether Kurt, Courtney, a combination of both, or neither, was responsible for the writing.

There is also a growing underground industry in both Europe and the USA of songwriters churning out songs for a fee that will be 'fronted' by established artists. The songwriters are paid a one-off fee and the artist who records them is credited as the sole author. While such practices have been commonplace in pop music for years, rock bands have always been believed to be somehow above such fakery. One senior American record company marketing executive told me, 'You won't get anyone who will say this out loud. Record companies are not some Medici-like patrons of the arts. Record companies are more like bookies. They want a return on their investment and they don't really want to take too much of a risk. Signing a band to your label is a risk. They may be good songwriters or good performers or whatever. They may just have the right look. A lot of bands talk about artistic freedom. Let me tell you, there is no artistic freedom. The artist has been signed to the label because we can sell the music, we can plan ways to do it, strategies. And the sad truth is that if a record company signs either five bands who sound exactly like Marilyn Manson or Limp Bizkit or Britney Spears or one that's an original, a one-off, they will always go for the five that sound like something else. The one-off is a risk. The original needs more investment.

'Too many people have sunk too much money into artists that maybe only the rock critic on *Rolling Stone* likes. Then they have to answer to the people above them in the company who in turn have to answer to the shareholders. It's like the scene in *Goodfellas* – you made a great album that didn't sell? Fuck you, pay me. You made a great piece of art? Fuck you, pay me. They want the money and they want it now rather than in five years when the artist or band has had a chance to mature and learn the craft of songwriting. All bands have a producer. All bands are given advice by management. All bands bring in professionals. I guess it's only a short step away from having bands put together by professionals. In future I think labels are going to be less interested in finding bands and more interested in finding band members who they can match up.'

The idea of major labels, management companies and marketers being involved in assembling bands according to current trends, with cold analyses of demographic data, honed using focus groups, songs written to a formula, performed in studios by session men and engineers, is anathema to anyone brought up on the idea that rock and roll should be about passion, intensity and talent. It even seems a million miles away from Tamla Motown, whose manufactured pop seems innocent by comparison.

There is, of course, another adage in the music industry, that because you have to spend so much money to 'manufacture' and launch a pop band, it takes five years before all that outlay is recovered and the band makes a profit. But the average lifespan of a pop band is three years at most before their teenage fans get bored and move on. Would it make sense to start 'manufacturing' rock bands when the 'authentic' ones are actually doing rather well on their own?

The fact is that despite healthy sales, record companies have been feeling the pinch; artists such as Madonna, Prince and Courtney Love have highlighted the unfairness of the contracts artists are forced into signing early in their careers. The record industry is under threat from digital music, which bypasses copyright and royalty collection. It is experimenting with alternative business models, some of which look like sharp practice, though they remain within the law and are essentially no different from techniques used by other companies to cut costs and boost returns.

In the past ten years there have been scandals in the UK about records being 'bought in' to the Top 40, of record companies using strategic marketing techniques such as price cutting in targeted chart return record shops to get records into the charts, forcing radio stations to add them to their playlists. Radio stations, too, have interests in record labels now, skewing their programming unfairly in favour of artists in which they have a financial stake. The Limp Bizkit pay-for-play scandal (see Chapter 4) was the legal manifestation of 'payola' – literally cash bribes to DJs, producers and radio station executives in return for airplay – which has dogged American radio since its early days in the 1920s. People tend to believe that the music industry is 'rigged'.

Perhaps this is the cynicism that makes people ready to think the worst of bands like Linkin Park. They're young, energetic, good-looking with killer songs, their album went straight into the *Billboard* charts at Number One – there must be something up. But even if it transpired that Linkin Park were actually as genuine as Britney's breasts, that still doesn't detract from the fact that *Hybrid Theory* is a genuinely good album, and the critics agree.

Britain's now-defunct *Melody Maker* called it 'an absolutely storming debut'. CMJ wrote, 'You could be standing in the middle of NYC's Grand Central Station on the busiest travelling day of the year and still hear the pre-release buzz generated by this debut. And the young Linkin Park has definitely lived up to the massive hype. The rhythmic-without-rapping *Hybrid Theory* is a solid hit machine, combining the catchy with the crisp, the melodic with the monstrous.'

There were few dissenting voices; if the people in the know who work in the music press believed Linkin Park were manufactured, it didn't stop them from putting them on the covers of their magazines or jamming the guest lists for their increasingly frenzied gigs. The live Linkin Park experience is a genuinely exciting one for the kids who pay their money to go mental in the moshpit.

Yet the live Linkin Park shows are also grist to the rumourmongers' mill. They are, we are assured, 'all on DAT'. Most major touring bands now use at least some backing tracks on DAT (Digital Audio Tape). Often the drums will be a prerecorded backing track with the live drummer doing only fills, rolls and solos live. This is down to logistics and the difficulty major bands have in reproducing live the sound they get on record. As they rely more and more on technology, bands are increasingly at the mercy of bad acoustics and dodgy microchips. DAT is a solution.

Again, stories about pop stars like Victoria 'Posh Spice' Beckham, who was pelted with missiles thrown by an angry crowd at a Radio 1 show in Leicester in September 2001 after it became obvious she was miming, just seem to confirm how 'fake' pop is. But if the true extent of how many 'credible' rock bands are not actually playing their instruments live onstage became widely known, the backlash would be tremendous. Record company press offices and band management become incredibly defensive when the subject arises; as a news editor on a major music weekly once told me, he was threatened with a 'hitman from the Lower East Side' if he pursued a story about a major American act cancelling European dates because of their inability to mime convincingly.

Certainly, hip-hop artists have been performing to backing tapes, records scratched by DJs, drum machines and DATs for years without anyone accusing them of being fake. So if Linkin Park do utilise DAT for some of their backing, they are certainly not alone, nor are they in the major league of fraudsters, if indeed fraud it is.

In a *Shoutweb* interview with Mike Shinoda, Linkin Park's alternate frontman, he dismissed any suggestion that the band were a studio creation: 'They're going to have a lot of questions when they see us live. They are going to start to realize that a lot of things that sound like samples are not. Brad [Delson, guitarist] plays full melodies that are only harmonics on his clean guitar that sounds like a keyboard or sounds like a harp or sounds like bells. People have said that it sounds like 100 different things and they're always thinking that it's not guitar and it is. The whole verse for "In The End" is harmonics. That high-pitched noise is Brad playing.'

Perhaps the only real problem with Linkin Park is one of communication; they are still a young band, they have little to say in interviews and this can sometimes be misinterpreted. And like most bands they are reluctant to admit to being part of any movement, to being influenced by those bands they are so obviously influenced by. They are particularly irritated by any suggestions that they are in the same mould as Limp Bizkit or Korn, though they admit to a hero-worship relationship with The Deftones, the band they sound least like.

'They are a big influence. Everything from hip-hop stuff like Black Star, The Roots, Mos Def to more electronic-sounding stuff. Roni Size, The Aphex Twin, even Depeche Mode. All of those bands we really like,' Mike Shinoda told the UK's *Dotmusic* in January 2001.

Although they maintain that they are one-offs, Linkin Park can't escape the fact that they are very much in the tradition of Limp Bizkit, right down to the onstage DJ. Lyrically they bear an uncanny similarity to Korn: songs about paranoia, loneliness, fear, anxiety. Their sound is inescapably drawing on the same rock and rap roots, though Linkin Park have the edge in terms of slicker, catchier songs.

In many ways the best comparison that can be made is with Depeche Mode. During the 1980s, this well-scrubbed electronic band were always condemned as lightweights in comparison with the other big post-punk bands like New Order, The Cure and The Psychedelic Furs. They straddled the 'fake' world of pop, teen magazines and the fledgling MTV, and the 'authentic' serious rock world of *Rolling Stone* interviews, big-concept albums and quality songwriting. They were bland in comparison with other bands, yet it was precisely their knack of balancing the 'fake' and the 'authentic', of taking some profoundly left-field material and blanding it out ever so slightly to suit the palates of middle-

American arena concert-goers and record buyers that ultimately gave them the edge over the hipper bands. Depeche Mode are still playing while the rest are either in semi-retirement or disarray.

But Depeche Mode were also a conduit to other things: their largely teenage audience went on to listen to 'hard stuff' like Chicago industrial metallers Ministry or Skinny Puppy, Front 242 and Nine Inch Nails. The early Detroit techno scene was heavily influenced by Depeche Mode, which was rather a slap in the face for the more 'credible' names in electronic music such as Cabaret Voltaire who never really extended their music beyond a limited cult following. 'When I was a kid I used to have a recurring dream that Depeche Mode flew a jet into my schoolyard and asked me to be their fifth member,' Chester told *Metal Hammer* in February 2001. 'I've always wanted to be a singer and I was so excited. So we performed a concert in front of my schoolmates and then we flew off on the jet and did a world tour together.'

Linkin Park are a much easier listen than Korn or Limp Bizkit. Chester has an appealing, tuneful voice, which contrasts with his more abrasive moments when it sounds as though he is singing through a bank of electronic effects. It's loud and scary, but only in short bursts. For a 16-year-old who is tired of pop but not ready for the real rotgut rock and roll, Linkin Park are an accessible conduit. They can pass as a rock band, there is some hip-hop in there, some left-field dance music, some pop. It's like a jumping-off point for their teenage listeners to discover something else. Their videos look like boy-band videos; they are a pretty-boy band; they look like an unthreatening street gang, how their 16-year-old fans would like to think that they and their friends look; there is nothing about the music or the lyrics that is too taxing. They are unquestionably tailored for this demographic, though that is part of the marketing process of every rock band, not evidence that they are manufactured.

Indeed, the people who most often manufacture bands are bands themselves. They are, after all, their own creation. All rock bands are art by committee. All rock bands are formed with a target audience in mind. All rock bands have some sort of plan. All rock bands tailor and compromise their songs to get them across to the fans in the most effective way. Singling out Linkin Park is a bit like handing out a speeding ticket to one car at the Indianapolis 500.

6 The World's Biggest Cult Band
The Deftones

One of the main pillars of nu metal are The Deftones, a band who have been around in one form or another since the 1980s, but who first made their impact on the contemporary rock scene around the same time as Korn, and whose rise has been in parallel with contemporaries Limp Bizkit, Slipknot and Coal Chamber. They are not, they insist, a nu metal band. 'We wanted to detach ourselves from any label,' Deftones singer Chino Moreno told the *New York Post*. 'Honestly, I don't think there's any band out there that does rap metal correctly, except The Beastie Boys. The rest just seem silly to me. It's hard to turn on MTV and see all these bands on *TRL* [the popular audience request show] doing really shitty versions of a sound we helped pioneer, while our video gets played once, at three in the morning.'

Of course, all nu metal bands deny that they are nu metal bands, just as all grunge bands denied that they were grunge bands and all new wave bands denied that they were new wave bands; but the association with the other bands has undeniably helped The Deftones sell a few records and concert tickets: the band's exceptional third album, *White Pony*, entered the *Billboard* charts at Number Three, went gold (500,000 sales) a month after it was released and subsequently sold over a million.

Bill Clinton famously chose his first cabinet 'to look like America' in its ethnic make-up. The Deftones look like a 21st-century Californian rock band: 'We're two Mexicans, a Chinese and a white boy. Metal and punk don't have to be white, anymore than rap has to be black.'

As we will discuss later, American music is still segregated between black and white artists, but there has been a surprising and welcome growth in the number of musicians of Latin-American and Latin-Caribbean descent involved in contemporary rock. Brazil's Sepultura and Max Cavalera's band/project Soulfly were the trailblazers; others include Dino Cazares of Fear Factory, Mexican band Titan and the heavily Latino east coast band Ill Niño.

But the other major faultline in contemporary music of all genres is that between music perceived to be 'intelligent' and that which is not. 'Intelligent' music, with complicated – some would argue pretentious – lyrics, difficult song structures and knowing references to other aspects of pop music and popular culture, is always in demand by college students, small-town existentialist intellectuals and wannabe dissidents with 'angst'. By extension this means that the more 'blue-collar' fans who do not appreciate such fine subtleties and nuances in music and lyrics are into 'dumb' music.

Just as music was divided between 'rock' and 'pop' in the mid 1960s, so within the more elitist world of rock there was another level of snobbery. It was no use just being into some lumpen boogie band like Mott The Hoople or Grand Funk Railroad, the 'discerning' listener went for 'difficult' music like Frank Zappa, Emerson, Lake And Palmer or Yes – bands with aspirations to classical composition and jazz musicianship. Even though this was every bit as much a mass-market phenomenon as 'pop' or 'rock', it allowed adherents to believe, smugly, that they were members of some enlightened intellectual fraternity, gazing down patronisingly at the baser elements below. 'Intelligent' music is always big with rock critics; 'dumb' music is always big with the kids.

Today, Radiohead, The Aphex Twin, Massive Attack and Smashing Pumpkins are bands that, by consensus, would be regarded as 'intelligent', while Limp Bizkit, Destiny's Child or

Britney Spears, for example, would tend to be regarded as 'dumb'. A counter-argument, of course, is that it takes more genuine intelligence to craft slick and timeless pop songs, with a wide appeal to a lot of fans, whether that pop is The Beach Boys, The Ramones, Eminem or Destiny's Child. What is so intelligent, you may argue, about a band such as Smashing Pumpkins deciding to make a record so pretentious it requires a Herculean effort to listen to it in its entirety? History tends to rehabilitate the 'dumb' bands and damn the 'intelligent' ones; most of the same critics now agree that there is more 'intelligence' in three minutes of The Ronettes than in all 80-odd excruciating minutes of Yes's *Tales From Topographic Oceans*.

'Intelligent' music also tends to be unhappy music, troubled music, angry music or depressing music. Leonard Cohen, Joy Division and The Cure are held to be in some way superior to 'good-time' bands and musicians. Misery is felt to have depth while happiness has only shallows.

The Deftones are tailor-made for this fanbase; even the guest appearance from Tool's Maynard James Keenan on 'Passenger' sealed the connection with rock and roll's cutting edge. They are not, of course, a band with 'issues' in the way that Korn are; The Deftones, musically, are a lot more complicated, almost impressionistic, providing a musical canvas on which the listener can splatter his or her own emotional responses. And despite the drunken penis-exposing incident in Holland, The Deftones are not a band on the edge like Nirvana. All the evidence points to a hard-headed and in-control unit, fronted by a shrewd and competent singer and songwriter, rather than an unpredictable genius wrestling with his inner demons.

With their abstract, surreal lyrics, Chino and The Deftones were certainly able to tap into the all-important fanbase of troubled teens and 20-somethings who felt they were too sophisticated to identify with Jonathan Davis of Korn. As he told *NY Rock* magazine, 'I want to express my feelings. I want to express what I feel without actually having to spell it out, without actually having to sing the words. I don't want to use the words to express myself. I think the music should express it all. I've always been a huge Cure fan, especially when Robert Smith was really abstract and cryptic, like in *Pornography*, where the lyrics were really cryptic, but definitely intense, and everybody understood and felt what he was trying to say.'

When he sings on 'Elite' through a vocoder adding a menacing, subhuman quality to his voice, Chino's actual words seem meaningless. He sings, 'When you're ripe you'll bleed out of control/You'll bleed out of control/You like attention/It's proof to you you're alive/Stop parading your angles/Confused?'

The words to 'Change (In The House Of Flies)' are almost Kafkaesque: 'I watched you change/Into a fly/I looked away/You were on fire/I watched a change in you/It's like you never had wings/And you feel so alive.'

In the *NY Rock* interview, Chino says, 'I think our lyrics are rather introverted and sometimes really complex. A lot of people describe Jonathan Davis's lyrics this way but I don't think our lyrics can be compared. The lyrics of Korn are quite different. For example, if you hear Jon singing about something, you know what he means. He's not talking around something. He's getting straight to the point, while I'd rather give you a feeling of what I'm trying to say. I prefer using metaphors and just giving you the general feeling about what I'm trying to say. It isn't necessarily something that has anything to do with my real life. It isn't necessarily autobiographical. It's the music that demands certain lyrics.'

Nonsense words have been effective for bands as diverse as The Cocteau Twins to '70s French progressive jazz outfit Magma, who actually made up their own language.

By the time they released *White Pony* in 2000, The Deftones already had extensive touring, recording and writing experience under their belts, something that occasionally gives them the edge over their contemporaries/competitors. They have toured with Ozzy Osbourne, Kiss, Anthrax, White Zombie, Pantera and Bad Brains, winning hearts and minds in the hard rock heartland. They also tend to be the band that people who don't like nu metal (or metal in general) make an exception for; older fans, traditional metal buffs and snooty critics will all sing the praises of The Deftones when it comes to putting down Limp Bizkit, Korn and Slipknot. It's the perceived 'intelligence' of The Deftones that is attractive to these admirers.

In a review of *White Pony*, the UK's *NME* said, 'Deftones started off as just another promising rap metal act that came from the skateparks and rock clubs of California. A band that grew up on Iron Maiden, Metallica and Faith No More but listened to the sensitivity-enhancing, girlfriend-securing sounds of The Cure and The Smiths. After the release of two albums, it soon became clear to see that Deftones were more than just another bunch of no-brainer rap-rock chancers, and buried within their machine-like riffing and cheeseball rapping lay songs of greater depth and, ultimately, mass appeal... If Marilyn Manson had half their feel for writing affecting songs for the masses, he'd be President of the USA by now.'

Rolling Stone writer Ann Powers was equally enthusiastic in her review of the album: 'Passion arises in the space between tenderness and brutality, where the longing to succumb meets the impulse to control. Rock & roll expresses these paradoxes, often without much forethought. But some artists do tackle them head on, in music that not only feeds primal hunger but tries to unravel it. *White Pony* is that kind of effort. The Deftones have always skirted the arty edge of hard music. They've long been threatening to stray from the head-and-booty-banging pimp-rock style they helped to invent. But few could have expected such committed experimentation from a band that has everything to gain from keeping things obvious.'

Formed in Sacramento, California, in 1988 by Chino Moreno,

guitarist Stephen Carpenter, drummer Abe Cunningham and bassist Chi Cheng (DJ Frank Delgado joined the group much later), who had all known each other since school, the group's initial influences were the usual '80s thrash and metal acts, as well as bands like Bad Brains, Smashing Pumpkins and Jane's Addiction (some of Perry Farrell's high-tension vocal phrasing can still be heard in the modern incarnation of the band). They played relentlessly, criss-crossing the state, recording demos and apparently getting nowhere until one arrived at Maverick Records, a Warner Brothers-distributed subsidiary set up by Madonna.

Terry Date (previous credits include Soundgarden and White Zombie, later ones include Limp Bizkit and Staind) worked with the band on their debut album *Adrenaline* in 1995. The follow-up, *Around The Fur*, also produced with Terry Date, built on the success of the first release, capturing the band's taut sound, veering between subtlety and brutality.

Max Cavalera played guitar on 'Head Up' while 'My Own Summer (Shove It)' picked up radio and MTV play, something unheard of in the past for a sound as abrasive as theirs. Their music is dynamic as opposed to just loud and energetic; there is a focus to their sound that other bands lack, a maturity and sophistication to their lyrics (for all their cryptic qualities) that bands like Staind have yet to acquire, and an openness to their boundaries that allows them to move on once they have exhausted all the musical possibilities. They have gone from hardcore punk on *Adrenaline*, through razor-sharp rap metal on *Around The Fur*, to the searing millennial rock of *White Pony* quite seamlessly. They combine this punk rock attitude with a sense of a rock aesthetic that few bands since The Pixies have accomplished. They invented a lot of nu metal clichés, such as the whisper-to-a-scream vocal phrasing, the soft verse/screamed chorus that Nirvana pioneered but The Deftones refined, the onstage DJ and the edgy post-punk/skater look of the band. Their live show can be incendiary, if unpredictable: during their 2001 European tour, Chino was noticeably the worse for wear at the Waldrock Festival, in The Netherlands, and spent most of the show stumbling around the stage, insulting the crowd and briefly coming alive only during a duet with Mike Muir of Suicidal Tendencies, exposing his genitalia to the crowd, finishing up with 'Bored' and stumbling offstage after telling the audience, 'At least I'm not Fred Durst!'

The band later admitted they had reached a low ebb on that tour, Chino telling reporters that he began drinking in the morning as soon as he got up and hadn't stopped. Yet, while this behaviour might seriously anger fans, in the case of The Deftones it actually added something to their allure. They may just have been overworked, jet-lagged and homesick, but their reputation as 'troubled souls' actually went down rather well with fans. One American fan gave me his insight into why The Deftones are the best band in modern America. 'They don't suck, dude!' he assured me.

The Deftones are the band most often mentioned as an influence by many of the second-generation nu metal bands. But although they remain friends with Korn, a band whose path they crossed in their early days when both bands were touring heavily around California, they have avoided signing up for franchise tours like Family Values, despite repeated lucrative offers. The Deftones have kept their distance from other nu metal bands, eyes wide open to the disastrous consequences of being associated with something when it inevitably sinks. Chino Moreno told the *Washington Post* in July 2000, 'Family Values would be good for us – we could play in front of a lot more people, it would be good money. But the decision has to do with the longevity of our band. I want to continue to make records for as long as we can. And if they don't sell, it should be because of us, not because we were attached to this whole music scene...and once it went down the drain, we went down the drain with it. Music goes through phases. No matter how many people like Limp Bizkit this week, I guarantee you five years from now all them five million people that bought that *Significant Other* record aren't gonna be buying their new record. It's already become a formula. Honestly, I can hear a Limp Bizkit song and I can already tell you what the next part's gonna be. What Limp Bizkit can do is progress, and change their sound a little bit, but they already kinda have their feet in the mud. This is what they are. They're just this party frat-rock kind of band. When that gets old and people see through it and are done with it, I don't want them to write us off just because we are associated with that scene.'

But regardless of whether they want to be associated with the scene, the fact is that they are always namechecked as a huge influence on bands who patently are part of it. Linkin Park, dedicated Deftones fans, supported them on their European dates, after pinning their hearts to their sleeves in a biography on their website admitting how much they loved the band.

'The bio we wrote a long time ago says that The Deftones are one of our influences,' Linkin Park's Mike Shinoda told me. 'It wasn't like we were trying to kiss ass to get a tour, it was just like, hey, these are our favorite bands. Now that we are actually touring with them...well, we're kinda star-struck.'

Chino was, however, underwhelmed by them, telling Britain's Radio 1, 'Honestly, I don't listen to their music at all. But, I think our fans, especially the younger ones, dig it. Whether those bands will admit it or not they are the epitome of nu metal. They are good bands, I'd take them over a lot of other stuff. If you listen to the stuff I listen to it's different.'

The Deftones are undoubtedly a band starting to chafe within the confines of the formulaic rock and roll world they inhabit. Their single 'Elite' won the 2001 Grammy Award for Best Metal Performance, critical reaction to *White Pony* was universally favourable and sales were rising. They were in a strong position to take their music wherever they wanted.

To some extent The Deftones are the band who fill the void left in American rock by the demise of Smashing Pumpkins, doyens of the '90s alt.rock scene. Even more than Nirvana, Smashing Pumpkins helped to patent the quiet verse/blustering chorus formula and listening to any number of singers, from Brandon Boyd of Incubus to Korn's Jonathan Davis, you can tell that they would give anything to be able to be Smashing Pumpkins singer Billy Corgan, who practically patented that 'whine' in the voice that is a trademark of so many nu metal vocalists.

Corgan steered his band away from this tuneful, angsty direction towards a more experimental though still approachable and recognisably rock and roll sound on their 1995 album *Mellon Collie And The Infinite Sadness*, also their best-selling record. But Billy Corgan wanted to move things on, telling people he had a 'certain sound mulling around in my head', hinting that he wanted to make something radically different, influenced by the challenging trip-hop emerging from artists like Tricky, Portishead and Massive Attack. Subsequent releases *Adore* and *Machina: The Machines Of God* were certainly ground-breaking recordings, but they were hard to listen to, dense and moody, and they alienated a lot of fans. Coupled with other internal problems in the band, related to heroin abuse and personal animosity, this spelled the end for what had been the great hope of American rock. An object lesson in the pitfalls of wanting to 'progress', of hearing sounds in the head.

The Deftones' 'Change (In The House Of Flies)' from *White Pony* was like a plan for an alternative music they were on the verge of exploring, heavily psychedelic with samples and FX adding to the uncomfortable tension in the track. Compared to the later Smashing Pumpkins or post-*OK Computer* Radiohead, it was hardly revolutionary, but in the confines of a band who had to keep their fanbase supplied with a ready supply of bombastic rockers and emotional punk, it was a bold step. But the fact that it was a successful single and a live favourite seems to have heartened Chino to take it further. In 2001, Chino announced that he was working on a solo project called Team Sleep, which would involve former Hole/Smashing Pumpkins bassist Melissa Auf Der Maur, and which he described as being 'like Portishead, except with my voice'. He also announced that he was going to collaborate with left-field British experimental band Mogwai, doing vocals for one of their post-rock instrumentals, something that looks like forging a new direction for The Deftones. Art metal? Nu progressive?

The spirit of experiment and progress has been central to the band from the start. Although he only officially became the fifth Deftone before the release of *White Pony*, DJ Frank Delgado - one of Sacramento's best-known DJs - had played live with the band since before their debut album *Adrenaline* was released in 1995. Frank was, and still is, a member of Sacramento hip-hop crew The Socialistics, who shared rehearsal space with the band, started jamming and found some common ground. Talking to music website *The PRP* in 2000, Frank said, 'There was no preconceived way on how to add me into the mix. It's not like we were going to have a metal-hip-hop thing with scratch breakdowns. I just interweave myself into the songs.'

Frank played a big part in the evolving Deftones sound, contributing to all of the albums but actually being an integral part in the recording of *White Pony*, adding the atmospheric samples and 'found' sounds.

The role of the onstage DJ - such as Limp Bizkit's DJ Lethal, (hed) pe turntablist DJ Product, DJ AM from Crazy Town, DJ Kilmore of Incubus, DJ Homicide of Sugar Ray and Joe Hahn of Linkin Park - has evolved in such a way that it now seems natural to see someone scratching behind decks onstage. Occasionally the DJ role is to provide rhythmic flourishes, occasionally it is to add samples, and sometimes it seems actually quite mysterious since all the samples actually seem to be supplied by an onstage keyboard player.

Rock bands have tried at various times over the past ten

years or so to integrate DJs into their onstage set-up. Offstage, DJ remixes are now commonplace. This has opened up new vistas for rock bands as well as breaking down barriers between musical genres.

In 1990, British rock band Primal Scream teamed up with a DJ on the British house scene, which had flourished during 1987/88 and the so-called 'Summer Of Love'. Primal Scream at that time were dedicated rock 'classicists', plundering the music and image of American garage rock bands like The MC5, The Byrds and Big Star. Compared to the energy of the house scene, however, they looked and sounded as out of touch and old-fashioned as Led Zeppelin and Rod Stewart during the upsurge of punk a decade earlier.

DJ Andrew Weatherall – one of the new breed of DJs who had helped forge a uniquely European style of house music in London clubs such as Shoom and in the Balearic Islands, notably Ibiza – was invited to remix a track from Primal Scream's second album *Sonic Flower Groove*, called 'I'm Losing More Than I'll Ever Have'. The resulting track, 'Loaded', was a landmark, revitalising the band, who spearheaded this new, vibrant hybrid, spawning a host of imitators and changing the face of British and European rock forever.

The so-called 'indie dance' boom, like all such movements, produced some genuinely innovative music as well as some dross. But this meant little in the United States where, despite having spawned house music, hip-hop was still the dominant DJ-centred music. Collaborations between rock bands and hip-hop crews tended to involve MCs rapping over rock tracks, such as on Run-DMC/Aerosmith's 'Walk This Way', or performing live, such as Chuck D and Flava Flav joining Anthrax onstage. Changing the line-up of bands changes the music: just as rock and roll's sound was created by the traditional four-piece (bass, drums, vocals, guitar) – a line-up that became standard out of necessity, to allow artists like Elvis to tour cheaply – so the addition of a DJ to the line-up is expanding the horizons of even the very 'dumbest' of bands.

Nu metal's DJ involvement represents a potentially explosive sea-change in American rock, whose influence may long outlive the genre itself.

7 What It's Like To Be A Heretic
Slipknot

Slipknot said goodbye to nu metal in mid 2001 with the release of *Iowa*, an album that cast a vast shadow over rock and roll, setting the bar several notches higher for any would-be competitors. They weren't a nu metal band, a death metal band or an anything else band anymore. They were Slipknot. Full stop. In the two years since the release of *Slipknot*, bands like Mudvayne, Hatebreed and Disturbed had all been able to shift some records to 'knot fans eager to feed their death-metal theatrics habit. There was also a rediscovery of the great 'lost' death metal bands in whose music Slipknot were rooted; you would see the hipper kids wearing Carcass, Morbid Angel and Immortal T-shirts at gigs. The album wasn't just important for Slipknot, their legion of 'maggots' (as their fans are affectionately termed), for producer/I AM label boss Ross Robinson and for Roadrunner, the parent company. Privately, people who worked in the field of metal, such as record company staff, journalists, DJs, TV and radio producers, promoters and magazine editors, admitted that they were nervous. *Iowa* was the most eagerly anticipated album in a year that seemed to be the apex of a great 'bull run' in the hard rock market. In 2000, Limp Bizkit's *Chocolate Starfish And The Hotdog Flavored Water* had come as a relief in terms of critical and popular acclaim. Marilyn Manson's *Holy Wood*...had stiffed in the shops (but he was never a big seller anyway – it was only the MTV coverage and *Newsweek* covers that gave that impression), but Slipknot were a band on the way up, multi-platinum sellers with the potential to turn some really big bucks, to establish their own tour franchise and to shake things around a little. A lot was expected of them because their debut album and live shows had led everyone to expect a lot. A duff record from a high-profile act like Slipknot could herald the end of the era, signifying the end of a particularly febrile period in rock and roll's evolution.

Rock and roll is akin to the stock market, with its boom years and recessions when growth slows. The period following the death of Kurt Cobain was a recession that started to turn around with the release of Korn's debut and peaked in 2000. Just as poor performance by a major company such as Microsoft could have disastrous consequences for tech stocks and ultimately for the whole economy, so a disappointing album, if that's what *Iowa* turned out to be, would shake the confidence of labels in their own acts. If rock CD and concert ticket sales declined, rock magazines, radio stations and websites would see sales, listeners and traffic fall. There would also be less advertising from the labels who would be hurriedly divesting themselves of bands and artists. Livelihoods were quite literally at risk. But Slipknot delivered. The world was saved. Temporarily...

Like its 1999 predecessor, *Iowa* wasn't an original ground-breaking album, it was just better. Better sound, better songs, better sales. Better. Slipknot are a band who, thus far, have managed to do everything better than any of their contemporaries, from live shows to albums to onstage theatrics. *Iowa*, the follow-up to their world-shaking eponymous debut, was the culmination of that.

Immediately before the album's release, hyperactive band spokesman drummer Joey Jordison (#1) told me, 'I have absolutely nothing to prove with this record. This record is a middle finger stuck up to every other band and they know who they are. A lot of these bands we like and respect, but this record is the musical equivalent of a kick in the face. It's the musical equivalent of having your fuckin' throat cut. The new Bible is out this summer!'

Producer Ross Robinson, who allegedly made the album while he was zonked out on potent painkillers after suffering a back injury said it was '...going to go out there and destroy everything. This real shit is going to just destroy what else is out there...super, super, super perfect and extreme and kick-ass!'

Iowa is one of those albums that every home should have. It is a *Zeitgeist*-defining album in the same way that The Sex Pistols' *Never Mind The Bollocks*, Metallica's 'Master Of Puppets' and Pink Floyd's *Dark Side Of The Moon* are albums that capture the mood of the times.

After hearing the album only once at their British record company office – as part of a new strategy to stop MP3s of tracks turning up on the Internet, record companies often no longer send out review copies to journalists – I wrote in a ten-out-of-ten review for *Metal Hammer*: '*Iowa*, in case you were in any doubt, is a solid fucking masterpiece; there have been some good albums this year, but few with that elusive "wow factor" and none with the absolute sheer perfection of this record... It's a fantastic record, the *Sergeant Pepper* of negativity, and an album that will be a benchmark that everyone else will be measured against for years to come. Most, of course, will fail to come close. This album is visceral and horrible and you want to just flip it back and start listening to the whole damned thing yet again as soon as the silence at the end kicks in.'

There was almost universal praise of the album even from the mainstream press. The *New York Times* called Slipknot 'one of the most exciting and enigmatic of rock's current crop of new bands'. *Rolling Stone* rolled out the heavy guns in the form of senior critic David Fricke who wrote, '*Iowa* is not just the first great record of the nu-metal era – it's better than that. In fact, Slipknot's second album may be the only platter of its day and subgenre that, in five or ten years, we call "classic," with the same awed breath we reserve for Black Sabbath's early monsters, Metallica's *Master Of Puppets* and Rage Against The Machine. Next to *Iowa*'s hell-hop polydrumming and nail-bomb showers of soprano-drone guitar and sampled squeal, nearly everything else in modern doom rock sounds banal, the empty yap of mall gangstas.'

Iowa entered the *Billboard* chart at Number Three and sold over a million copies in the USA in just over three months.

Slipknot, the terrifyingly garbed nine piece, seemed to spring fully formed, like Athena from the head of Zeus. They actually formed in Des Moines, Iowa – 'the middle of nowhere', as they describe it – in 1995. Iowa, a pig-farming state, has little in the way of a rock and roll heritage. There are no great bands from there, no memorable artists. Joey once joked that while Cleveland has the Rock And Roll Hall Of Fame, they ought to build the Rock And Roll Hall Of Obscurity in Des Moines.

The members wore masks – at first crude, home-made affairs – and adopted numerals as performing aliases. The stabilised line-up, in order from 0 to 8, included DJ Sid Wilson, drummer Joey Jordison, bassist Paul Grey, percussionist Chris Fehn, guitarist James Root, sampler/programmer Craig Jones, percussionist Shawn Crahan, guitarist Mic Thompson and vocalist Corey Taylor. The band sought to protect their own identities in the hope that Slipknot would be thought of as a single unit, not as a product of individuals.

'We never put on the shit we wear to try and get people into us,' says Joey Jordison. 'We did it because, after being degraded constantly for trying to play music or do something in Des Moines, it just came to be like we were an anonymous entity. No one gave a fuck, no one cared, so we were never about our names or our faces, we're just about music. So we just put it on and it started gettin' people, and it just started to turn into this big thing. The music's the most important, though. The coveralls and masks happened, and for some reason it worked, therefore we had to kind of continue with it. We got stuck with it.' Although the immediate comparisons were with Insane Clown Posse – a rap-metal act who dress as clowns, inspired by serial killer John Wayne Gacy's alter-ego, Pogo The Clown – as well as Kiss and Alice Cooper, who all incorporated theatre into their acts, Slipknot were at pains to prove it was the music not the masks that people came for. Backstage at a show when they throw off the masks they do so with a great deal of relief; they are uncomfortable to perform in. Yet they always put them back on to go and wander around among the crowd or to go to clubs afterwards.

As Corey Taylor told *HitParader* magazine after the band unveiled their 'new look' masks and costumes following the release of *Iowa*, 'Let me give you some insight into exactly how stupid we are. You might think that after experiencing everything that we went through the first time, and knowing that we were going to kick off this tour with more than 30 shows outdoors in the heat of summer, we'd have made lighter, more comfortable coveralls. Well, we went the exact other way. We made 'em thicker and of a harder material. We went on stage some days when it was like 90 degrees outside, and it must have been twice that temperature in our suits. Oh well, it's a great way to lose weight. Maybe we'll go on late night TV and offer the Slipknot Diet Plan – put on the heaviest coveralls you can find then run around in 90 degree heat for an hour.

'[The masks] changed to reflect the changes in our emotions. They're darker and more menacing than before, and that goes right along with the music on *Iowa*. We wanted the masks to really be extensions of both our personalities and of the new music. My goal was to have my mask be devoid of emotion. That way it's totally up to my movements and my voice to convey the way I feel.'

Masks have a long history in performance. In classical Roman and ancient Greek drama, masks were used for the portrayal of characters. Each mask had its own shape and colour to denote the character or emotion being depicted. The most well known of these are the masks of Comedy and Tragedy, which still symbolise the theatre today. In ancient times, without sight correction, many

Jonathan Davis, as sponsored by Adidas, shortly before he threw them over for Puma

Fieldy, whose guitar style shaped every other nu metal band

The album that started it all, Korn's eponymous 1994 Ross Robinson-produced debut. Their anti-logo was scrawled in magic marker in a couple of seconds

System Of A Down, Armenia's greatest contribution to rock 'n' roll

Limp Bizkit's Fred Durst, the poster
boy for nu metal celebrity

Limp Bizkit's Wes Borland, the musical talent
behind the band. His departure leaves a
gaping hole

Sepultura, roots mapped out new directions for metal

Great goth almighty! Coal Chamber, nu metal's dark side

Rage Against The Machine, whose 1992 debut probably had more influence on future directions in rap metal than anything before it

Slipknot, the overloads of negativity

Faith No More, whose seminal hit album included the rap-rock standard 'Epic'

Linkin Park, manufactured? Can you see the joins?

FAITH NO MORE

THE REAL THING

The Deftones, the biggest cult band in the world

Industrial scum rockers Ministry, forerunners of Static-X

Sugar Ray, famous for having famous friends

Staind, the big breakthrough band of 2001

Disturbed's Dave Draiman lives up to his band's name

Godfathers of funk metal The Red Hot Chili Peppers

Taproot, hopefuls from the next generation of nu bands

Static-X, industrial crazy men bringing techno to nu metal

Nirvana's *Nevermind* – much imitated, seldom equalled

Spineshank, the best of the rest and top of nu metal's division two

Mudvayne, theatre of blood and guts

(hed) pe, exhilarating high-energy hopefuls for 2002 and beyond

Papa Roach - Coby Dick, insects
and bugs and rock and roll

Incubus - cutting edge theatrical metal

of the audience must have had blurred vision and needed the 'coding' the masks lent the actors in order to understand what was going on. In Greek theatre, which was actually closer to a religious ritual than the way we understand theatre today, the actors represented gods and heroes, and were supposed, literally, to transform themselves. Japanese Noh theatre employed a similar tradition. When we look at masks in tribal religious rituals – beast masks and human masks, monsters and complicated head-dresses – all find their use not only in Greece and Rome, but also in China, Tibet, India, Ceylon, Siam, among the old Mexicans and Peruvians, as well as Native Americans, Inuits and traditional African tribes.

Way Of Life, an extreme Baptist sect, also made this connection, citing Slipknot as part of a conspiracy to brainwash America's youth: the masks were evidence that they were, in fact, a voodoo sect. Although Slipknot have been controversial, they have never attracted the same level of hysteria that has been directed against other bands. On the Ozzfest tour in 2000, most of the protests were directed against Marilyn Manson, who has perhaps served to keep the heat from Slipknot.

If the Christians looked a bit deeper into the background of Slipknot, they would find more than just some Hallowe'en masks to link them to the Horned One. Slipknot were inspired by a multitude of death metal bands from the late 1980s and early 1990s, particularly Venom, a band from the north-east of England who practically invented the genre with their 1981 track 'Black Metal': 'Black is the night, metal we fight/Power amps set to explode/ Energy screams, magic and dreams/Satan records the first note/ We chime the bell, chaos and hell/Metal for maniacs pure.'

Venom, then a trio fronted by a man called Cronos, with bandmates Abaddon and Mantas, recorded three cult albums in the early '80s *Welcome To Hell*, *Black Metal* and *At War With Satan*, which were fast, manic and infused with Satanic lyrics. This was a new departure for metal. Later bands – like Slayer, Exodus, Sodom, Nuclear Assault, Destruction, Kreator, Bathory and Celtic

Frost – accelerated metal to the level of a firefight with high-velocity automatic weapons, blending the comic-book occultism of the first three Black Sabbath albums with an ultra-nihilist aesthetic that seemed to revel in blood and mayhem. Of course, the difference between Black Sabbath and Slayer was really only the difference between Hammer horror films and *The Exorcist*; at heart, for all its supposed realism and seriousness, *The Exorcist* was still entertainment.

All of Slipknot, particularly Joey, were death metal fans, but they had other mutual interests that are obvious in Slipknot. Speaking to *Metal Update* in 1999, Joey dismissed those who wrote Slipknot off as some kind of sell-outs: 'The weird thing about this band was...underground people have certain bands that are so special to them – the whole thing really means so much. And then like, some fucking eighth-grade kid wearing a Korn shirt has the record and they feel the band has cheapened. A lot of times that's not the band's fault. If you listen to a song like "Eeyore", which is a bonus track on the record, or if you listen to "Get This" from the digipack or "Surfacing" or "[sic]" or even like fucking "Scissors", the roots are death metal, thrash, speed metal, and I could go on and on about all those bands. I know all the songs, and I know every fucking label... The underground metal kids should also be happy because the current success of Slipknot, on songs like "Surfacing" and "[sic]" that have super-fast 16th-note double-bass – none of those other fuckers in the other bands they lump us with could contend with that. Wait till you hear our fuckin' next record...'

There is still a vibrant international death/black metal underground, which ranges from Norwegian band Emperor's cosmic doom rock to My Dying Bride's gothic pseudo-classical stylings. The main reason anyone outside of the underground became aware of the existence of death metal was the high-profile murder case surrounding Burzum frontman Varg Vikernes, currently serving time in prison for the murder of rival

Euronymous amidst stories of church burnings, neo-Nazi connections and bloody rituals.

None of these bands, however, have much common ground with Slipknot. For a start, Slipknot avoid all the old occult clichés: Slipknot's imagery is rooted in the grittier world of mass murderers and serial killers, of the real-life monsters who stalk America. These are white trash demons, the Gacys, the Geins, the Mansons (Charlie, not Marilyn); their characters are the crazed rednecks hopped up on strychnine and moonshine who go on senseless killing sprees. Their fictional world was the gruesome world of *The Shining* (the video for 'Spit It Out' is based on Kubrick's twisted and disturbing vision), *The Texas Chainsaw Massacre*, *The Last House On The Left*, *Friday The 13th* and *Halloween*. This is about evil that has less to do with any supernatural devils or demons than it has with the twisted psychology of isolation, abuse and normalised violence. Slipknot don't actually defy categories, but they have much more going on in their sound than just reviving old death-metal riffs with some rapping and scratching on top.

As Jordison told *Rolling Stone* in October 2001, the band had no idea what they were going to sound like when they formed: 'I was a night manager at a Sinclair gas station from 1995 to 1997. That's where most of Slipknot was conceived. I'd get off band practice at about ten, and I'd bring a radio and TV and fucking crank metal. Shawn would come down at about 11:30, and we'd start plotting things out. He'd split at about five in the morning, and we'd have all these ideas. That's how we did it. Until I got fired. My bosses were cool, but I was scaring the customers away. We literally had people pull up, see me and Shawn sitting in the window, floor it out of there and go to the Amoco across the street. We were looking for a style. We had one song called "Bitchslap" that went from, like, metal to jazz to disco to thrash.'

Shawn Crahan said, 'Our philosophy had always been we

wanted to do something really different. Back at that time, there was no metal going on, there was no hardcore, nothing, so we decided to be true to ourselves. We had all been in bands that had opened up for each other, and the scene had become just terrible. No one really gave a fuck about music, so we formed Slipknot, and we played this all-reggae bar. It was in a terrible part of town, we could only get Thursday nights, and we used to flyer so much in this town, we were putting up 3,000 to 5,000 flyers. The bar owner would get a call from the city saying they were going to fine him for every flyer.' 'Then it just got sicker and sicker...' said Corey Taylor.

The band recorded a series of demos, releasing their eight-track debut *Mate. Feed. Kill. Repeat.* 'That's what Ross Robinson got a hold of, and he came to see us practise in 1998. He was standing right by me in Shawn's parents' basement, and I'm counting off the first song. I get to 'three' and I drop the drumstick. I blew it,' Joey told *Rolling Stone*.

After hanging out with Robinson in a series of strip bars – 'the single most popular form of entertainment in Des Moines' – he was convinced enough to want to record the band's new album for his newly formed I AM records. 'I used to have to get up every morning and work out to do that record,' Robinson recalled in early 2001. 'I would run, I would have to get myself physically and mentally at my peak so that I could go into the studio and make that album.'

'We're a highly, highly aggressive band,' said Crahan. 'And very seldom do we meet people who are in the realm of our aggressiveness when we play as a unit, and Ross took us into the recording room and he was throwing punches at us. He was into it.'

The recording and mixing of *Slipknot* is said to have left Robinson exhausted. The resulting album was, however, the most intense music he had ever captured on tape.

Not everyone 'got it' right away; there were the inevitable

comparisons with Limp Bizkit and Korn, and debate as to where they stood in relation to those groups. Even at one of the band's first high-profile appearances, at Ozzfest '99, nobody quite knew what to make of them. Yet with virtually no press, radio or MTV support, the album went platinum in the space of about three months.

It was a brutal, desensitised catalogue of rage and despair. There was none of the angst of Jonathan Davis about Slipknot's words. In the raw blast of 'Eyeless' Corey Taylor screams, 'Insane – Am I the only motherfucker with a brain?/I'm hearing voices but all they do is complain/How many times have you wanted to kill/Everything and everyone – Say you'll do it but never will/You can't see California without Marlon Brando's eyes/I am my father's son/He's a phantom, a mystery and that leaves me/Nothing!/How many times have you wanted to die?/It's too late for me/All you have to do is get rid of me!' The song was inspired by the schizophrenic ravings of a street dweller the band met in New York when they were visiting the offices of Roadrunner records to sign their contract. According to Mic Thompson, 'He was running around, screaming it at everyone. Though I think his choice of actor was pretty cool. He was off his shit.'

In the more defiant 'Surfacing' he sings, 'Fuck it all/Fuck this world/Fuck everything that you stand for/Don't belong/Don't exist/Don't give a shit/Don't ever judge me.'

But the truly terrifying 'Scissors' – an unconnected, rambling stream-of-consciousness outpouring, evocative of a deranged killer – was the album's equivalent of Linda Blair's 360-degree headspin in *The Exorcist* or the chest-burster in *Alien*: 'I play doctor for five minutes flat/Before I cut my heart open and let the air out/Three bugs, a pound of dust/Some wind spilled before me/In the strangest manner that had/Broke away my tear spout.'

It may have sounded like horror-comic stuff to some critics, but there was a basis in the very real human pain that some of the band's members had suffered. Rumours of childhood abuse, suicide attempts and a mania for self-slashing added to the band's mystique.

In an interview with former *Metal Hammer/Kerrang!* editor Robyn Dorrean, Joey Jordison said, "'ou stick nine guys together who have had no outlet for their whole lives, and you live in Iowa and you come out on a fucking stage then you have some shit to portray. We were walking around like ghosts, slitting our wrists open saying, "Please take a look at this, look at what we are trying to do." When we put it together and came to doing a live show all the elements of being downgraded, not appreciated, being given nothing because we live in such a shithole, all that came out. There is no way you can go through life thinking everything is great because it is not. Look at all the fucked-up shit that goes on. The world is a sick fucking place. The fact is you can come to our show and get all your aggressions out and go away feeling relieved. I want everyone to get a rush of emotion from it.'

Slipknot went out on the road, playing the major tour franchises Tattoo The Planet – a sort of halfway house between Family Values and Ozzfest – and Ozzfest 2001. The band struck up a good relationship with Ozzy Osbourne's son Jack on the 1999 tour and were hailed as conquering heroes on their return. According to Joey, 'I've always been a big Black Sabbath fan ever since my parents used to blast that shit out at me as a kid, 'Master Of Reality' and all. And Jack, Ozzy's son, is a big Slipknot fan. The last time we played Ozzfest, Jack took me to introduce me to his dad and I was so overcome that I gave him a hug and spilled Coke all down his back. He was cool but the rest of the band were going "Are you fucking nuts?"'

They also landed a slot in John McTiernan's remake of *Rollerball*, a film that was shaping up to be a disaster even as they filmed their contribution at an arena show in July 2001.

Despite their massive success, Slipknot eschewed all the

trappings of nu metal success. There was no sportswear sponsorship. Apart from instruments – '...'cos we can't fuckin' afford our own, dude!' Shawn Crahan explained to me with extreme prejudice – they steered clear of Adidas, Puma and their ilk. They were a real *No Logo* band, though their very anonymity and uniformity became the greatest 'brand' of all. This resulted in a spate of cheesy merchandise, from 'action figures' to trading cards.

'I don't know what happened. We had just changed merchandising companies or something,' Joey told me. 'The next thing I knew you were seeing Slipknot on lunchboxes, which was the sort of crap you used to get with Kiss. I know we're a band for the kids, but all of that stuff in the stores made us look like some sort of kiddie-shit band. It misrepresents the band so we're going to keep a tight rein on that shit from now on. Slipknot became more like a line of clothing and less like a band. But you live an' you learn.'

IGN For Men magazine asked Corey Taylor if we were ever likely to see a Slipknot Gap ad: 'Fuck no! Negative. You will not and if you ever do see us, dude, shoot us in the face 'cause we don't know what the hell we're doin'. We're not in this for the fuckin' modeling. We're not in this for any of that shit, dude. The music mainly and fuckin' foremost. We don't give a shit about all that crap.'

The inevitable public feud with Fred Durst – something that, it seems, no major player in the world of rock and entertainment in general can avoid – flared up when a friend of the band (alleged to have been Ross Robinson) saw a posting or a transcript of a webchat where Durst is supposed to have called Slipknot 'maggots' 'fat and ugly kids'. Corey Taylor responded angrily, 'You might have a lot of money and be famous, but the next time you talk shit about Slipknot and its fans we'll kill you.' Slipknot then upped the ante by burning, or otherwise destroying, Limp Bizkit paraphernalia live onstage at every show.

In another interview, they widened the net to include Korn:

'Some people may think that we hate Korn and Limp Bizkit, but that's not entirely true, we just hate Korn's third album and Limp Bizkit's second album. Their first albums, however, did greatly influence us. We do, however, like Korn's album *Issues*, some of it does sound like the first one, but they still could have perfected it. We've never met either of them, but we'd like to.'

Whether Ross Robinson had fuelled this war, or whether it was stoked up for publicity is unclear. In fact Durst made a few peace moves, saying publicly how much he loved Slipknot and denying that he had ever said anything disparaging about their fans. But Corey, characteristically, responded by saying that he didn't give a shit what Fred Durst said.

When the band came to do *Iowa*, some of the songs had already been previewed live, most notably 'People=Shit', which was bootlegged and found its way on to the Napster and Audiogalaxy sites, at the time the premier file-trading protocols on the web. But nobody knew what the album would be like; there were some rumours that it would be a poppier record and others that it would be an almost unapproachable extreme death metal collection.

The songs for the album were actually written very quickly in a space of only a few months. Recording seemed to go quickly, the band ensconced at Robinson's Indigo Studios near Malibu. The release was slated for early summer 2001, with the provisional titles being *People=Shit* and *Iowa*. As it turned out, the mixing and remixing of the album by Andy Wallace in New York took longer than anticipated and the album was put back until August. This delay, coupled with the speed at which it had been recorded, suggested that it may actually have been a problematic release. Robinson talked up the album in interviews as did the band to everyone they met, but the completed record was kept under wraps as long as possible.

It was, as we now know, a huge record, an epochal event.

Lyrically, musically and production-wise, *Iowa* was even better than their debut. The opening instrumental '(515)' (which is the Iowa telephone area code) and the segue into the pulverising 'People=Shit' is one of the most exhilarating beginnings to any rock album in the past ten years. 'Here we go again, motherfucker!' Corey spits. The pure rage of 'The Heretic Song' ('Throw a suicide party and I'm guaranteed to fucking snap/It's evilsonic, it's pornoholic/Breakdown, obscenities it's all I wanna be/If you're 555, then I'm 666/What's it like to be a heretic?') and the rabid 'Left Behind' were among the strongest and most memorable rock and roll songs to have emerged from the nu metal scene.

Songs like 'I Am Hated', mercilessly mock their cry-baby contemporaries: 'Welcome to the same ol' fuckin' scam/Same ol' shit in a dead fad/Everybody wants to be so hard/Are you real or a second-rate sports card?/They all lost their dad or their wife just died/They never got to go outside – SHUT UP/Nobody gives a fuck/It doesn't change the fact that you suck.'

And the closing track, 'Iowa', a bleak and disturbing glimpse into the head of a killer, a slow and menacing track that builds up through samples, disembodied voices and half-audible noises, evokes The Stooges' *Dirt* and The Velvet Underground's *The Gift*. 'Relax...it's over, you belong to me, I fill your mouth with dirt/Relax...it's over, you can never leave/I take your second digit with me...Love.../You are...my first, I can breathe/I find you fascinating/You are...my favorite, lay you down to sleep.' This was visceral. It wasn't a joke, a parody or even mere sickness for sickness sake. This was something that was intended to unsettle and disturb, like a James Ellroy novel or a David Lynch film. It was one of the darkest rock and roll songs ever because there wasn't even the hint of pretension that it served some moral purpose. It was evil, in a real sense.

Speaking to me in late September 2001, Joey admitted that *Iowa* had inadvertently presented them with a problem: 'Nobody is saying it right now, but it wasn't really so hard to top the first record. This record is gonna take some doing.'

Having raised the stakes for everyone in rock and roll, by presenting them with the standard they must at least aspire to beat, Slipknot and their rivalries, their taunting of other bands, may have spurred on the rest to try to top their achievement. Nobody - not the band, not Ross Robinson - is even talking about the next album as yet, but *Iowa* threw the ball into Limp Bizkit, Korn and Marilyn Manson's court. If they meet the challenge, that's good for rock and roll. Period.

8 Girls' Skool
Kittie

Kittie, Coal Chamber, A Perfect Circle, Defenestration and My Ruin are exceptions in nu metal because they include women members. Kittie, an all-female band from London, Ontario in Canada, are unique in that they are currently the only all-female band on the scene. From a period when women seemed to dominate the Top 40 and the alternative charts in the early 1990s to the present day, which is dominated by angry, loud guys, it seems there has been a major seismic shift in the position of women in rock. Kittie, like Slipknot, could only be considered a nu metal band by stretching the boundaries to fit them. As well as being a girl band, they have little in common with the rap-metal-derived boy bands other than their youth, energy and reinvigoration of rock's abandoned corners – in their case glam rock. Neither do they really fit into any of the other prevailing subgenres.

American rock is male dominated; that has always been the case and probably always will be. But in the current climate, it is almost a reversion to some 1950s college fraternity mentality or one of those dreadful '80s 'comedies' like *Porky's* or *Revenge Of The Nerds* that prevails. There's a sniggering porno mag-reading attitude to sex and a streak of blatant homophobia that runs through youth culture ('totally gay' is one of the worst insults you can pay a person or thing), which seems to have been dredged up from the Eisenhower years. And women don't so much play a secondary role as much as seem to be completely absent. Of course, if you go to see Korn or Limp Bizkit or Slipknot, at least half of the audience will be girls. Once, metal was an all-male preserve, though there were a few female bands and female-fronted bands. Now, the stage is the only place you are unlikely to see women.

Courtney Love, when asked about the abiding influence of Nirvana on bands today, responded with a characteristic outburst, calling nu metal bands 'boring sexists'. She said that nu metallers access black male American culture, without the pain of being a black male in America: 'They are such pain in the ass, old skool, boring sexists that it's actually starting to hurt the culture of females in the US.' Courtney has recruited an all-female band called Bastard – featuring former Hole drummer Patty Schemel, Nashville Pussy/The Masons guitarist Corey Parkes, ex-Veruca Salt guitarist Louise Post and ex-Rockit Girl bassist Gina Crosley – which she describes as a 'female Megadeth' and claims that there is an urgenct need for a female supergroup like this, given the anti-woman climate in rock. On a posting on her website she said, 'I'm not trying to do a real pop-rock record again, because I did that. The Bastard demo is really raw and really rock and really personal. I don't write songs about the business or deconstruct celebrity; they're more emotional, internal songs. I have really high standards, and it's not a joke anymore. I love Kittie, but it needs to be Zeppelin-level. And if we can't kick Fred Durst's ass, I don't want to do it. I'm not happy unless it's going to be fucking great.'

Interestingly, she also noted that the success of Limp Bizkit may be down to the fact that sensitive women's music like that of Alanis Morissette, Tori Amos, Joan Osborne, Jewel, Sarah MacLachlan and other artists associated with the women-only tour Lilith Fair, dominated so much of mainstream music in the early 1990s and claimed that if she were a testosterone-drenched adolescent male then she would go for them too. 'Maybe,' she wrote in a widely circulated newsgroup posting 'somehow all of a sudden the boys got really fed up with all the singer-songwriter girls and all the gentle emo-alternative bands. I would if I were raging with testosterone.' Other observers have suggested that it is this separatism – the creation of events like Lilith Fair – that has given the 'masculist' rockers the excuse they need to exclude women. By coralling them in a neat sector, it leaves the market clear for men's music, which is what is really important.

Criticism of Fred Durst's attitude to women has already been noted. But nu metal's rival genre for the hearts and minds of America's youth, the contemporary 'punk' of Blink-182, The Bloodhound Gang and Weezer, sort of like the dumber, more inbred cousin of nu metal, makes Fred look like a sensitive new man. It's a far cry from self-styled 'male feminist' Kurt Cobain onstage in a dress.

A few (all-male) bands at least seem to buck the trend of beer-drinking boys screaming about how much women have hurt them, huddled together like a bunch of schoolboys with a porn mag, as though seeking protection in gangs. Orgy flirt with androgyny, something that – with the exception of Marilyn Manson – has all but disappeared from American rock. There are few openly gay artists in American rock, never mind in nu metal: Orgy, who let it be known that they are strip-bar *habitués*, may dress like the transvestite crew of the Starship *Enterprise*, but they seem to want to spell out in the clearest possible terms that they are all straight men. They even appeared in a notorious porn video, *Backstage Sluts*, directed by self-styled Gen-X pornographer Matt Zane.

As Zane told *Kerrang!*, 'The films have the biggest rock bands in the world in them. They explain their backstage stories, which we then re-enact. We've had people like Mark McGrath from Sugar Ray, Jay Gordon from Orgy, and the Sevendust guys telling stories. Limp Bizkit's Fred Durst appeared on camera as Vinnie "The Weapon" Malone, disguised by a fake porn-star moustache and wig. He was actually interviewed while a name girl had her hands down his pants and he was sucking on her nipples and spreading her ass and pussy. We even had the late Lynn Strait from Snot actually fuck one of the girls in a movie. She was in a three-way with his girlfriend.'

Zane's films may be post-modern pornography, and may be seen to celebrate a more liberated, rock and roll attitude to sex, contrasting with the puritanism of American feminist writers such as Andrea Dworkin – who equates all heterosexual acts between a man and a woman with rape – and Catherine McKinnon, a liberal-left anti-pornography crusader who has made common cause with the Republican and Christian right. However, his films can also be seen as simply old porn in new videos, and the bands who participate in them are colluding in the exploitation of women.

Of course, not all of the new bands share the 'frat boy' mentality. Speaking in the November 2001 issue of *Spin* magazine, Incubus singer Brandon Boyd said, 'Most of my favorite artists are women – Björk, PJ Harvey, Ani DiFranco. Men have a lot less to write about, unless you're somebody like Tom Waits or John Lennon. And the female voice is much more suited to melody. Men have this barky thing – we're domesticated apes with a microphone.'

Rap, for all its misogyny, has some strong female voices, such as EVE, Li'l Kim, Lauryn Hill, Da Brat, Foxy Brown, Lady Luck and Gangsta Boo. R&B is almost wholly dominated by women. Rock and roll, though, has always been a man's world. There have always been female singers, but more often than not they have been the mouthpieces for male producers, songwriters and managers. In the 1960s, a new school of female singer-songwriters such as Joni Mitchell, Carole King and Joan Baez broke through, though this was more as an outgrowth of the folk scene. Credible female performers like Grace Slick and all-woman bands like Fanny, The GTOs, The Chicago Women's Liberation Rock Band, The Runaways and Bertha were rare. In the post-punk era, it seemed that more and more women were breaking into music, playing in mixed or all-female bands. The Slits, Siouxsie And The Banshees, X, The Mekons, The Delta 5, The Au Pairs and The Raincoats all brought a new female-centred consciousness to rock that challenged the prevailing orthodoxy. Suddenly, the inherent sexism in songs by artists like The Rolling Stones was questioned: why were women in rock and roll songs all honky-tonk women, bad-ass bitches, stupid girls or drippy mystical virgins?

Metal always seemed to be the worst offender. Whitesnake, for example, used an air-brushed painting of a large-bottomed naked women straddling a giant hissing snake on the sleeve of their *Lovehunter* album. The world was changing, but metal seemed to be holding out against the tide. In the 1980s, the term 'metal fan' was almost like shorthand for 'sexually inexperienced adolescent white male retreating into a fantasy world with few opportunities to vent his sexual frustration'. But this, too, began to change as metal itself mutated: all-female bands like L7, The Lunachicks, Babes In Toyland, Bikini Kill and Seven Year Bitch were all mainstays of the metal/grunge scene in the early 1990s. Bands like Throwing Muses, Kim Deal's The Breeders and The Amps, Luscious Jackson, Veruca Salt and Tanya Donnely's band Belly created music that transcended any notions of 'novelty act' sometimes associated with all-woman bands and demanded to be taken seriously. There was no compromise, the music was not 'de-sexed' in any way. It was challenging and exciting in a way that Liz Phair, Jewel, Natalie Merchant, Sarah MacLachlan and other menstrual-cycle poetesses weeping into their acoustic guitars were not.

Kittie, then, are the inheritors of this lost age of female rock bands. In interviews they have always avoided singling out any of these groups as influences and, given their age, it's likely that until they were asked questions about them, they had never heard of them. But there is too much in common to be ignored. They too stand on their own merits and demand never to be treated as a curiosity, their sex being their unique selling point but never in any way something to hide behind as an excuse or to exploit. They should be treated as a rock band rather than a girl band. The trouble is that, because they are the only one, the latter is unavoidable.

The band themselves steered clear of any women-in-rock clichés, taking it for granted that there was nothing unusual about four girls forming a hard rock band. Their sound and attitude owes more to bands like Pantera and Machine Head than to L7 or Bikini Kill. Bassist Talena Atfield told the *NY Rock* website in 2000, 'I think there are a lot of people who are still really ignorant. They're like, "Girls can't play." They hear it and most times their minds are changed but it's a lot different. I mean, you don't look at most bands and say, "Oh look, it's a guy band." But they do that to us. They're like, "It's a girl band." We're about our music. We don't want to be known as a "girl band". We want to be known as a band. People take that word "female" and automatically have preconceived ideas that we can't play and that we're gonna go up there and try to sell sex. But that's not what we do.'

Morgan Lander told *Metal Hammer* in December 2001, 'Our first experience of the British press was very bad. I think Mercedes was ready to deck the guy! He obviously had his own idea of what the band should be about and he kept trying to make us agree with him. He thought that everything we did had a sexual slant to it. The fact that we wore big boots onstage meant that we were promiscuous and we wanted sex! It's a stage costume, lots of people wear different clothes to go onstage, but because we're female he was trying to drill it in that it had to be about sex.'

Formed by drummer Mercedes Lander and guitarist Fallon Bowman, Kittie met in a gym class at their high school, and began playing Nirvana and Silverchair covers with Morgan on vocals before being joined by Talena Atfield on bass. Like Slipknot, the band are second-generation metallers; they recount how they were taken to see Bon Jovi by their parents when they were younger, and Morgan and Mercedes' father is the band's manager. These are hardly rock and roll rebels, out raising hell on the road and driving Mom and Pop to drink.

After playing local battle of the bands shows, Kittie got a demo to producer GGGarth Richardson through a friend who worked as an engineer in his studio. Richardson, whose previous work had been with Rage Against The Machine and The Red Hot Chili Peppers, loved the band and, rather as Ross Robinson has done with Korn, Limp Bizkit, Amen, Slipknot and numerous other bands, took them under his wing as well as producing their first record. The band signed to New York independent label Artemis (labelmates include rapper Kurupt and country legend Steve Earle). *Spit*, their debut album released in 1999, was a potent combination of Kiss-era glam and the darkest death metal; the single 'Brackish' was almost shocking when people realised that this was four teenage girls.

Kittie don't have a feminist agenda like Sleater Kinney, Bikini Kill or Courtney Love; they just want to be respected for their music, and they get irritated by constant questions, particularly from the mainstream press, about Britney Spears or whether they have a favourite member of N'SYNC.

'We write songs, we perform live, we play our own instruments, we make records,' said Morgan when I interviewed the band in 2000. 'What do we have to do to be credible? Why do they always ask us about Britney or who we have sex with?' Morgan Lander's vocals alternate between the demonic death metal growl of a latter-day Glenn Benton of Deicide and straight, sweet little-girl singing. In person and offstage, they are fairly typical sulky late-teens/early-20s North American kids. Onstage they are possessed. The lyrics are like an angry feminist riposte to Durst & Co On 'Spit', Morgan sings, 'Why do I get shit all the time?/From you men/You are swine/You think dick is the answer/But it's not.' 'A lot of guys don't want a bunch of little girls to get in the way of their music,' said Fallon, who wrote the song. 'That song's about someone telling you that they love you so much, and they put you up on a pedestal and make you feel great, then they turn around and say, "Screw you."'

On the even more brutal 'Choke', Morgan berates her – real or imagined – abuser: 'There's only one word to describe you, and that's a hypocrite/I looked over you, I looked over me/Look at you and smile, you fucking paedophile/I looked over you, I looked over me/Look at you and smile, paedophile!'

Actually, the lyrics might have been more shocking if it was possible to make out what she was actually singing: Lander's voice is reminiscent of the voice of Linda Blair in *The Exorcist* (though the voice of veteran hard-smoking actress Mercedes McCambridge was the one actually dubbed on), possessed by the devil, bellowing, 'The sow is mine!'

Touring with Slipknot in the USA and Europe in summer 2000 – something of a baptism of fire – Kittie hardened up their sound and forged themselves into a much tighter musical unit. This is evident from the fact that second album *Oracle* – also produced by GGGarth Richardson – is a much more brutal and vicious record than its predecessor, something of an achievement in itself, albeit with better songs and less desire to rely on 'shock tactics'. It is almost an emerging pattern amongst the nu metal bands that it is the group's sophomore album that is the most accomplished work (with the third as the mega-seller) and so it is with Kittie. Reduced to a power trio in late 2001, following the departure of founder member Fallon Bowman, Kittie seemed defiant and confident with the new album.

The album saw Kittie struggle to break out of the short, sharp and brutal rock song prison. 'Pink Lemonade', a slow and evil long song to close the album, in the manner of Slipknot's 'Scissors' or 'Iowa', was a partly successful attempt to map out a new direction, while their cover of Pink Floyd's 'Run Like Hell' bucked the trend for metal bands doing '80s pop covers.

But if anyone was looking for Kittie to make any bold feminist pronouncements, they were to be disappointed. But perhaps their statement was just in being themselves; they looked like normal teenage-girl rock fans going through their goth phase. They were not packed off to plastic surgeons, make-over artists or couturiers by their record company A&R staff to mould them into something else – a fate that has befallen many female performers in the past – nor were they encouraged to exploit their sexuality for publicity. Obviously having Dad as a manager means they are less likely to appear in a *Maxim* celeb nudie spread. There's a cliché which says that women have to try twice as hard as men to be thought of as being half as good. And no matter how good their music is, they will be judged on what they look like. Speaking to *Metal Hammer* in early 2001, Talena Atfield said, 'You wear one thing and you get called this, you wear another and you get called that. You wear a short skirt and a tank top, which is pretty natural for girls our age and people say you look slutty; or you wear jeans and a T-shirt and people say you look like you just rolled out of bed.'

Morgan Lander said, 'The sad thing is if you are a female and there is an unflattering picture of you in a magazine then people start talking shit about you. That even happens to guys these days. Look at Chino from The Deftones – he gained a little weight and people said, "The Deftones suck 'cos Chino's fat!"'

There are early signs that the male domination of rock is about to be challenged again; mixed bands like Defenestration and SugarComa, still at a very early stage in their development, are none the less winning fans. But it is early days and their numbers are few. Whether Kittie are the first of a new wave of girl bands or the last of them remains to be seen, but given the preponderance of frat boys in rock, they may merely be an exception that proves the rule that rock is strictly a men-only business.

9 The Second Wave And The New Nu Breed
Tomorrow's Major Playas

As well as the major players like Korn and Limp Bizkit, nu metal has produced a strong second wave of bands who are less obviously in the rap-metal mould, and who appeal to a smaller and more defined fanbase. These are not underground bands by any means – many of them enjoy success on the *Billboard* charts, gold and platinum sales and headlining tours – but they are names that are less likely to be recognised outside the confines of those fans in the know. They are all bands, to be sure, who receive heavy rotation on MTV, though they are more likely to appear on the specialist rock strands than sandwiched betwixt Britney and J-Lo during peak hours. Spineshank, Orgy, System Of A Down and Static-X are all bands with roots in the industrial scene from the 1980s and 1990s, while acclaimed west coast band (hed) pe take the Limp Bizkit rock-rap blueprint to a new level, refining it even further, cranking up the energy and adding a healthy dose of sexuality. When genres die, there are bands who survive and bands who are dragged screaming into oblivion. Some of these bands are likely to be the stadium acts of the next 147five years and are likely to develop in such a way that it will scarcely be remembered that they were in any way associated with nu metal.

There is a veritable plethora of second-wave bands, ranging from the good (Dry Kill Logic, Ill Niño, Papa Roach, (hed) pe) to interchangeable clones of the more successful groups. Every movement, whether or not it recognises itself as a movement, follows this pattern. Movements contain the seeds of their own destruction. They also inspire opposition, which often uses their own success against them. Eventually the onslaught of a profusion of third-rate hack bands will destroy nu metal, leaving only a handful of devotees to write their fanzines, buy their small-scale singles and turn up at shows in their hundreds rather than tens of thousands. In this chapter we'll look at the best of the emerging division two, the newcomers and a few bands who still inject excitement, energy and guts into their music, even if originality is not their strong point.

Others point the way to some sort of life beyond nu metal – the next phase in the music's development. Predicting the future of rock and roll is trickier than tackling the stock market and the race track combined. If there *is* any pattern, it tends to follow VI Lenin's adage of 'Two steps forward, one step back', becoming increasingly sophisticated and intelligent, then renewing itself by reverting to a more primitive form and starting again. Rock and roll is like a South American banana republic, beset by popular uprisings, palace coups and Marxist revolutions every few years, with Year Zero looming just around the corner as soon as any kind of stability seems to have been achieved. But it's safe to assume that some of these bands – particularly Coal Chamber, Static-X and System Of A Down – will form the backbone of the major league in the next five years.

GODSMACK

A Boston four-piece consisting of Sully Erna (vocals), Tony Rambola (guitar), Robbie Merrill (bass) and Tommy Stewart (drums), Godsmack's independently released 1997 debut, *All Wound Up*, was recorded for two and a half thousand dollars. Universal records picked up the band and re-released the album – this time simply entitled *Godsmack* – a year later, with extra tracks. To date the album has gone platinum. Godsmack would be just another second-division success story were it not for the controversy that surrounded this release when self-appointed clean-up-rock campaigner Kevin Clarke started a campaign to have the album removed from the shelves of retail chain Wal-Mart. In the late 1990s, even before the Columbine High School shootings, America was experiencing one of the frequent moral panics – about rock, rap, movies, video games and TV – that grip the nation from time to time. Sometimes it is sex, sometimes violence. In the case of Godsmack, Clarke, whose other targets have included Powerman 5000, objected to the swearing and the lyrics encouraging suicide.

Getting albums banned from Wal-Mart has been a ploy of the Christian right for some years, allowing them to take the moral high ground and argue that they are not calling for censorship over an artist's right to free speech. Since banning records and books from Wal-Mart amounts to the same thing in some areas, it is censorship.

But this was a difficult case to make: the artist does not have a moral or legal right to distribution or sale in privately owned stores. Christian magazine *The World* was jubilant: 'The model of persuading the salesmen, rather than the manufacturers, is an intriguing tactic for cleaning up the culture without censorship. It may be impossible to police the Internet, but what if the major search engines that choose which sites they link to could be persuaded not to carry pornography? People are free to write what they want, but publishers are not obligated to buy it and print it. Maybe those who manufacture entertainment for our young people could develop a sense of shame, so that their conscience would not allow them to corrupt children as they have been doing. A number of filmmakers have been saying that they would not let their children see the movies they have been making. So why are they doing this to other people's children?'

Wal-Mart founder Sam Walton was a devout Christian who continued to teach Sunday school long after he became one of the richest men in America. Wal-Mart also knows its customers. The big department store chains concentrated on upscale urban shoppers, but Walton realised that most Americans live in small towns. By targeting this under-served market, Wal-Mart eventually dwarfed every other retailer, driving local mom-and-pop stores out of business and ensuring an almost undefeatable monopoly based on its pile-'em-high-sell-'em-cheap philosophy. Wal-Mart believes that being a 'family' store is the key to its mass appeal. Wal-Mart knows where its middle American customers stand on 'culture wars', and the move to 'censor' music by refusing to stock material it deemed offensive was actually a popular one in the US hinterlands, away from those big-city folks with their clever talk about the Constitution and freedom of expression.

Wal-Mart accounts for ten per cent of US CD sales, and has effectively forced artists and record companies to produce 'clean' versions of their works so that they can go on sale in its stores. Nirvana, for example, changed a song title from 'Rape Me' to 'Waif Me' for the Wal-Mart version of *In Utero*, which Wal-Mart also objected to because its sleeve portrayed foetuses. Kurt Cobain and Krist Novoselic agreed to the changes because – as we saw in an earlier chapter – as kids growing up in Aberdeen, Washington, their local Wal-Mart was the only store where they could buy records. *Playboy* magazine is banned from the store and *Cosmopolitan*, *Rolling Stone* and *Vibe* have all been taken off the shelves because the store regarded their covers as too provocative. The *Godsmack* album – which contains 'profanity' and the word 'fuck' throughout, though no more than any other release – was removed from the shelves because it did not carry the Parental Advisory sticker, which supposedly guarantees that it will not be sold to minors.

But there were other contributing factors: Sully Erna is a high-profile practitioner of Wicca, a 'practising witch of the Celtic religion under Salem witch Laurie Cabot, continuing to weave the Wiccan arts and rituals into the fabric of daily life. It's been my salvation. A lot of people are confused about witchcraft; it's simply about worshipping the power of the earth, and that's it! It's a positive religion that has helped me through a lot of bad times.'

Although Satanism has long been associated with metal, only the most deluded fans and detractors take it in any way seriously. Yet here was an articulate and informed high-profile spokesman for a faith that has long been targeted by Christian fundamentalists.

Then there was the name: it was originally a song by Alice In Chains, a cute conflation of the Lord Almighty with a '70s street-slang term for heroin. In an interview with *NY Rock* website, Sully spoke about the origin of the name and elucidated further about his beliefs: 'We don't worship Satan or the devil because we don't believe in it. We believe that the earth is a mother to us all and we should honor and respect her, and live a harmonious life. We don't own the earth but we are part of it and to destroy it means to destroy ourselves. We respect life above all. Respect for life and free thought I'd say are the basics for Wicca. We respect every other religion because we think all gods and goddesses are the same. People just worship them in a different way. Wicca is often mistakenly associated with evil, but we believe in Karma and if we do something bad it comes back to haunt us, as a "Godsmack"! I was making fun of somebody who had a cold sore on his lip and the next day I had one myself and somebody said, "It's a Godsmack." The name stuck. We were aware of the Alice In Chains song but didn't really think much about it. It's a cool song and the name had meaning for us.'

In the end, the Wal-Mart incident may have consolidated support for the band and offset some of the sales lost when the album was removed from stores. Like many of the second-wave bands, Godsmack's sound is a little too close to 'Enter Sandman' era Metallica, Soundgarden and Alice In Chains for comfort, though second album *Awake* saw them go some way towards carving out their own identity. It was also clear that despite being mired in their grunge roots, Sully was a talented and charismatic frontman and songwriter, struggling to rise above leaden riffs and monoculture bass.

STATIC-X

When Wayne Static described the band's second album *Machine* as 'two parts Ministry, one part Pantera, one part Donna Summer and maybe with a little Joy Division sprinkled on top' before it was released, people assumed he was joking. He wasn't. *Machine*, released in May 2001, is the band's second album and while it never made the sort of big-bang impact of Staind or Slipknot on the charts, Static-X's slot on Tattoo The Planet and Family Values 2001 saw them comfortably breach the walls of that rock and roll Premiership. Energy, guts, passion and a jackhammer beat, which cracks the bones in your sternum and forces the air out of your lungs will always win through in the end; and people are always going to want great disco records. Offstage, Static-X are real regular-guy types; onstage they catch fire together.

Comparisons between Ministry and Static-X had been drawn, even before the release of debut album *Wisconsin Death Trip*, not just because of the nature of the music – a fusion of the hardest-edged techno, riff-laden speed metal and machine-gun industrial beats – but the sheer mad-to-exist craziness onstage. Their cover of Ministry's 'Burning Inside' is still one of the high points of their live set, investing the already manic classic with an injection of energy that pushes the needle on the speedometer off the dial. But if you're looking for a band who snort meals straight from a mirror balanced on top of a real human skull then maybe you should look elsewhere.

The Ministry story is funny as hell but a little bit tragic at heart. The band formed by demonic Al Jourgensen, aka Buck Satan, and slightly less demonic partner Paul Barker began life as a post-goth electro outfit in Chicago in the early 1980s, pushing at the boundaries bands like Depeche Mode had set, making electronic pop that was a bit less sweet and a bit less nice. Early albums like *Twitch* barely hint at the dark madness that was to come on albums like *The Land Of Rape And Honey*, the awesome 1989 release, *The Mind Is A Terrible Thing To Taste*, and the most magnificent heart of darkness itself *Psalm 69*. Other bands, like Skinny Puppy, The Young Gods, Front 242 and Nitzer Ebb, also made fantastic, still unsurpassed pulverising tech-metal music during the same period, but it's Ministry who epitomise what we mean when we talk about industrial music.

At their peak they created a sort of apocalyptic *Mad Max* universe involving flaming gas jets, flame-throwers and genuine, certifiable onstage insanity. Unfortunately, they also epitomise the very real dark side of the genre, the nihilistic quality that took its toll in many ways on main(line) man Jourgensen.

On the cusp of major mainstream success – Ministry were selling albums, getting written about in the press and pulling in huge crowds – Jourgensen lost it. It's not fair to call Al a junkie, because that implies he was taking heroin and, in fact, Al was an equal-opportunities drug abuser. Another journalist once told me a story about interviewing Al in Texas. They were put in a limo together to do the interview after Al had been frisked for drugs. As they closed the door, he produced a pipe and a rock of crack from the hollowed-out heel of one of his cowboy boots and proceeded to get high. The interview consists of disconnected ramblings, one-word answers and long, long silences...

Naturally, relentless negativity and copious drug abuse make for a great story but not necessarily a great album, and *Dark Side Of The Spoon*, the much-anticipated follow up to *Filth Pig*, was a bit of a disappointment.

Yet there are bands that are important because they sold a few million records and there are bands that are important because although they only sold a few thousand records, most of the people who bought a copy were inspired by it to form a band. Fear Factory, Stabbing Westward and Nine Inch Nails are just a few of the countless bands who have heard Ministry's dark gospel and gone forth to preach it themselves. The Static-X story, on the other hand, is a little less eventful and a little more concerned with making music, touring and recording.

Wayne came from Shelby, Michigan, Ken from Jamaica, Illinois. Both moved to the comparatively cosmopolitan city of Chicago, hog butcher to the world and original home of the whole Wax Trax/Ministry axis as well as house music and Chicago blues. Ken played in metal bands and Wayne started a goth outfit called Deep Blue Dream who shared a rehearsal studio with a then unsigned Smashing Pumpkins. Wayne was introduced to Billy Corgan's record store co-worker, Ken, who joined Deep Blue Dream, before the two decided to move to the sunnier climes of LA in 1994 and eventually form Static-X.

'The whole theory behind this band was that we wanted a constant driving beat, much like what Ministry did with their early recordings out of Chicago, we wanted to extend that sound and make it even more accessible like on the song "Push It",' said Wayne in an earlier interview and, in a sense, that's exactly what Static-X have done. They have filed a lot of the rough edges off the sound, made it acceptable to MTV and mainstream as well as 'alternative' and rock radio. In other words, take the blueprint and bland it out ever so slightly.

That's not a criticism of Static-X, suggesting they are doing something immoral. Far from it; they've done what every great rock and roll band over the past 50 years has done, taking something extreme, obscure or very raw, and refining it into the stuff of classic Top 40 hits. Elvis, The Rolling Stones, The Jam – the best-known exemplar of the technique today would be Limp Bizkit, plundering a whole raft of underground hip-hop and punk influences, and getting the whole shebang on MTV.

Things could, however, have taken a slightly different course and, in their earliest incarnation, Static-X experimented with a very different sound. 'We're far too white to go into rap metal,' says Ken. 'Wayne actually tried rapping for, like, a day and we thought, God, this sucks. That was years before anybody else was seriously into rap metal.'

Other groups have borrowed liberally from hip-hop but there

aren't too many places where rave and metal have dovetailed; Static-X are unmistakably a rock and roll band, albeit one laden with samples, synth effects and cybernetic basslines. Even the name suggests some late-'80s studio collective in smiley T-shirts luv'd up and monged to the tits on disco biscuits.

Living in Chicago, was house music a big influence? 'How could it not be?' says Wayne. 'It was born in Chicago, it was the headquarters for house.'

'I was a dance music buyer for the record store I worked in in the late '80s, so I think we were all aware of what was going on,' says Ken.

'I listened to a lot of techno for a while,' says Wayne. 'There's nothing new that has caught my imagination but '94, '95, '96 I was listening to a lot of stuff like Prodigy and Crystal Method. There are a lot of bands today trying to copy Prodigy, but to me the whole thing got really boring. It's a lot of the same stuff. When I heard that last Prodigy album I thought, "Wow, this is so different." But then it was like nobody else stepped up.'

Why move from Chicago, which seems to always have been a musical hotbed? 'Chicago was a big city filled with small-town people,' says Wayne. 'It's very closed minded other than a very very small underground scene. Everyone's from the Midwest and is very conservative. LA is much more open minded.' 'LA is like a collection of small cities all in one, very culturally diverse,' says Ken. They still have a lot of gratitude for LA and the LA scene, particularly bands like Coal Chamber and Fear Factory who famously took the band under their wing during their formative years. 'One of the best things that happened to us was when we went on tour with Fear Factory,' remembers Ken. 'We just learned so much from them. In fact, all the LA bands. We always had fun on those tours and it was always an easier tour for us to do because it was like taking a piece of home along with you. There was a higher comfort factor. That's not to say that we have anything against bands who are not from LA. We've just finished touring with Godhead, from Washington DC...but they're moving to LA.'

Static-X are, as we've noted, real down-to-earth regular guys and don't have the toxic cloud of sheer negativity that surrounded Al Jourgensen. You don't exactly have to roll up their sleeves to tell that there are no major narcotics disasters in the group. They even believe in setting a good example to their fans. 'Oh, we're such dads,' laughs Ken. 'I tell them not to smoke. I see all these kids out there at our shows and they're smoking. I tell them that it's not cool.'

'I remember one girl in Philadelphia and she's just standing at the front yelling at the top of her lungs, "Fuck me!" After the show I went out to the bus and she was standing there waiting with all her other friends, smoking and I was like "How old are you?" and she said "I'm 11." And all her friends were, like, 13. I was just like "What the hell is wrong with you? Gimme those..." and I'm taking their cigarettes and their beer away,' says bassist Tony Campos.

'The bad thing is that I had already lectured them inside and she was going "Sign my boobs" and I was like "No, you don't *have* any yet..."' says Ken. "These kids are in such a hurry to grow up and when it does happen it's like "Where the hell did my childhood go?"' says Tony.

This is interesting; a band influenced by Ministry who get pissed off at under-age smoking? 'Al's a really good role model,' sniggers Tony. 'The difference is that I wasn't into Ministry when I was 12 years old,' says Wayne. 'I was 18 and that's a whole different story.' 'Look at how far we've come since The Land Of Rape And Honey was released. Look at how far the media coverage of this music has come,' says Ken. 'Drug use is now widely publicised and we know statistics. I know rock and roll is supposed to be "dangerous" but there's a whole lost generation of kids out there that the media have dubbed Generation Y right now, like a marketing thing. And these kids need help...' 'And we're gonna give it to them,' says Wayne.

Are Static-X fans obsessive? 'Some,' says Wayne. 'A few,' says Ken. Maybe the wholesome influence is making some progress. Apparently, fanatical Static-X fans are now more likely to use glue as hair gel than to sniff it.

'This kid came to one of our shows and he was, like, "You gotta get me in to meet Wayne. He's my god!"' recalls Ken. 'But when he finally got into the dressing room he was like this [sullen, eyes downcast] just standing there between us.'

'This kid had his hair sort of like Wayne and he used Elmer's Glue [a well-known US brand popular with DIY types] and not just Elmer's, it was Elmer's Wood Glue he used, the yellow stuff. And he asked Wayne, "So you use Elmer's on your hair?" And Wayne was, like, "No." And this look of dread came on the kid's face: "How can I explain this to my mom?"' 'He was gonna be like that for the rest of the school year, unless he shaved it off,' says Ken. 'Yeah, with a chainsaw,' says Wayne.

To call Static-X the 'new' Ministry is to do a disservice to both bands. Static-X are already forging something new and fresh out of their goth/industrial roots and Ministry themselves are back in action. OK, they're on the nostalgia circuit with their *Greatest Fits* collection, but their appearance in Spielberg's *AI* is one of the most exciting things about that mushy sentimental disaster area of a movie. If everything they do on their next album is as good as 'What About Us?', then a 'new' Ministry might be surplus to requirements.

Paul Barker recently acknowledged that Static-X do stand out from the herd in American rock.

'You know what, I've seen 'em a couple of times and I was introduced to them a couple of years ago. They're doing "Burning Inside"? I heard the cover of "Burning Inside" that they did with the singer from Fear Factory. And to me it wasn't radical enough, as far as doing a cover is concerned it was a little bit too safe. But then when I listen to Static-X, I just have to laugh because it's like they have heavy-riffing guitars and everything else about the music is totally disco. So to me it's comical.'

But it's not all faint praise. 'I like some of Wayne's vocals, his vocal phrasings and stylings, that's kind of unique,' says Paul. 'And that's hard to do, it's hard to be unique. I don't know what it's like in Britain, but here in the States, all these horrible bands are interchangeable, absolutely interchangeable. Just pick a genre and then you have five bands that are all vying for the same thing, the same style. They all sound exactly the same. So at least Static-X have something that's slightly different and that's their blatant humour. To me anyway. When I hear them I just end up laughing.'

But Static-X are hardly a po-faced band. Industrial music has always taken itself very seriously indeed, to the point of being utterly humourless and dull. That's why many of the profoundly underground bands, particularly from Scandinavia and former communist countries, often end up promoting genuine fascism. Ministry – and offshoots like Revolting Cocks, Lard and 1,000 Homo DJs – always burst any bubbles of pretension that the band or audience may have felt and in many ways Static-X do the same thing. Can you take a band with songs like 'Shit In A Bag' – about the heartbreaking dilemma of being on the road in a bus with no lavvy and having to, er, pass solids urgently and being unable to stop – 100 per cent seriously? They open *Machine* with a Mariachi band; this is not a band who aren't in it for a laugh. 'I definitely don't want people to take us seriously,' says Wayne. 'We take ourselves seriously onstage, but outside of that, it's entertainment.'

Spoken like a true disco diva.

SPINESHANK

They have what has to be one of the all-time greatest rock and roll names. They look a bit like a well-scrubbed boy band who would sit nicely alongside N'SYNC on MTV or on a teenage girl's bedroom wall. But Spineshank make a sound more akin to a great door slamming in the deepest pit of hell. A pop band they are not.

Like Orgy, Static-X, Coal Chamber and System Of A Down,

Spineshank are unlikely to cross over to the mainstream A-list world of Limp Bizkit (celebrity parties with Britney and Madonna *et al*) and are more likely to survive the inevitable 'death' of nu metal. They are a working rock and roll band who have benefited as well as suffered by being branded as part of some nu metal 'movement'. Spineshank are seen as the favoured sons of Fear Factory, an established west coast metal band who are a sort of early hybrid between resolutely old-school thrash metal such as Pantera and Slayer and the cooler, '90s incarnation of metal.

Spineshankers Jonny Santos (vocals), Mike Sarkisyan (guitars) and Tom Decker (drums) broke up their previous band, Basic Enigma, as soon as they heard Fear Factory's seminal 1996 album *Demanufacture*, reforming almost immediately, with new bassist Robert Garcia, as Spineshank.

Fear Factory are in some ways a fairly traditional metal band and in others almost avant-garde in their approach. They brought industrial music into their sound, working with samples and cut-up tape loops, creating an uncomfortable form of techno metal that was steeped in the cyberpunk imagery of William Gibson's *Neuromancer*, the bleak decaying future Los Angeles of the films *Blade Runner* and *Terminator 2*, and dark predictions of a world ruled by universal surveillance and genetic manipulation. They experimented with remixes by Canadian industrial duo Frontline Assembly – hitherto the preserve of the house scene – and in 1997 released an album called *Remanufacture*, for which electronic artists such as Frontline Assembly's Rhys Fulber, DJ Dano, Kingsize and Dutch 'gabba' DJ Junkie XL all reworked tracks from their earlier album *Demanufacture*. It was a bold step, but Fear Factory have always been at the cutting edge of music, technology and ideas.

Dino Cazares of Fear Factory heard Spineshank's demo and immediately offered them a support slot at one of Fear Factory's LA shows. They have spent the five years or so since supporting bands like System Of A Down, (hed) pe, Coal Chamber, Snot,

Soulfly, Sepultura, Danzig and Static-X, pounding their brand of slick, melodic hard rock into the ears of anyone who will listen. They signed with Fear Factory's label Roadrunner, which has been at the forefront of credible hard rock for well over a decade, releasing music by Sepultura, Machine Head, Slipknot and Dry Kill Logic amongst others. Their debut album *Strictly Diesel* was released in 1998 and featured Fear Factory vocalist Burton C Bell singing on closing track 'Stain', which perked up the interest of a comparatively indifferent metal world.

It was an abrasive record, which seemed to be packed with decent ideas but few that were properly executed. In retrospect it was a bit half-formed, something the band themselves are the first to admit.

Drummer Tommy Decker, speaking to east coast fanzine *Romper* said, 'Truthfully, we would not say anything bad about the first record. It's definitely a step we had to take to get here. *The Height Of Callousness* is actually really the first Spineshank record. I mean, this one we made for ourselves. We made no apologies about anything, we didn't care what was the cool thing at the time ya know. We just really did it for ourselves and we ended up being really happy with it and so far it seems like the response is really good, which is very relieving because we didn't know what was going to happen. It was such a departure from the first record. We were afraid the fans we gained on the first record would be so pissed off because we changed so much and everyone else, like, couldn't understand it. But, it's worked out pretty well and we're just happy because we have a record that if it sold five copies, we'd still be proud of it. If it sold five million, it's the same record to us, it's real for us.'

But it pointed the direction they would take; the cover of George Harrison's 'While My Guitar Gently Weeps' might have been done as a joke by other bands, but Spineshank are eager to inject some serious melodies into their work.

New album *The Height Of Callousness* followed in 2000, a

much more extreme animal, which built on the solid industrial foundations inspired by Fear Factory but with driving techno beats worthy of Prodigy. Produced by GGGarth Richardson (Rage Against The Machine, Kittie) at Mushroom Studios in Vancouver, British Columbia, the songs really gave Jonny's voice the space it needed to reach the soul-crushing vocal crescendos he was capable of. It was, apparently, a struggle to make. Jonny Santos told UK magazine *Metal Hammer*, 'Jesus, we literally went through mental breakdowns making this album, one night I packed my bags and I even booked a flight home saying that I couldn't cope any more and that I wasn't equipped to deal with making a record and dealing with all the other shit that was going on. We had a huge drag-you-outside fistfight with each other too... We were so pissed off making it. The circumstances in which we recorded it were perfect to make us that way. The fact that the label just fucked with us constantly and the distressing things going on in our lives propelled us through like a fuel. I think we must've written about 50 songs but recorded 16 and selected the 11 most vile and disgustingly pissed-off ones for the record. We made exactly the album we wanted to make, a record that no one else told us what we could or couldn't do – we basically left the planet to make it – we weren't connected to anyone whatsoever.' Like fellow LA-based industrial metallers Static-X, Spineshank are adding a new dimension to a sound that was dismissed as played out after Ministry went off the boil. Bringing an MTV sensibility to what was once profoundly underground music, Spineshank are tipped to wildly surpass their mentors, Fear Factory.

'When we started in '96 there really weren't any metal bands other than Fear Factory using samples in their songwriting,' Santos told *Metal Hammer*. 'There were hundreds of industrial bands like Godflesh, Ministry and Foetus, but as for metal bands there was just us, Fear Factory and White Zombie. Now you look around, and I'm not naming anyone, but they're fucking everywhere! So now we have to look at a third album and be true to what we do without looking like we're copying anyone. But the one thing I know, and the thing that those bands should watch out for, is that Spineshank are still years ahead of the rest of the pack!'

ORGY

As Korn begat Limp Bizkit, who begat Staind, so they begat Orgy. 'I think they'll appeal to a lot of kids, a lot of different people. They're fashionable pretty-dudes, so all the chicks will dig 'em. And they're real heavy, so hopefully a lot of our friends will like them, too,' Jonathan Davis said of the first band that signed to Korn's label Elementree. Orgy haven't begotten anyone else yet, but their cover of New Order's 'Blue Monday' highlights something that has become a great nu metal cliché, the reworking of a song from the '80s.

Many of these songs are obvious choices, betraying the band's roots, like Static-X's version of 'Burning Inside'. But more often than not they are sort of metal-kitsch reworkings of pop hits like Limp Bizkit's version of George Michael's 'Faith', Disturbed's rather pointless revisiting of Tears For Fears' 'Shout' and even Marilyn Manson's ghastly Eurythmics tribute 'Sweet Dreams Are Made Of This'. It's something this new breed of rock bands has in common with their dumber 'nu punk' cousins – witness Alien Ant Farm's 2001 hit version of Michael Jackson's 'Smooth Criminal', which sold rather better than Jackson's latest single – as well as with those pop, rap and R&B artists intent on mining the decade of shoulder pads, mullets and cap-sleeved T-shirts for inspiration.

Orgy's 'Blue Monday' was less of a novelty song than these; it fitted well with the band's overall hi-tech sound and in any case would have been unrecognisable to many of their fans who had not even been born when the song was originally released in 1983 or had been toddlers when it was remixed and re-released in 1991.

Formed in 1997, singer Jay Gordon, guitarist Ryan Shuck, synth-guitarist Amir Derakh, bassist Paige Haley and drummer Bobby Hewitt were signed in the studio with producer Josh Abrahams and had their debut album *Candyass* out within six months. They joined the bill on the first Family Values tour with Korn, Limp Bizkit and Ice-T and had their version of 'Blue Monday' included on the soundtrack for quickie *Scream* clone teen horror comedy sequel *I Still Know What You Did Last Summer*. The Jonathan Davis connection ensured a healthy amount of interest in the album, particularly because he sang on 'Revival', one of the album's stronger tracks. Guitarist Ryan Shuck had been Davis's bandmate in SexArt, then singer in LA punk band Lit. The two had kept in touch despite Jonathan feeling that he had in some way let down SexArt by joining Korn. Just as Fieldy and Head were instrumental in the discovery of Limp Bizkit, so Davis was associated with Orgy. Had the band had their own label at the time and been able to sign Limp Bizkit, they would have been able to share in the massive profits that their protégés generated. Orgy were a less instantaneous sensationalist band than Bizkit, though fans expecting another band full of angsty lyrics and detuned riffs were in for a surprise.

'Nobody wants to hear Korn Part Two and nobody wants to be a Korgy, well, we don't want to be Korgy, we're pretty happy being Orgy. Whoever wants to listen to Korn Part Two has enough to choose from,' Jay told *Circus* magazine in February 1999.

'At the moment it's pretty horrible in LA, because everybody is trying to sound like Korn. I think somehow we crossed British rock with hardcore trash and industrial, *Star Wars* with James Bond and came up with our very own thing! I think Orgy is a pretty good name for our style. It's not sexual, it's a musical orgy. James Bond, Slayer, Psychedelic Furs and Duran Duran...'

Their gloomy, quasi-industrial sound was dubbed nu goth, gothcore and death pop. The band, who wore too much make-up on MTV, looked like they were making a pitch for the growing horde of Marilyn Manson devotees in white face foundation and black lipstick.

Jay sang in an inexplicable English accent, sounding like a sort of industrial version of Dick Van Dyke's unconvincing cockney chimney sweep in *Mary Poppins*, though oddly the style seemed to work very well for the band. They were like a dumbed-down Fear Factory, a prettier Nine Inch Nails, a more approachable Skinny Puppy. This 'death pop', as they styled their own sound, was often compared to Duran Duran covering songs by Ministry.

Critical reaction to the album was mixed. Jason Pettigrew writing in *Alternative Press* said, 'The cynic in me says that Orgy are nothing more than hype victims dressed up with hi-tech digital gear and flash wardrobes. But as modern rock gets even more regimented in its factions, Orgy have the ability to hold their ground in front of a moshpit or a dance club, drinking their competition under the table while receiving hummers from the girlfriends of myopic nitwits who still wear KMFDM T-shirts.'

The band's second album, *Vapor Transmission*, a more consciously futuristic image for the band and Fear Factory-lite concept resulted in disappointing sales. The album debuted at Number 18 on the *Billboard* Hot 200, quickly going gold, but then dropped out without trace. Although Orgy could hardly be described as a cutting-edge avant-garde outfit, their death pop was, it seemed, just a little bit too much for the still rather conservative American market. As noted in an earlier chapter, the climate in rock became decidedly 'male' in the latter part of the 1990s. Orgy were a decidedly androgynous band, harking way back to the golden age of glam rock gender-benders like David Bowie, Marc Bolan, Cockney Rebel, Roxy Music and The New York Dolls on one hand and the modern glam-goth manifestations of Marilyn Manson, Nine Inch Nails and Rammstein on the other. They lacked Manson's shock tactics, which kept him prominently in the mainstream press, on MTV news and on the cover of music magazines. Orgy were trying to appeal to fans on the basis of their music and image, an image that was actually going to alienate a large section of their potential audience who would dislike the band for looking 'gay'. Singles 'Opticon' and 'Fiction' sold poorly despite the latter's impressive *Matrix*-style video and there was some talk of the band being dropped before it was announced that they were back in the studio at the end of 2001 working on new material for their third album. Orgy guitarist Amir Derakh was also splitting his time between the band and Coal Chamber (he and Jay produced their debut release) to help them work on demos for their follow-up to 1999's *Chamber Music*.

Whether a rethink of the image, the music or both is in order, Orgy were left under a lot of pressure to repeat and build on the success of their debut album. A difficult feat, and given the notorious short-term tolerance of record labels for 'failure', Korn or no Korn, friends or otherwise, they have found themselves working on album number three in the last chance saloon.

PAPA ROACH

Papa Roach demand that you take them seriously. Seldom smiling, clad in black with a raft of songs like 'Last Resort' ('Don't give a fuck if I cut my arm bleeding/It all started when I lost my mother/No love for myself, no love for another'), 'Never Enough' ('Life's been sucked out of me/This routine's killing me/I did it to myself/I cannot say this would not be/Somebody put me out of my misery') and 'Broken Home' ('Broken home/All alone/I know my mother loves me/But does my father even care?'), this is not a party band.

Lyrically they have more focus for their anger and frustration than Korn's verbal lash-outs; the songs are first-person vignettes running the full gamut of emotions from existential discontent to suicidal despair. These are emotional songs that obviously come from deep within the psyches of the band and strike a chord with America's teens, though delivered in a pulverising and brutal package of rapid-fire rock. They, and the crowd, jump around and mosh furiously to songs about lives wrecked by alcoholism, family break-up and profound emotional scarring.

Rock and roll traditionally deals with escapism and fantasy: the perfect eternal love of pop balladeers, the sword and sorcery/sci-fi of prog rock and '80s heavy metal, the bad-ass superpimp alter-egos of Kid Rock and Fred Durst. Even the negative fantasies of violence, murder and torture in the songs of Slayer and Slipknot are still dealing in fantasy, escapism. Few bands have the capability of being 100 per cent honest all of the time, though Papa Roach try harder than most. They hold up a mirror to their fans that exposes some of their own pain. Of course the feel-my-pain school may be just another fantasy, with well-adjusted and prosperous rock stars cashing in on teenage angst for kudos. But if the fans perceive it as truth, then it becomes their truth.

Although they are often written about as a rap-rock band, Papa Roach sound more like a meat-and-potatoes rock and roll band who could have come along at any time in the past 30 years. There is nothing fancy about them, no frills or flourishes in the sound and no erudition in the lyrics. What you get is raw and upfront. There's a minimalism about them, right down to the identical black clothes onstage and the stark high-speed guitar riffing that leaves more to your imagination, almost forcing you to fill in the sound in your head and make it bigger than it actually is. There are turntable scratches on the record but onstage they perform as a straight four-piece with no DJ, singer Coby Dick speaking the verses in a rapid stacatto – which is more like Mike Patton on Faith No More's 'Epic' than it is like 'real' rapping – then belting out the choruses.

Talking to *Shoutweb* in early 2001, Coby Dick firmly eschewed all other definitions of their music: 'Just rock 'n' roll man. I think to call it 'rap rock' is fuckin' gay, and I think to call it 'pimp rock' is gay, ya know what I'm sayin'? So we're just, like, rock 'n' roll.'

Hailing from Vacaville, California, a nowhere town that most people drive through without stopping, Papa Roach have that same ruthless work ethic and ambition born of the misery of small-town life that also fed Nirvana and Korn's thirst for success. Vacaville has a prison where mass murderer Charles Manson was incarcerated; apart from that, Papa Roach are the most famous thing about the town.

Coby Dick assures me they had no choice but to form Papa Roach because there was no way they could possibly have spent the rest of their lives there. With Jacoby Shaddix, aka Coby Dick, on vocal, guitarist Jerry Horton, bassist Tobin Esperance and Drummer Dave Buckner, Papa Roach formed in 1993, and began to gig around northern California, supporting rising stars The Deftones, Downset and Incubus along the way.

The band were heavily influenced by Faith No More, Nirvana and Primus, though as they played and wrote solidly over the following three years, they forged their own sound, which was recognisably Papa Roach's short, sharp power rock as we know it today. There are a lot of other influences lurking under the surface: names like John Coltrane are dropped alongside the inevitable Deftones. Coby Dick recalls listening to Pink Floyd's epic double album of depression and madness *The Wall* in his mother's car when he was a child. All of these bands – Papa Roach, Staind, Korn – appeal to exactly the same sort of kids who were reared on Pink Floyd during the '70s and '80s. Intelligent, well read, they may not have excelled in school and may have felt themselves to be misfits, outsiders and loners; but while Roger Waters dealt in convoluted metaphors, Papa Roach's words say exactly what they mean.

While there are no obvious parallels with Pink Floyd, another interesting aside is that while the psychedelic/prog rock dinosaurs took their name from conflating those of two old bluesmen (Pink Anderson and Floyd Council), the name Papa Roach was suggested by a CD by jazz musician Pancho Sanchez called *Papa Gato*. Coby Dick's grandfather's last name was Roatch – he was Papa Roatch. It also tied in with their loudly proclaimed underground status. In 2000, Coby Dick told MTV, 'The cockroach represents longevity. Like when the bomb hits, what's going to be around? Cockroaches. That's like us. We're dirty, underground. When you see one of them, you know there's a million of them, and that's our plan: to infest. That's Papa Roach.'

The band recorded and released their debut album *Potatoes For Christmas* in 1994, along with a stream of singles and EPs, and second album *Old Friends From Young Years* on their own Onion Hardcore Recordings label, but it is their major-label debut, *Infest*, that fully captures the sound of Papa Roach and reduces the band to its essence. The honesty of the songs, rather than alienating potential fans, touched a nerve.

Speaking to *Metal Hammer* magazine in March 2001, Coby Dick said, 'What I hope we can always avoid being is escapism. For me that's what's wrong with pop music and rock music and entertainment and pretty much the whole of America at the moment. The whole thing is about pretending that everything is fine, that the world is a wonderful place, that we can all escape through music to this bullshit world where nothing can hurt us. Papa Roach aren't about escaping reality, we're about facing it, diving into it, sucking it all up then letting it all go. It's not so much therapeutic as just letting it all out, sweating it all out, dancing it all out, rocking it all out, forcing it all into a ball of energy and letting it explode. That's what we do and we don't bullshit about the pain. We admit it and try to find a way to deal with it. That makes us more honest than a lot of bands and it also makes us open to people who wanna be cynical about it.'

INCUBUS

Incubus were very nearly called Chunk-O-Funk, a name – along with that of their debut album *Fungus Amongus* – that would have blasted this Calabasas, California, band right out of the water before their career even launched. Fortunately they chose the name of a mythical medieval European priapic demonic entity who sneaks into the bedchambers of women and has sex with them while they sleep.

The band started out heavily influenced by the free-form funk of Primus, one of rock's genuinely original left-field bands, proving the truism that if you must base your sound on somebody else's, it's a good idea to pick a band that are comparatively obscure and whose sound suggests a few other avenues to explore. Incubus, at least, sound like a band who are comparatively cliché-free in comparison with many of their pressed-tin-toy contemporaries.

They were formed at high school in an affluent suburb near Malibu after singer Brandon Boyd and drummer Jose Pasillas, who had been friends since elementary school, and guitarist Mike Einziger, met their future bassist Alex Katunich. At first they played Megadeth and Metallica covers, performing at neighbourhood parties, until Brandon started writing his own songs. The band began to play gigs at all-ages clubs in the San Fernando Valley, at the Roxy on the Sunset Strip – apparently they were so nervous before performing that Brandon's mother taught them how to meditate to relieve their anxiety – and recording demos in a Santa Monica studio. The demos fell on deaf ears, so they recorded and released their debut album independently on their own Stopuglynailfungus Music On Chillum label.

The band added a rapper, DJ Lyfe (Gavin Koppel – replaced by DJ Kilmore before the release of 'Make Yourself'), to their line-up, gradually mutating away from Primus clone into an original, soulful though still heavy rock band. The band garnered obvious comparisons to Limp Bizkit because of their onstage DJ, and despite sitting comfortably in the nu metal section in the record stores, or on the modern rock radio playlists alongside Slipknot, Korn and Staind, Incubus detest the current scene.

Speaking to *Mean Street* magazine in November 2001, guitarist Mike Einziger said, 'I think rock music is at the lowest point I've ever experienced. During the making of this record I kind of rediscovered old bands that I listened to as a kid, like Led Zeppelin and The Doors. Those were the bands that were doing something cool. And more recent bands like Pearl Jam, Nirvana and

Soundgarden have done something creative and real. But now, this rock/rap metal that's all over the place just makes me want to throw up. I mean, how many times can you really tolerate listening to someone tune up their guitar so loudly that it's just noise? I don't like to insult others, so I won't mention any names, but I just don't find any intelligence in the music any more. How angry can you really be living in the suburbs?'

Lyrically, too, the band eschewed the mom-and-pop rage of their contemporaries, opting for a more sensual and even spiritual view of the world. They were even – shock horror – capable of optimism. In 'The Warmth' from their double platinum-selling third album *Make Yourself*, Brandon sings, 'Don't let the world bring you down/Not everyone here is that fucked-up and cold/Remember why you came and while you're alive experience the warmth before you grow old.' On 'Warning', from the 2001 follow-up *Morning View*, he sings, 'What's so wrong with/Being happy/Kudos to those who/See through sickness/When she woke in the morning/She knew that her life had passed her by/And she called out a warning/Don't ever let life pass you by/I suggest we/Learn to love ourselves before it's/Made illegal.'

By the time the band had signed to Korn's label Immortal and released their debut major-label album *SCIENCE* in 1997, the sound had moved on sufficiently for the band to be considered originals themselves, particularly in a climate that saw a distressing number of soundalike bands emerging. Scott Litt, who has been REM's long-time producer, as well as working with Nirvana, actually tried to sign Incubus to his independent label Outpost. But he remained a fan of the group and worked with them on their breakthrough album *Make Yourself*. The Incubus sound really gelled; his production opened up the band to showcase Brandon's voice. Not only did Incubus sing intelligent and optimistic lyrics, but you could tell that they did because they had a singer who could actually sing. Critical opinions were mixed – one reviewer described them as 'the nu metal Backstreet Boys' while another called them 'bourgeois metal' – and sales were healthy. Again, as with many bands of their generation, if Incubus could be said to have a major failing it was in trying too much to be all things to all people, balancing the needs of a rock audience with the pop sensibilities of the mass market. The sound veered from crunching rock riffs to jangly Byrds-like passages on to acoustic ballads and back to pulverising funk, often in the space of the same song.

Live, Brandon had developed into a charismatic performer, combining boy-band looks with a snaky, sub-Perry Farrell sensuality that appealed more to female fans, a fact reflected in the crowds turning out for their shows.

In the flesh, the band have an aura of 'niceness' that is at odds with the surliness of their generation: if Korn are a band with issues, Incubus are a band who have not only confronted those issues, but have undergone therapy to learn how to deal with them. Their fourth album, *Morning View* – also produced by Scott Litt – entered the *Billboard* chart at Number Two and, while this is not exactly evidence of a phenomenon, it's proof that it isn't just anger, angst and anxiety that sells.

MUDVAYNE

Occasionally dismissed as Slipknot-lite, Illinois band Mudvayne do seem to fit the bill. Midwestern monsters performing in horror-movie make-up, singing songs about alienation, mutilation, torture and murder, their major-label breakthrough album *LD-50* was actually produced by Slipknot percussionist Shawn Crahan. While Slipknot style themselves after movies like *The Texas Chainsaw Massacre* – they are like a whole band of leatherfaces – Mudvayne's look is more sci-fi and fantasy, a bit supernatural. They also wear make-up as opposed to masks, looking like demons or aliens in ways that Kiss could never have imagined. Along with Chicago's Disturbed, they differ from most nu metal bands in that they have introduced these elements of theatre into their live shows, though this is something Limp Bizkit also explored with their giant toilet stage set at Ozzfest.

Mudvayne formed in 1993, releasing debut album *Kill I Oughtta* in 1997, though it was on their 2000 release *LD-50* that the line-up of vocalist Kud (Chad Gray), Gurrg (Greg Tribbett) on guitar, Ryknow (Ryan Martinie) on bass and drummer Spag (Matthew McDonough) finally gelled.

They cite influences like Stanley Kubrick, Quentin Tarantino, ee cummings and Aleister Crowley 'because of their courage to challenge', though the album itself sounded like Pantera, Fear Factory and Slipknot, with jazz-bass flourishes from Ryknow giving some individuality to a sound that somehow seemed to jar with their onstage image. Their rock theatrics have precedents in Kiss, Alice Cooper, Peter Gabriel-era Genesis and stalwart shock-rockers GWAR, all of whose music, to varying extents, was overshadowed by masks and costumes.

The subject matter of Mudvayne's songs was killers, mass murderers, alienation and fear. In 'Nothing To Gein', a paean to '50s serial killer Ed Gein, upon whose life story the film *Psycho* was based, Kud sings, 'Sheltered life innocence/Insulated memories, spark reflections of my head/Duality in my consciousness/Caught in the war of hemispheres/Between the love lost in my head/Mommy do you still live inside of me? ...Blame mother for the sickness/Mutilate and sew my new clothes for masquerading/Aprons of flesh corpse scalped hair with skin upon my face/Dance and masturbate in night light by myself...'

Stripped of the sensationalist inside-the-mind-of-a-serial-killer ramblings, the song is at heart an update of poet Philip Larkin's observation, 'They fuck you up, your mum and dad.' The evil absent parent crops up again in 'Cradle', which according to Kud '...is about my bad dad. Fuck off, Dad...' He sings, 'Here I stand now and I'm alone/With no one to comfort me/One set of footprints in the sand/No one to take my hand/I'll walk through as long as I need/I'll drift through my life though I'm alone/Outgrown the cradle that once housed me/And I've found that all I need is/Me.'

In addition, the excessive use of the word 'motherfucker' on the album would give Freudians a field day.

Critical reaction to *LD-50* was mostly favourable. *Q* magazine described the album as '...a clever amalgam of Korn, Tool and Mr Bungle...the Slipknot you can actually listen to'.

Mudvayne's album went gold, though they never quite ascended to the stratospheric levels of mentors Slipknot and, short of a major overhaul of their sound and image, it seems unlikely at the time of writing that they will escape from under their shadow.

(hed) pe

As many bands are inevitably distancing themselves from rap-rock, others are going deeper into the genre, mining every last ounce of sonic possibility, and there's none more exciting than (hed) pe.

(hed) pe (the 'pe' stands for 'planet earth' for the moment but the meaning changes from time to time) formed in 1993 in the conservative Los Angeles suburb Orange County. 'Our name was just hed, then the legal people said that hed wasn't going to pass, so we put the pe and people thought that it stood for "head pee", not that "pe" is a word, so then we changed it to Planetary Evolution, which is a cool meaning in kind of a universal-consciousness way, but on this record we didn't want to confuse anyone so we spelled it out "hed planet earth" because we didn't want the kids to be standing there chanting "head pee head pee", which does happen in some territories. But to us we're just hed,' DJ Product told me.

The six-piece drew its players from the worlds of rap, punk and metal – honing a style that's experimental but not so much so that it alienates the kids in the moshpit – and comprises a band (Westyle and Chad on guitars, Mawk on bass, BC on drums) with an onstage DJ (DJ Product who resembles a psycho Vietnam vet with a turntable) and rapper/singer Jared, aka MCUD. Jared is one of the few black artists involved in nu metal on a full-time basis. Many rappers have collaborated with bands, ranging from Cypress Hill's forays into metal on their acclaimed double album *Skull & Bones* to Wu-Tang-associated artists Method Man and Red Man teaming up with Limp Bizkit, but Jared is here for the long haul.

'I'm way too black for MTV,' he tells me. 'You can have a white guy fronting a rock band rapping and they're fine with that. It's when you have a black man doing it that they find reasons why you can't be on the show.'

Writing in the April 2000 issue of *Metal Hammer*, Neil Kulkarni said of them, 'Where so much rap-rock seems to labour under the illusion that genre-fusion means reducing each genre to its lowest common denominator, (hed) pe can genuinely execute rap's sonic ambience and rock's punka aggression in a way that sells neither genre short. Here be beats and rhymes that could stand toe-to-toe with the most cutting-edge current hip-hop (instead of the decade-old Run-DMC/Public Enemy fixation that seems to occupy, say, Limp Bizkit's sound world) rock and roll noise harder and heavier than anyone else is playing it. The seamlessness of their sound is of crucial importance to (hed), if only because they've seen so many people get it so wrong.'

In frontman Jared they have one of the most exciting performers in rock today and despite the reluctance of MTV to allow him to intrude on its white-bread world, the band's relentless two years of touring has paid dividends in the number of fans who saw the band during 2000 and 2001.

After touring extensively with Korn, Slipknot, Kid Rock and System Of A Down, they recorded their current album, *Broke*, wherein their self-styled g-punk sound gelled to perfection, before going back on the road, visiting Europe with Papa Roach and playing a few headlining dates of their own.

DEADSY

Deadsy's image of band as monied prep school secret society crossed with teenage fascist group isn't too far from the truth. Fronted by Elijah Blue Allmann (son of southern rocker Gregg Allmann and Cher during their brief high-profile marriage in the '70s), who was given his first guitar by his mom's then boyfriend Gene Simmons, Deadsy were a band born with a silver spoon in their mouths (or rather, under their noses).

Formed in 1997, the band came complete with a striking image, a sound they describe as 'Gary Numan and Duran Duran getting run over by Morbid Angel', and a manifesto that parodies college fraternities and secret societies like the Skull And Bones Club.

'Deadsy is an institution that was developed to purify and primify the human solution of sound and vision. It is adamantly committed to the realization of a comprehensive conveyance of simplicity and complexity's synergistic unions – a sort of "simplexity" or "complicity", if you will. This institution is comprised of five separate entities: academia, leisure, horror, war and science-medicine. These ingredients are the core basis of the Deadsy formula and the keys to the equation of this plight. Each of the members (fraters) has been designated one of these entities in accordance to their natural predisposition and most primal congruencies to best exhibit the root aspects and essential constants of humanization.'

Like Kiss, they wear make-up and have 'secret' identities: P Exeter Blue, aka Elijah Blue (vocals and guitar); Dr Nner (keyboards); Carlton Megalodon ('Z-tar'); Alec Pure (drums); and The Beast Craig (bass). They have been the secret weapon of the west coast's nu metal scene since 1997. Orgy's Jay Gordon was Elijah's one-time bassist in an early incarnation of Deadsy and, as well as a guest appearance on their album *Candyass*, he has also guested on Coal Chamber's *Chamber Music*. Deadsy's debut album, *Commencement*, was actually finished in 1999 and has circulated in demo form among the rock cognoscenti and their rapidly expanding LA fanbase. But it was the patronage of Korn's Jonathan Davis – a stint on the Family Values tour and a deal with Davis's label Elementree – that finally unleashed them on the world. The band were signed to Warner Brothers but dropped before the release of the record; Davis hooked them up with legendary death metal producer Scott Burns who re-recorded some of the tracks.

They told *Kerrang!* magazine in 2001, 'With Scott's help its gonna be way more super-radical. I think that there's a real kindred spirit between our band and the Tampa bands like Cannibal Corpse and Six Feet Under. I think that Deadsy will be the trojan horse of death metal – we're going to bring it to the masses because we have that goth-and-bubblegum element to our music.'

Along with the much-hyped Andrew WK (whose band includes Obituary drummer Donald Tardy), the massive success of Slipknot and Kittie, Deadsy may actually be part of a movement back towards the brutal negativity of death metal in the coming months and years.

ADEMA

One band that has not received patronage from Jonathan Davis is Adema. They do have a lot of ties with Korn, however. They're from Bakersfield, and bassist Dave DeRoo and guitarist Tim Fluckey were in Juice, the band that grew out of the ashes of SexArt, which included Davis as singer in his pre-Korn days and guitarist Ryan Shuck who went on to form Orgy. Kris Kohls was in Videodrone, whose debut album was released on Korn's Elementree label and was produced by bassist Fieldy. More importantly, Adema singer Mark Chavez is Jonathan Davis's half-brother.

In the Arista records biography of the band, Mark plays down any connections with his brother, despite the fact that Davis was originally tipped to make a guest appearance: 'His biggest influence on me, and absolutely the best thing he could have done for me, was telling me when I wasn't good enough. I'm the type – and this is something that's instilled in our family – that when I want something, I go for it; there's no way you're gonna deny me or tell me I can't have it. But as far as being there and being supportive and stuff, he was awesome.'

The other members of Adema – guitarist Mike Ransom and drummer Kris Kohls – had all paid their dues in other bands (including, in Mike's case, a well-thought-of local ska-punk band, Mento Burro) and despite initial speculation that the band would sound like Korn, Adema are a far more commercial-sounding outfit and have more in common with the slick, poppier sound of Linkin Park.

While they never made too much of the connection, it was obvious that a lot of the initial curiosity around the band was about the Chavez/Davis connection. Even before they actually had a record out, fans were trading live MP3s, demo tracks and advance copies of the album on Napster, turning up to shows able to sing along with all the songs. But rock star siblings traditionally fare badly – one thinks of Chris Jagger and Simon Townshend – unless they were in the same band, as in the case of Johnny and Edgar Winters' White Trash, The Allmann Brothers Band, Red Kross or Kittie.

And while Adema made a respectable debut album and held their own in live shows, there was little to separate them from the countless other second- and third-on-the-bill bands trawling across the States in the last quarter of 2001, all hungry to follow in the wake of Linkin Park, Incubus and Staind.

Rolling Stone said of the band's debut album, 'Singer Mark Chavez focuses on alienation, sure, but unlike his half-brother Jonathan Davis of Korn, he's conventionally troubled rather than rewardingly twisted. Nothing going on here that some Paxil couldn't fix.'

Critical reaction was almost universally kind to the band,

though quite how far this, the Korn connection and their nu-metal-by-numbers songs will carry them in the 'real' world remains to be seen. What is clear is that Chavez is a gifted singer and frontman in his own right, though the also-ran bands of rock and roll are littered with singers as good as and better than him.

APARTMENT 26

Apartment 26 are one of the few British bands to make any sort of dent on the seemingly impenetrable US rock market, though this may have something to do with the fact that they are favoured sons, part of the second generation of metal. Formed by Biff Butler, son of Black Sabbath bassist Geezer, Apartment 26 have enjoyed advantages over the competition, like a slot on Ozzfest '99 and a guest appearance from Fear Factory's Burton C Bell that few other bands were ever lucky enough to get. But debut album *Hallucinating* proves they have created a buzz on their own merit, which is just as well considering that you can't be born into rock stardom.

Formed in Leamington Spa by Biff, keyboard player and programmer AC Huckvale, guitarist Jon Greasley and bassist Louis Cruden just after leaving school, the band quickly moved from a derivative grunge sound to a more experimental electronic one, similar to influences Nine Inch Nails and, in particular, Fear Factory.

Deaf to cries of nepotism, Apartment 26 signed on for a gruelling opening slot on the 1999 Ozzfest tour along with Biff's dad's band, the legendary reformed original line-up of Black Sabbath. As well as Biff, Ozzy Osbourne's son Jack has a growing influence on the scene, not least because he has the ear of his parents when they come to selecting bands for Ozzfest. Taproot got on the bill this way.

But a defiant Biff is adamant the band got on the bill on their own merit: 'Ozzy and Sharon are like family to me, but there isn't any chance they would have us on the Ozzfest bill if we were going to be embarrassing. We had to do what all the bands who go on the tour had to do in terms of submitting demos.'

Although a strong Sabbath influence is unavoidable in any modern metal band, *Hallucinating* evoked comparisons with everyone from Prodigy to Korn and The Deftones. Most of their touring has been in the USA, where they hope to imitate the success of Bush by breaking America before making it at home, they have supported everyone from Papa Roach, Pantera, Soulfly and (hed) pe to Fear Factory (whose frontman Burton C Bell making a guest appearance on the track 'Void' on their debut album) and had a track on the *Mission Impossible II* soundtrack.

Like most British youth, the influence of 'rave' culture – the single biggest youth pastime over the past decade or so has involved dropping ecstacy and dancing in a club to pounding electronic music – is unavoidable and Apartment 26 are unique in working this into their sound, something that bands like Pitchshifter and Static-X have also done, though less successfully. Techno, it has often been said, is the heavy metal version of house and disco, and the fact that Apartment 26 are one of the few bands to make this link puts them in a strong position. Whether this techno-metal fusion represents the future direction the band will take will be revealed on their second album.

GLASSJAW

This band are often called Phase III of Ross Robinson's masterplan to destroy Limp Bizkit and Korn, and their myriad of imitators. Although they are often lumped in with Inkling, Far, Cleanse, Blind By Choice, Tenfold, Helen 55, Codeseven, Will Haven and other so-called emo bands – a subset of hardcore, originally known as 'emotional hardcore' then 'emo-core' but more often just 'emo', whose meaning has since become as diluted and catch-all as that of the term nu metal – they inevitably claim that they defy all categories.

'We don't know where the hell we fit in. You got your shitty, crappy pop, and then you have your shitty, crappy 'Yo wassup dawg', like, rapcore, Adidas Rock, whatever you wanna call it. And it's kinda like, we're not a heavy metal band, we're not a pop band, we kind of pave our own little path, and where we're gonna land I don't know,' Justin Beck said.

Long Island teenagers Daryl Palumbo and Justin Beck formed Glassjaw at summer camp, drawn together by a mutual love of bands and artists like Bad Brains, Quicksand, Black Flag, Morrissey, Depeche Mode, Niel Rubenstein and Anthrax. Six years on and they are already being talked about in the same breath as Radiohead and The Deftones.

Daryl Palumbo (vocals), Justin Beck (guitar), Todd N Weinstock (guitar), Manuel Carrero (bass) and Larry Gorman (drums) were discovered and signed to his own I AM imprint by by Ross Robinson. Justin Beck told me, 'Ross Robinson came to see us. So he comes to see us practise and after 15 seconds – we didn't even get to the chorus – he stood up and said, "Stop! You're signed." And we thought he was joking and said, y'know, "Eff off." And then he just said, "OK, start playing again and just enjoy it this time." So we did.'

The band recorded at Robinson's Indigo Ranch studio in Malibu, California, recording the album in around eight weeks. Robinson called Glassjaw 'the new post-millennial destroyers of Adidas rock' and coaxed some of the most intense and personal songwriting and performances out of the band on their widely acclaimed debut album *Everything You Ever Wanted To Know About Silence*. Described as a 'modern take on love' record, Palumbo's songwriting at times makes Thom Yorke sound like Weird Al Yankovic. It is intense and sometimes hard to take; dense, full of pain, but not the 'fake' pain of many of their contemporaries. With Palumbo having recently been diagnosed with Crohn's Disease, the suffering and depression is more than some middle-class kid's angst at not having a girlfriend; the howl of pain and rage is for real.

After a gruelling world tour with Soulfly, Glassjaw's intensity and honesty had crept into the souls of a lot of fans, inspiring an almost frightening dedication to the group. The album was not a big seller but the people who did buy it were fanatical about it, creating a strong word-of-mouth buzz and frantic anticipation of the follow-up album, whose release is scheduled for late 2002, with song titles heatedly being revealed on Internet newsgroups along with in-depth discussions of their lyrics.

TAPROOT

Michigan is America's greatest rock and roll state, the home of Motown, Iggy Pop, The MC5 and too many other bands to list. Ann Arbor natives Stephen Richards (vocals, programming), Mike DeWolf (guitar), Philip Lipscomb (bass) and Jarrod Montague (drums) formed a band after coming together and realising they shared a deep love of Rush, Faith No More and Tool, as well as a serious Bone Thugs-N-Harmony fixation.

Acclaimed as one of the brightest hopes of the next wave of rap-rock bands, Taproot famously crossed paths with Fred Durst early in the careers of both bands, giving him a demo, which Durst apparently loved. Durst promised to sign them and work with them when he set up his own label. In the meantime the band, on good terms with Fred, set about promoting their music, a febrile blend of staccato riffing with big, bawdy choruses, through their website, selling their self-released CDs, *Something More Than Nothing* and *Upon Us* via mail order. There was something of the punk DIY spirit about the band. Frontman Stephen Richards recalls, 'We burned them [the CDs] at the University of Michigan lab. I'd personally hand package them and send them out myself and we'd do it all at cost. Starting off, it was sending out a couple of CDs every week or two, but it slowly progressed to getting 25 orders a day. These kids would send cheques in my name, 'cause I was just using my personal bank account, and I kept getting all these cheques and money orders made out to me. Some were even sending cash, taking that chance just to get our music.'

The band sold over 10,000 CDs this way, all the while plugging away, sending out demos to record companies and eventually going out to Los Angeles to play a showcase for producer Rick Rubin. The day the band returned was the day the Family Values tour was in town. Stephen found a message waiting for him on his answer machine: 'Steve. Fred Durst. Hey man, you fucked up. You don't ever bite the hand that feeds in this business, bro... Took you under my wing, brought you to my house, fucking talked about your fucking ass on radio, in press and you embarrassed, like, me and the Interscope family. Your association with Limp Bizkit doesn't exist,' Durst berated him in a 30-second message, also saying that their manager had 'fucked' the band's career before it had even started, threatening that if Taproot were ever seen at a Limp Bizkit show they'd be 'fucked' and that if they used Limp Bizkit's name they'd be 'blackballed and erased'.

Sean 'Puffy' Combs also showed an interest in signing Taproot to his Bad Boy Records imprint but the band eventually signed with Velvet Hammer Records, an Atlantic subsidiary, and recorded their major-label debut *Gift* with producer/engineer Ulrich Wild (Pantera, Powerman 5000, Stabbing Westward, Static-X).

They went out with Ozzfest 2001 after impressing Ozzy's son Jack. Richards says, 'He'd heard of us and wanted to see us, so he came down and checked us out, and loved it. He was ranting and raving about us to his mom.'

They subsequently toured the USA and Europe with Papa Roach, The Deftones, Incubus and Linkin Park, starting work on their second album in late 2001 with producer Toby Wright (Korn, Sevendust, Alice In Chains).

SYSTEM OF A DOWN

As far as System Of A Down were concerned, 2001 had been a good year for them until events beyond their control got the better of them. When their free show in an LA parking lot ended with police firing tear gas and rubber bullets at an angry mob, they got the sort of publicity they didn't need, particularly since second album *Toxicity* had shifted a staggering 220,000 copies in its first week of release.

The band were set to play on 3 September 2001 at Club Vynyl on Schrader and Hollywood Boulevard, but apparently way too many fans showed up, prompting the authorities to pull the plug before the band were even able to take the stage. Amidst rumours that permits had not been sought, the crowd erupted, barricades were overrun and US$30,000-worth of the band's equipment was trashed.

On 11 September, they were set to appear on *The Conan O'Brian Show* before setting out on the Pledge Of Allegiance tour with Slipknot, Rammstein, Mudvayne, American Head Charge and No One. Following the World Trade Center attack, however, the tour was postponed, TV appearances pulled and, despite its having crashed into the charts at Number One, there seemed little impetus to build on the success of *Toxicity*.

Like contemporaries Static-X, Orgy and Powerman 5000, System Of A Down sound as white-bread American as apple pie and drive-by shootings. But they are a band whose roots are truly international: vocalist Serj Tankian and drummer John Dolmayan were both born in Lebanon and bassist Shavo Odadjian was born in Armenia; the band mixes Middle Eastern, Native American, Armenian and tribal rhythms in a forceful and engaging melting pot of contemporary metal.

'We play heavy music, which is essentially American,' Serj told me in late 2000. 'Armenian music isn't heavy music. There is some of that in there and some music of Mediterranean and Middle Eastern origin. But we're not an Armenian band, we don't play Armenian music. But it's a part, one part, of what and who we are.'

Formed in the mid 1990s, System Of A Down went into the studio towards the end of the decade with producer Rick Rubin to cut their self-titled debut. The album sold well despite the fact that there were no obvious singles and it received minimal radio and TV exposure. Slots on the Family Values 1999 tour and Metallica's

Summer Sanitarium tour in 2000 brought System Of A Down to the attention of a generation of malcontents. Like their contemporaries, they are powered by a dynamo of anger and frustration. But Korn's anger is largely apolitical. System Of A Down have a well-thought-out militant edge, which has led to comparisons with The Dead Kennedys; Serj Tankian's voice has also been compared with that of DKs singer Jello Biafra.

'PLUCK' on their debut album (it stands for Politically Lying, Unholy, Cowardly Killers) is about the Armenian genocide. Serj explains, 'The Armenian people had a genocide, just like the Jewish people had the Holocaust. Those who look the other way, such as Turkey, who committed it, that injustice itself has been a driving point of my life,' he admits. 'Because of that, I've been able to look at other injustices in the world. I know that injustice exists and it's always hidden, so it opens your eyes. It's been a motivating factor.'

Kerrang! called them '*the* next big agit-politicos'. But there is a lot more to System Of A Down than the politics; they sing about love, dope, angst and good times too. With other influences like jazz and traditional Van Halen guitar heroics, System Of A Down have an openness about their sound, their words and their live passion that actually recalls The Clash in their heyday.

DRY KILL LOGIC

Formed in Westchester, New York in 1995, Dry Kill Logic were originally known as Hinge, apparently taking their name from Winston Churchill's book *The Hinges Of Fate*. Citing Pantera, Tool, King Diamond, Sepultura and Fear Factory as their influences, they released their first EP *'Cause Moshing Is Good Fun* in 1997 before going into the studio with producer Andy Katz (Overkill, Rakim) to record debut album *Elemental Evil*. Support slots with Coal Chamber, Incubus, Anthrax, System Of A Down, and The Misfits followed, though with the departure of their original guitarist at the end of 1999, they decided to take time out to consider their next move.

With new line-up consisting of Cliff Rigano (vocals), Dave Kowatch (bass), Scott Thompson (guitars) and Phil Arcuri (drums), they started writing for the new record and went into the studio with Scrap 60 Productions (Eddie Wohl, Steve Regina and Rob Caggiano) to record their first album for Roadrunner, *The Darker Side Of Nonsense*.

At times, particularly on 'Assfalt', the album's stand-out track, they sound like the bastard offspring of late-'80s industrial noiseniks Big Black. There's also more than a hint of their New York hardcore predecessors Prong in the way that they make guitar riffs sound like offensive weapons.

'Tell you what I want, what I really really want, is to see you die!' Cliff spits on 'Rot', a sort of 'tribute' to The Spice Girls' 'Wannabe'. The album closes with 'The Strength I Call My Own', which hints at future directions, a more slow-burning and spaced-out direction, but still imbued with the same spite and guts of the rest of the record. A strong record, then. Everything seemed set for a big-splash debut when a phalanx of lawyers representing a club, also called Hinge, served cease-and-desist orders on the band.

As Cliff told music website *The PRP*, 'We went about trademarking the name, only to find out that there was another "music entity" with the same name that owned the trademark. Said "entity" wasn't into sharing the name at all when approached about obtaining consent to share it, and initially we all agreed that Hinge AD would be sufficient to all parties as an adequate replacement. Unfortunately, a week after we initiated the name change the entity changed its mind, and threatened an immediate lawsuit if *any* form of the word Hinge was included in the name of the band. It truly was a dick move, but whatever. The band, the music, the live show...it's all bigger than a name. Just remember what goes around comes around. *Ten*fold.'

The upshot was that the existing albums had to be repressed and reprinted with the band's new name, Dry Kill Logic, a major stutter in the momentum they had built since their earliest incarnation.

CRAZY TOWN

'Who the fuck is Crazy Town?' they asked on their first release. Seven-piece LA rap-rockers Crazy Town describe themselves as hip-hop kids who needed a bit of rock in their sound rather than a rock band adding a bit of hip-hop. Crazy Town are the band who seem to inspire most ire from metal purists, possibly due to the fact that as well as looking and sounding like a hip-hop crew rather than a metal group, they could also pass for a boy band when you see their videos on MTV. Formed by lyricists/vocalists/producers Shifty Shellshock ('Sid Vicious, Kurt Cobain and Biggie Smalls all trapped in one body') and Epic Mazur (producer of MC Lyte and Bell Biv DeVoe), Crazy Town are nothing if not a more brattish LA update of *Licensed To III*-period Beastie Boys. Their debut album *The Gift Of Game*, produced by close friend Josh Abrahams (Korn, Coal Chamber, Orgy), fell foul of the Federal Trade Commission in a 2000 report on the marketing of music with 'explicit lyrics' to children: TV advertisements for albums by Crazy Town, Ja Rule, DMX, Blink-182, Rage Against The Machine and other recordings with the Parental Advisory stickers were shown on MTV during early-evening and after-school programming, leading to calls for a more stringent system of censorship. The album included tracks like 'Revolving Door', which is about attempting to have sex with as many groupies as possible: 'My sex drive is kicking/I'm sexually exploring/So many possibilities/It seems my life could never get boring.'

'Do what you want to do,' Epic says in the band's official press release in a rudimentary flash of social responsibility. 'Go out with that girl, do that drug, go to that place. Just realise that you're going to have to deal with the aftermath.'

It is obvious to anyone, even after only a cursory listen, that Crazy Town's constituency consists entirely of 13-year-old boys vicariously living out their fantasies of being a bad-ass tattooed pimp through Shifty's raps. Despite their biggest hit being the almost ethereal 'Butterfly', a smoochy love song set around a sample from The Red Hot Chili Peppers' 'Pretty Little Ditty' from *Mother's Milk*, Crazy Town are unremittingly heavy, blurring the reality, as far as possible, between their affluent roots and their affected gangsta/criminal personas. Speaking about the early days, Shellshock told *Rolling Stone*, 'For nine years, we made music on drugs in a loft in downtown LA. We'd do one song and celebrate for six months. We didn't even think about a record deal until we started running out of money and going to rehab, and I got arrested.' As well as claiming that he was once on the LAPD's Most Wanted list, he got the band suspended from Ozzfest for throwing a chair out of a window.

But if he's a fake then that puts him in company with every other rock and roll star on the planet. Despite critical savaging of the band – 'Crazy Town are the rap Mötley Crüe, a band liked by idiots only. Look at their record sales and realise how fucked the world is,' said the *NME* – respected rappers and producers Red Man, Paul Oakenfold, Mad Lion And Dirty Unit and KRS-One have all worked with them, and any follow-up to *The Gift Of Game* will be one of the major releases of the next few years.

WILL HAVEN

Will Haven are not so much a critic's band as a band that other bands tend to like: The Deftones, Limp Bizkit and Max Cavalera of Soulfly all sing the praises of this Sacramento band, particularly with the release of their debut album, 1997's *Diabolo*, released on straight-edge hardcore label Revelation.

Tours with The Deftones, The Beastie Boys, Limp Bizkit and Vision Of Disorder followed and the band's European shows particularly excited the critics there. Comparisons were drawn between Will Haven and early Korn, The Deftones and Jawbox. Phil Alexander, editor-in-chief of *Kerrang!* magazine, said in his review of second album *WHVN*, '[It] is an uncompromising, dense affair which establishes Will Haven as the antithesis of the current crop of nu metal wannabes doing the rounds Stateside. If anything, *WHVN* is the missing link between the ever-fertile Yank noise underground (think Revelation, think Dischord) and straight-down-your-throat metal riffery.'

Grady Avenell (vocals), Jeff Irwin (guitar), Mitch Wheeler (drums) and Mike Martin (bass) are hardly master-musicians in comparison with the more polished works of Limp Bizkit *et al*, though their punk-rock attitude, putting ideas over ability and cranking the whole thing up really loud, is more attractive to Brit critics than their US counterparts. Certainly, a lot of the reaction from the hardcore purists was less than enthusiastic: 'A mall-metal girl blew me once. She'd probably like this' and 'Who signs these bands? Helen Keller?' were among the listener reactions posted on label Revelation's website.

After touring to promote *WHVN*, the band went back into the studio to record their third opus, *Carpe Diem*, an album that was originally hinted at as a double release with 'ambient' tracks inspired by Radiohead's 2000 album *Kid A*. With the release of Tool's magnificent *Lateralus* in the first half of 2001, the prospect of Will Haven making another *Zeitgeist*-defining progressive metal record was hotly anticipated. The resulting release was a more straightforward heavy record, almost a step back from the art metal hinted at on *WHVN* to a plainer, almost hardcore punk sound.

Songs like 'Alpha Male' seemed to poke fun at the testosterone rock-rap beach-bully jock-rock faction: 'Give up your identity/Become a slave and take one for the team.' On 'Saga' they hit back at the woe-is-me kids with 'issues': 'He cut his nose to spite his face/Because he thought it would bring a change/And cleans his heart of all its ugliness/And we just watch him bleed/He is a boy who hates himself/He is a boy who hates his surroundings/He is a boy who hates his future/Gather around and watch him bleed/He is a boy who hates me.'

Yet Will Haven insisted they were big fans of Slipknot, Limp Bizkit and particularly The Deftones, who they regarded as uncompromising in a world where they could easily make a straight rap-metal album and sell billions.

PUDDLE OF MUDD

Like Staind, Puddle Of Mudd are yet another band who have benefited from the patronage of Fred Durst. Like Staind, they sound nothing like their mentors, having more in common with alt.rockers Pearl Jam and Alice In Chains than rap-rock, though while Staind benefited from the advice and support Fred offered before going on to become one of the hottest and highest-grossing new acts, Durst held Puddle Of Mudd a little closer to his bosom.

Signed to his label Flawless, with frontman Wes Scantlin standing in for the departed Wes Borland at the 2001 MTV Europe Music Awards, where they played an acoustic cover version of Led Zeppelin's 'Thank You', Kansas City's Puddle Of Mudd got their demo to Fred by sneaking into the backstage area at a Limp Bizkit show with a forged pass. They give great myth, true or not.

The band's first album, *Come Clean*, mixed by Andy Wallace – who engineered on Nirvana's *Nevermind*, a connection underscored by the fact that Wes sounds at times uncannily like Kurt Cobain – sold half a million copies in its first few months of release.

Predictably, critical reactions were hostile, calling it derivative and dull, *Rolling Stone* even suggesting that, 'If the Who's *Who's Next* is the finest album ever made with a picture of someone urinating on the cover, Puddle Of Mudd's major-label debut, *Come Clean* (which features a child relieving himself in the bushes), could be the worst.'

But opening spots on tours by Limp Bizkit and Staind showed that there is an apparently insatiable market for the nu grunge of Wesley Reid Scantlin (guitar/vocals), Douglas John Ardito (bass), Paul James Phillips (guitar) and Greg David Upchurch (drums). While Staind are also heavily influenced by grunge, they have at least developed a more unique voice of their own. Perhaps there hasn't been enough of a decent interval between the death of grunge/Kurt Cobain and a band whose songs, particularly 'Control', 'Drift And Die' and 'She Hates Me', are so obviously derived from Nirvana songs that they could pass as one of the many 'tribute' bands who still litter the small-town live scene.

The trick with being derivative, basing your career on the greats of the past and recycling ideas, fashions and attitudes from previous generations is all in the timing. That REM could be hailed as a ground-breaking genius American rock and roll band for making music that blatantly borrowed and stole from The Byrds, The Band and The Beach Boys, though with a gap of 15 years or more between Stipe and those bands' creative peaks, shows that their real trick was to get the timing right.

At least Static-X and Orgy have the wit to steal from '80s sources like Ministry and New Order. It's not inconceivable that in another ten years or so a band exactly like this will be the darlings of the 'smart set' but, for the time being, Puddle Of Mudd are perhaps too hot on the heels of any grunge revival bandwagon for them to have any sort of a lasting artistic career.

COLD

Another group of Fred Durst protégés, Cold knew him from Jacksonville, Florida, where Fred offered them the use of his home studio to produce a demo and eventually persuaded Ross Robinson to work on their first album.

Drummer Sam McCandless and vocalist/guitarist Scoot Ward met up in high school in the mid 1980s, started jamming and formed a succession of garage bands before adding bassist Jeremy Marshall and forming Grundig, a metal/punk trio who based themselves in Atlanta, playing gigs until they wore themselves out. Ward returned to Jacksonville, hooked up with Fred, who had been a Grundig fan, demoed his songs, reassembled the band with the addition of Kelley Hayes and Terry Balsamo on guitars and recorded the eponymous debut album, which was released by Interscope.

Cold, despite the name, made dark, emotional music that recalled the negativity of Soundgarden's classic song about depression and life sickness 'Black Hole Sun'. The band betrayed the usual influences – the ubiquitous Alice In Chains and The Cure seem to have seeped into their souls as children. Scoot admitted as much but also claimed that their interests were much wider: 'We like Tool and Black Sabbath, but we also love Radiohead and even Sarah MacLachlan.'

While they lacked the 'arty' qualities that won Will Haven such respect from older fans, there is still an impressive dark quality about Cold that implies more than just the usual beer-fuelled testosterone-puppet high-school aggro or bedroom nerd contemplating the unfairness of life.

They went out on the road with Soulfly, The Urge and Gravity Kills, and visited Europe where fan and press reaction was extremely favourable.

In an unprecedented five out of five review, *Kerrang*! said of the album, 'There's nothing better than slapping a debut album on the deck and finding yourself swamped by an excitingly alien new sound... Cold songs are evil. They crawl under your scalp and build a nest. Before you know it you're overrun... Cold is the first brilliant album of the year.'

The music was actually uplifting. Nevertheless with song titles like 'Everyone Dies', 'Insane', 'Goodbye Cruel World' and 'Serial Killer' it was clear that with negativity in style, Cold weren't a band worried about being taken too seriously.

They played to legions of fans on the free Cypress Hill/Limp Bizkit Napster tour. Second album, *13 Ways To Bleed Onstage*, followed in 2000 as did a slot on the Tattoo The Planet tour along with support slots for Staind and Godsmack.

While the new direction was hardly a reinvention of the wheel, songs like 'Sick Of Man' on the sophomore record showed a willingness to experiment, layering studio effects to create a low-key psychedelic track, while the addition of a piano on 'She Said' hinted that they aspired to more than the most basic punk-grunge sound.

ILL NIÑO

The Latin-American diaspora is the fastest-growing sector of the American population; California and Florida are effectively bilingual states, while in the cosmopolitan environs of New York, Spanish and Portuguese are the most prominent languages you'll hear. There has always been a strong Latin pop scene, inspired by samba and bossa-nova rhythms from Brazil or the hotter Afro-Cuban salsa style. Few Latin artists, however, have crossed over into the rock and roll mainstream.

Mexican-born Carlos Santana was one of the few to make it in the white-bread world of '60s rock. Brazil's Sepultura and former member Max Cavalera's Soulfly blazed a trail for other bands to follow; Sepultura's 1996 album *Roots* pioneered a fusion between their brand of thrash and the tribal rhythms of rainforest natives.

The members of New Jersey's Ill Niño have their roots in South and Central America and in Puerto Rico; they are unique in the addition of flamenco, tango, bossa nova and salsa elements to crushing rap metal. 'The idea is to be as heavy as possible and as melodic as possible – with a Latin twist,' says drummer, Dave Chavarri.

Formed as El Niño, a hardcore thrash band singing in Spanish and English, it was a stint as temporary drummer in Soulfly that inspired ex-Pro-Pain sticksman Chavarri with the vision to take the band further. Returning to New Jersey, he changed the name to Ill Niño, and recruited Brazilian-born bassist and songwriter Christian Marchado to front the band.

With guitarists Marc Rizzo and recent Brazilian transplant

Jardel Paisante, bassist Lazaro Pina and ex-Ricanstruction percussionist Roger Vasquez, the band was unveiled in 2000 on a series of support slots with Kittie, Soulfly and Snapcase, and a co-headlining set at March's Metal Meltdown festival held in New Jersey.

The band signed with Roadrunner and went into the studio with producer Ron St Germaine (whose production credits include Soundgarden, 311 and Creed) to make their debut album *Revolution, Revolución*.

Reactions to the album were mixed: there were some rave reviews and others that compared them to Ricky Martin with dreads, piercings and tats. Despite the title, the album was not particularly militant in content. An exciting live act, Ill Niño are one of the most promising of the new nu breed.

DISTURBED

Chicago band Disturbed's Dan Donegan (guitar), Mike Wengren (drums) and Fuzz (bass) had been plugging away for years and getting nowhere before hooking up with frontman David Draiman, a softly spoken Jewish skinhead with a degree in philosophy whose onstage presence is charismatic and...disturbing. Ozzy Osbourne called them 'the future of metal' after they appeared on Ozzfest 2001. Their support slot with Marilyn Manson on his European tour had as many people coming along to check them out as came to see ol' red eyes.

It wasn't just the music as the presence of Draiman that won the punters over. Like Slipknot, Manson and Mudvayne, Draiman taps into rock theatre; his intense performances have camp flourishes about them, something that is otherwise completely absent from nu metal or 'heavy music' in general.

Their debut album recorded for Giant Records, *The Sickness*, suffers from sounding like an identikit nu metal record, with none of the nuances and humour of their live set. Disturbed's choice of obligatory '80s pop song to cover is the Tears For Fears hit 'Shout', a song inspired by Arthur Janov's 'primal scream' therapy.

Draiman, in an interview with *Voxonline* said, 'I think it is a masterpiece. We did want a song that is completely opposite to our sound, you know, coming from a completely different direction, but yet at the same time has the same meaning, has lyrics like something written by Disturbed. "Shout" is perfect for it. It's about voicing your displeasure and yelling it out, shouting it out, not sitting back and taking it. But if you remember when "Shout" was written – it's an '80s pop song from England – things were softer then. I think it really blends in well with our other songs and we play it almost every night and our audiences love it. Curt Smith of Tears For Fears told us that he thinks now finally the song has the aggression he envisioned when he wrote the lyrics. Wow, that was such a great compliment. We were floored. We could hardly believe it.'

SEVENDUST

After a gruelling tour that left the band emotionally drained and physically wrecked at the end of 2000, the four-piece from Atlanta, Georgia, returned home and took their first vacations after a period of almost two years continuously on the road. During this period, the songs that would form their brilliant third album *Animosity* were written, an outpouring of anger – and some joy – at the people who had crossed their path and the events that had befallen the band.

According to guitarist Clint Lowery, 'The title of the record says a lot. There are issues that we had with people who led us the wrong way and disappointed us, and this was a chance to get it off our chests. We finally felt some sort of closure with those issues by writing these songs.'

The most significant event was the break-up with their long-time manager Jay Jay French (formerly of Twisted Sister) who had been an integral part of the band since the beginning.

The band formed in 1994 when bassist Vinnie Hornsby and drummer Morgan Rose played in a band called Snake Nation. One night they played with Body And Soul, a local R&B band fronted by Lajo Witherspoon who had a reputation as one of the best frontmen on the local scene. They were blown away by his range, his presence and his sheer ability, and poached him for their new band, then called Rumblefish after the cult Francis Ford Coppola film (the name cropped up again as a track on 1999's *Home*).

A name change to Crawlspace followed, Clint Lowery joined the band and a demo was recorded in the back room of an Atlanta nightclub where the temperature allegedly rose to over 100 degrees. TVT records, home of Nine Inch Nails, liked what they heard and signed the band.

A further name change was forced by an existing band called Crawlspace, so their debut album was released as Sevendust, after the brand name of a can of pesticide. Combining sub-Korn riffing with Lajo's chilling soulful voice, the album was a strong collection of songs but a poor seller in its initial release period.

TVT Records president Steve Gottlieb bought airtime on TV to broadcast a live show by the band. Like the Limp Bizkit pay-for-play scandal, this move, though not illegal, raised a few eyebrows. It was an audacious move and a gamble that paid off: the album charted and eventually went gold.

Second album *Home* bore an uncanny resemblance to the output of Korn, thanks in part to production by Toby Wright who had worked with them on *Follow The Leader*. The album included the skate anthem 'Waffle' and 'Licking Cream', a duet with Skunk Anansie vocalist Skin.

Radio began to pick up on the band – this time without a cash inducement to do so – and their set at Woodstock '99 was one of the high points of that blighted festival.

Sevendust's brand of funk metal lacks any real identity. Despite their respectable sales, they are more of a workaday band, albeit one with good songs and a charismatic frontman.

COAL CHAMBER

Whether it was the events of 11 September 2001 or some other change of heart that prompted it, Coal Chamber altered the title of their third album from *Dark Days* to the more hopeful *Salvation* shortly before its completion. Then, they compromised and announced that it would be called *The Dark Salvation*.

Los Angeles band Coal Chamber, like Marilyn Manson, are one of the few flags left to which beleaguered 21st-century goths can rally. Projecting an image of morbid decadence and louche sensuality in a world of big shorts, beefy white boys with dreadlocks and fob chains, they seem to stand out as the inheritors of the legacy of Siouxsie And The Banshees, Bauhaus and The Sisters Of Mercy. They cite their influences as Black Sabbath, The Cure, Nick Cave and Mötley Crüe.

Musically, however, particularly on their debut release, Coal Chamber sound like a band at the heartland of modern heavy music. Their eponymous debut seemed to be more of an album for skaters than for absinthe-sipping black-clad wannabe vampires. Kicking off with the jolt-like 'Loco' and including the marvellous crowd-pleaser 'Sway', Coal Chamber were a band that promised great things with their synthesis of hip-hop, metal and punk. *Kerrang!* said of the album, 'It's like King Kong on a skateboard, walloping and flattening just about everything in his path.'

The band's image and imagery had them dubbed – albeit briefly – 'spookycore' and lumped alongside Marilyn Manson and several, mercifully forgotten, other bands as heralds of a new genre. There's some evidence to suggest that Coal Chamber were the first band to whom the tag 'nu metal' was actually applied, in a live review in *Spin* magazine.

Formed by frontman Dez Fafara, a former bricklayer and hairdresser (!) with drummer Mike Cox, guitarist Meegs Rascon and bassist Rayna Foss-Rose (who is married to Morgan Rose of Sevendust) in 1994, Coal Chamber produced a demo and quickly established a committed cult following through gigs at the Roxy and the Whiskey A Go Go. Both Ross Robinson and Fear Factory's Dino Cazares spotted the band and, independently, recommended them to Roadrunner label A&R man Monte Conner who snapped up the band straight away.

Things would have progressed nicely from there had not Dez decide to leave the band, unable to balance the responsibilities of leading a group like Coal Chamber with those of marriage and parenthood. After 18 months, Meegs went to his house and asked him to 'put the magic back together'. Dez reformed the band and signed a final deal with Roadrunner. Ross Robinson was originally set to be the producer for *Coal Chamber*, but after working with him at rehearsal for an hour Dez decided not to go with him, because they all felt he was trying to make them sound like something they were not. Instead, he roped in Jay Gordon of Orgy, a friend looking for a break, to produce the record. His wife left him the very day he went into the studio to start recording his vocals.

'She left me in the driveway of my home, taking the dog and everything I fuckin' owned. Everything I fuckin' thought was real,' recalled Dez. Her parting words to him were 'Are you all right?' His response 'Do I seem all right to you?' became the chorus to 'Unspoiled', which was recorded later that same day.

The band toured heavily, including a slot on Ozzfest '98 – Sharon Osbourne managed the band until recently – garnering rave reviews for their emotionally stimulating sound. In 1999, the band were at the centre of controversy over the death of a fan who committed suicide while listening to the track 'Oddity' from their first album. The band's alignment to the 'dark' side seemed to be coming back to haunt them. In an interview with *Guitar* magazine the following year, Meegs Rascon said, 'It's very sad because our music, almost all of it, is very positive. And many people can't go past the image, can't go past the harshness of our sound, so they automatically lump it into the whole satanic evil music genre. A lot of our songs are written for the kids, and only for the kids and the situations they're in. We always try to be positive in the end, instead of being all negative and "Oh, I hate my life." Because we're not complaining. We get paid to do what we love. I hate bands that complain about life. Why do you have to complain? You have millions of dollars in the bank, you have a beautiful wife or girlfriend, and a big fucking house. Stop complaining. And talk about issues that matter. I think we tackle a lot of issues that matter. I grew up with a lot of friends who were gang members, but I was never into that. It made me go, "I want to do something with my life." There were two options: college or music. And I chose music, because I was so into it. And now I listen to everything. Without music, I wouldn't be anything.'

But while the first album was the culmination of years of songwriting and was a comparatively raw outpouring of everything the band had to give at the time, they decided that with the follow-up they were going to raise the bar. Limp Bizkit and Korn had spawned numerous clones, and even bands that Coal Chamber admired, like The Deftones, seemed to have inspired countless imitators. *Chamber Music* was going to be different. With an orchestra, pianos and strings as well as guest appearances from Ozzy Osbourne on a cover of Peter Gabriel's 'Shock The Monkey', DJ Lethal (Limp Bizkit), Aimee Echo (ex-Human Waste Project, now theSTART) and Elijah Blue Allman (Deadsy), *Chamber Music* was, as Meegs described it, 'a record in three dimensions'.

As Dez told *Shoutweb* in 2000, 'I think *Chamber Music* was extremely ambitious; 17 tracks and various landscapes – we really wanted to get into some melody and break away from everybody, which I think we did.'

After more upheavals in the band – Rayna left temporarily to have a baby – they regrouped to work on their third album at NRG Studios in California with producer Ross Hogarth. With the nu metal sound they pioneered now an all-pervading force in American music, the resulting album was unmistakably a very heavy release.

'This is who we are,' said Dez. '*Dark Salvation* is the Coal Chamber bible.'

10 Nu And Non-Nu
Artists At The Edge Of A Genre

There's a wonderful 1969 episode from the last series of the original *Star Trek* called 'Let This Be Your Last Battlefield'. It's about a 50,000-year struggle between two aliens, Lokai and Bele. They are humanoid, their 'alienness' being that they are black on one side and white on the other. They hate each other, one seeing the other as an oppressor and a bigot, the other seeing his quarry as a subversive and a terrorist. The *Star Trek* regulars are bewildered to finally learn the prejudice that fuels their passionate hatred: Lokai's people, with their black half on their left side, are opposites of Bele's, who are black on the right.

It's a great metaphor for the tyranny of small differences, that stir up passions and prejudices within all genres of popular music. To one uninitiated into the freemasonry of metal, the genre seems homogeneous, with no obvious differentiation between an '80s soft-rock power ballad by Journey, a death-metal workout by Slayer or the latest MTV-friendly single by Crazy Town. Even to close observers, the categorisation of bands into nu and non-nu seems equally arbitrary. If nu metal is white hip-hop, then doesn't Eminem count? Why Orgy but not Marilyn Manson? Don't Slipknot have an onstage DJ, lyrics about angst and anger, elements of rap and Ross Robinson as a producer?

The fact is that nu metal is changing rapidly, evolving, sucking in other influences and throwing out others. It does not necessarily mean the same thing now as when it was first applied to describe

Korn, Limp Bizkit and Coal Chamber in the mid 1990s. The term is becoming wider and is essentially describing new metal. And nu metal is not the only thing happening in metal. The biggest alternative is music derived from punk, a sort of *National Lampoon's Animal House* take on The Ramones, centred around Blink-182, Bloodhound Gang, Everclear, Pennywise, Wheatus, Weezer and Green Day. This is a dumbed-down version of punk, comedy punk with more in common with novelty acts like The Dickies than with The Sex Pistols or Black Flag. There is still a living museum of 'authentic' punk rock – bands like Rancid, Earth Crisis and AFI who tour and release records independently to a large but stable or even declining market of fans.

The success of Queens Of The Stone Age, a band formed from the remnants of acclaimed early '90s standard-bearers for ultra-heavy blues Kyuss, heralds a growing underground phenomenon called stoner rock (variations include desert rock). Stoner rock is a drug-fuelled return to the very early roots of metal, with the bands looking and sounding like it's still that ephemeral era between 1968 and 1972. Nebula, Spirit Caravan and Unida all draw on this immediate post-psychedelic imagery and sound for inspiration, citing influences like Blue Cheer, Cactus and early Black Sabbath. Stoner rock, as a form that is essentially revivalist, may be a dead end in American rock, metal's equivalent of ska-punk, but there is a freshness about the sound that attracts a growing cult of followers.

LA's Buckcherry also take their inspiration from another era, in their case the various incarnations of glam rock and classic early '80s hard rock, particularly AC/DC. Looking like Keith Richards wannabes, Buckcherry evoke a vanished world of hotel-wrecking drug fiends from The New York Dolls to The Faces. There isn't quite enough in the way of compatriot bands to call this 'nu glam' a movement yet – we have Hardcore Superstar and Backyard Babies from Sweden, arguably Nashville Pussy and possibly ex-Wildhearts man Ginger's band SG5 – though, strangely, the classic '70s/'80s rock-chick look has started to appear on catwalks and in high-fashion stores, with rhinestone-spattered AC/DC T-shirts selling for over US$100.

There is also an 'ironic' rediscovery of bands like Mötley Crüe, Ratt, Hanoi Rocks and Skid Row by LA teens, which goes under the name 'Classic', though thankfully this has not yet spread from the borders of the state of California.

But none of these subcults has anything like the selling power of nu metal. The term may actually be meaningless – one of the many transient labels attached to a disparate group of bands and artists that outlived its usefulness a few seconds after it was coined – but like all such labels, we know *exactly* what we mean by it, even if, when you come to define the term in words, it becomes ephemeral and seems to lose the meaning that was intended.

As has been noted elsewhere, there are many bands lumped alongside nu metal who definitely are not part of that scene. Marilyn Manson, Slipknot, Amen, Eminem, Kid Rock, Bubba Sparxx and A Perfect Circle have all at some time or another been filed alongside Limp Bizkit, Korn, Coal Chamber and their ilk. They are not nu metal acts: like them or loathe them, they are all successful bands and artists who either arose in isolation from nu metal (or any other kind of metal) or stand in direct opposition to it. Visit any of the thousands of online forums, chatrooms and websites where fans discuss the minutiae of metal with all the passion and intensity of the Inquisition rooting out heresy, and it's clear that there are serious faultlines between one group, who perceive themselves as fans of 'true' metal (usually older-school bands such as Pantera, Slayer and Metallica) and the younger fans who like the bands they see on MTV, such as Staind or Mudvayne.

Sometimes the rivalry looks very much like hatred, with everything that one group stands for – clothes, hair length, age – being savaged by the other side. While there is little or no actual violence – unlike in the '70s and '80s when punk rockers were often targets for more reactionary rock and roll elements – there is a very real divide.

Yet there are more similarities between Marilyn Manson, Slipknot, Amen, Eminem, Kid Rock and the nu metal bands than there are differences. They interact with each other, have often appeared on the same touring bills together, they are all part of a greater set of contemporary American rock and roll bands, they come from the same roots. All genres provoke the creation of others; some movements are spawned that are even more radical, others that are reactionary. In the 1970s, out-of-touch 'progressive rock' was ultimately responsible for punk, punk in turn was responsible for a plethora of revivalist cults (Mod, 2-Tone, Skinhead/Oi!) as well as creating a 'siege mentality' amongst traditional hard rock fans that actually defined and energised '80s heavy metal. So nu metal contains the seeds of its own opposition, its own death, and the bands and artists out there, known and unknown, who would be its executioners.

In an incendiary 1999 rant on his website, Marilyn Manson savaged the nu metal mentality: 'We are constantly shoveled milky mounds of unchallenging, moronic impotence disguised as entertainment, but really only designed to lower our standards and make us passive and content on being dumbed down. Why do we watch the things they give us on MTV or *Jenny Jones* or *The 11 O'Clock News*? We have been conditioned to have low expectations and our standards have become less than primitive. The illiterate apes that beat your ass in high school for being a "fag" now sell you tuneless testosterone anthems of misogyny and pretend to be outsiders to a world that they were born to wear their ADIDASS-FILGERING uniforms in. And we buy it up, helplessly.'

Ross Robinson, producer of Korn and Limp Bizkit, is still generally perceived as the man who somehow 'invented' nu metal, a label he has worked hard to shake off. The first two bands to sign to his label I AM were Amen and Slipknot, bands he intended to use to knock over the post-Korn/Bizkit axis. 'The new Slipknot record is going to go out there and destroy everything. This real shit is going to just destroy what else is out there,' he said on the eve of the release of Slipknot's second album *Iowa* in 2001. 'That hip-hop, stupid metal kinda thing is now finished, and I wanna drive the final nails into its coffin and utterly destroy it.' Although he said that he is still proud of the Korn record and still on good terms with the band, his relationship with Fred Durst did not survive his turning down the opportunity to work on Limp Bizkit's second album *Significant Other*, preferring to publicly announce his intention to sweep away 'Adidas rock'. To understand further what nu metal is, then, it's worth looking at what it is not and at what stands in opposition to it.

MARILYN MANSON

Marilyn Manson is either the *bête noire* of American rock or a *Rocky Horror Show* tribute that got out of hand, depending on your point of view. In the wake of the 1999 high school shootings in Columbine, Colorado, when Dylan Klebold and Eric Harris, two students, went on a rampage, shooting dead 12 students and a teacher, Marilyn Manson became a national symbol of hatred for middle America. Desperate to explain why two teenagers would turn into mass murderers, commentators sought scapegoats in the usual places: violent films such as the recent hits *The Matrix* and *The Basketball Diaries*, video games such as *Doom* and *Mortal Kombat*, and 'the gothic movement', the decades-too-late discovery that some kids dress in black, listen to depressing music and try to look like vampires. Obscure industrial bands such as KMFDM, Filter and Thrill Kill Kult turned on their TVs to discover that they were part of a sinister Satanist plot to brainwash the youth of America because their albums were included in Klebold and Harris's record collections.

But it was Manson who was singled out for special treatment: despite the fact that the two misfits had been the victims of bullying at the hands of the school's 'jocks' and had easy access to guns, it was the fact that they were fans of Marilyn Manson that seemed to be more of a motive as far as the investigators were concerned.

When Manson cancelled his Colorado show 'out of respect for the dead' (a statement by the promoter, not Manson), it was like an admission of complicity. His concerts were picketed by born-again Christian groups, there were calls for stricter censorship and even in 2001, when he joined the bill for Ozzfest, there were calls for him not to be allowed to perform in Colorado. He even received death threats.

In George Bush's home state of Texas, the Crime Prevention Resource Center, a spin-off of the Fort Worth Chamber of Commerce's Code Blue Crime Prevention project, declared that school officials should monitor closely any students who were fans of Marilyn Manson or were attracted to 'gothic' fashions. The group suggested that student lockers be searched, and that officials even examine their art work, and track which books they were checking out of the library.

Columbine, Manson said, 'is probably the only event since the Kennedy assassination to really shock America... It's grotesque that they used it as a toy to toss around to set up the election – the only thing Bush and Gore were talking about was violence in entertainment and gun control. I may have nihilism in my music, and it may not be pretty, but at the same time I don't think I behaved in such a disrespectful way as these other people.' In his song 'The Nobodies', Manson sang, 'Some children died the other day/You should see the ratings,' expressing his disgust at the capital made by the media and religious groups.

Manson made it easy for them. Like all of his band (Madonna Wayne Gacy, Daisy Berkowitz, Twiggy Ramirez), he took the surname of a notorious American mass murderer or serial killer and conjoined it with the first name of an American female icon. He was ordained into the Church Of Satan (who do not, despite the name, literally believe in the existence of the devil) and was an unapologetic and intelligent critic of the conservative 'family values' lobby centred around right-wing churchmen such as presidential hopeful Pat Robertson.

Formed in 1989 by Tampa, Florida-based music critic Brian Warner, Marilyn Manson And The Spooky Kids built up a strong local following before signing a deal with Nine Inch Nails mastermind Trent Reznor's Nothing Records in 1994, supporting their mentor on tour with a now abbreviated name. The band's initial sound was jokey, goth metal with overtones of other 'dark side' bands such as horror-rockers White Zombie. Many critics immediately recognised Manson as a rallying flag for a new generation of goths, many too young to remember bands like The Sisters Of Mercy, The Mission and Fields Of The Nephilim.

Goth was a romantic tradition that flourished in the '80s in the wake of bands like Siouxsie And The Banshees, New Order/Joy Division and Bauhaus, who had all emerged from the British punk rock scene but soon eschewed its minimalism and anti-intellectualism for a dreamier, almost psychedelic, music heavily influenced by David Bowie and imagery informed by German expressionist cinema, Weimar cabaret, horror movies and a hint of Luciferianism. Manson, painfully thin and pale with long raven-black hair, was in the mould of Byronic goth pin-up boys like Peter Murphy of Bauhaus and Andrew Eldritch of The Sisters Of Mercy.

The band had a minor hit in 1995 with their Eurythmics cover 'Sweet Dreams Are Made Of This', taken from their Reznor-produced debut album *Portrait Of An American Family*. Manson was often seen as merely Trent Reznor's puppet, a sort of 'Mini-Me' clone who followed his master around. It was advantageous – the tours with Nine Inch Nails and David Bowie brought Manson to a huge audience. Reznor, who composed the soundtrack for David Lynch's *Lost Highway*, was instrumental in having Manson appear in the film. During the recording of Manson's third album, the breakthrough *Antichrist Superstar*, however, Reznor and Manson's relationship broke down, resulting in an ugly public feud.

Reznor took exception to tell-all revelations in Manson's autobiography, *The Long Road Out Of Hell*, which describes in lurid detail on-the-road escapades involving groupies, which would make Led Zeppelin blush, including one in 1995 that involved burning a woman's pubic hair, and a party with the Jim Rose Circus Sideshow where they held a contest to see which groupie could hold an enema the longest before ejecting into a bowl of Froot Loops.

Ironically, when Reznor and Manson supposedly buried the hatchet in 2000, with Trent directing the video for Manson's 'Starfuckers Inc', a song attacking the cult of celebrity-at-any-cost, it drew him into the ongoing cold war with Fred Durst, who took exception to seeing his image smashed in the clip.

Durst told *Revolver* magazine, 'Trent Reznor is pissing me off. I'm a huge Nine Inch Nails fan; *Pretty Hate Machine* was a huge part of my life. Big. Trent really took industrial music to another level. So to have him smashing a plate that's got my image on in his "Starfuckers, Inc" video for no other reason than jealousy is really small. I understand his record isn't doing what he'd hoped it would, but that doesn't mean he has to bring everyone else down with him. Despite everything, I'd like to collaborate with him. That would be fantastic and our fans would love it. But instead, he's out there talking shit, and he's hurting himself.'

Durst responded with the refrain 'You want to fuck me like an animal/You want to burn me on the inside/You like to think I'm your perfect drug/But just know that nothin' you do will bring you closer to me' – all references to Reznor songs – on 'Hot Dog' from *Chocolate Starfish And The Hot Dog Flavored Water*, over a sample from Nine Inch Nails' 'Closer'.

Durst and Manson were the polar opposites of contemporary pop culture. One was a hard-headed small-c conservative businessman whose brand of music was rooted in gritty gangsta rap, a hero to the sort of 'jocks' – the beer-drinking football players – who date-raped cheerleaders, the sort who bullied Harris and Klebold. The other was a standard-bearer for the misfits and outcasts, not merely for the goths, but the sensitive kids who wrote poetry in their bedrooms and felt at odds with the world, the ones who didn't join in, who stood apart. But, as with all enemies, they were actually remarkably similar characters.

Both were singled out by the media, unfairly, to represent something that was none of their doing. Manson accused Durst (and by implication Jonathan Davis) of being like 'the illiterate apes' who pick on the 'sensitive' outsiders in high school, yet Durst could hardly be described as a 'jock', one of the goody-goody sports types who is 'popular' at school. Both were shrewd media manipulators, great communicators and, when the mood took them, intelligent and articulate commentators on the state of America and their generation.

Manson played with the same negativity, the same discontent, the same anger as all of the nu metal bands, but while their anger was directed against parents, girlfriends and friends, Manson had a nihilistic message of rage against society. His songs showed the influence of a host of literary sources, such as the Marquis de Sade, Charles Baudelaire, Isidore Ducasse (aka le Comte de Lautremont), JK Huysmans, Friedrich Nietzsche, Pier Paolo Pasolini and Oswald Spengler. If he had any predecessor, it was less Alice Cooper or WASP's Blackie Lawless and more Aleister Crowley, Britain's self-styled Great Beast, magician, poet, novelist, occultist, Orientalist, mountaineer, painter, opium addict and aesthete, whose scandalous exploits involving sex, drugs and magick guaranteed him constant attention in the 'yellow press' during the 1920s and 1930s. Like Crowley, Manson delights in 'bourgeois baiting'. On 'I Don't Like The Drugs (But The Drugs Like Me)' from *Mechanical Animals*, the acclaimed follow-up to *Antichrist Superstar*, he attacks perceived middle American bourgeois conformity when he sings the lyrics, 'Norm life baby/"We're white and oh so hetero and our sex is missionary."/ Norm life baby/"We're quitters and we're sober our confessions will be televised."/You and I are underdosed and we're ready to fall/Raised to be stupid, taught to be nothing at all/I don't like the drugs but the drugs like me.'

His 'Beautiful People' from *Antichrist Superstar* is a darker song where he perceives himself and the listener as part of a Nietzschean elite besieged by the less evolved people around them ('It's not your fault that you're always wrong/The weak ones are there to justify the strong/...If you live with apes, it's hard to be clean,' he sings) with a message that this world was created by capitalism but will be swept away by fascism. Like Durst, Manson offers no real solutions; the words give the impression of being political, of being protest songs, but the message is often contradictory and ends up in the sort of 'just be yourself and have a good time' cop-out so beloved of rock and roll stars who can't take their ideas to a logical conclusion.

But while Durst courts a safe, daytime TV showbiz controversy, a sort of two-fisted hard-drinking womanising hellraiser image, Manson does at least pick fights with real targets, particularly with Christianity. In *The Long Road Out Of Hell*, Manson describes how years of being indoctrinated by Christian teachers with bizarre conspiracy theories and descriptions of the 'end times' caused him, eventually, to reject it.

In a 1996 interview with *Alternative Press*, Manson spelled out his 'Nietzschean' line and his fear of the growing fundamentalist influence in politics: 'I think Christianity itself is self-destructive because it's based on weakness, and I think as people are raised in this country, you're meant to have faith in something you can't put your hands on. As you get older maybe you feel cheated, and you start to develop your own ideas of morality. So in a sense, for Christians, morality hasn't declined; it's just merely taken a different shape. The more you get government involved with religion, the worse off you are. They don't even see the irony in the Romans murdering Christ, if you want to buy into that story. It was because there was no separation of Church and State.'

The Christian right is a potent force in the USA today and the censorship lobby has grown. Even before Columbine, bands such as Ozzy Osbourne, Judas Priest and Slayer were the targets of lawsuits, brought and backed by Christian fundamentalists, blaming them for inspiring teenage murders, suicides and rapes through their music, lyrics and alleged hidden messages in the songs. Manson baited them relentlessly. He told *Rolling Stone* in 2000, 'Christianity has given us an image of death and sexuality that we have based our culture around. A half-naked dead man hangs in most homes and around our necks, and we have just taken that for granted all our lives. Is it a symbol or hope or hopelessness?'

Part of his stage act consisted of Manson dressed up as a gigantic fascist pope; he attacked Christianity in interviews and in articulate and well-thought-out rants on his website; his post-Columbine album *Holy Wood (In The Shadow Of The Valley Of Death)* was steeped in imagery about the Kennedy assassination and an absent God.

Durst, on the other hand, picked a fight with Christian rock band Creed, who had upstaged him at a gig. They challenged him to a boxing match, which Fred declined. But if the rivalry between Durst and Manson was anything other than media jamming, then it was a rivalry where Fred Durst had the upper hand. *Holy Wood*...was a disappointing album compared to its two immediate predecessors, both in terms of critical reaction and in terms of overall sales. *Rolling Stone* critic Barry Walters said, 'On *Holy Wood (In The Shadow Of The Valley Of Death)*, Manson is as ambitious, personal and heavy as he's ever been, but the album is not, as he has proclaimed, the band's *White Album*. The music of these LA scenesters, though still evolving, can't hope to match The Beatles' level of eclectic experimentation or melodicism. But you have to respect Manson for addressing real-life issues with a theatrical verve and genuine vitriol that no other mainstream act can match. *Holy Wood (In The Shadow Of The Valley Of Death)* won't win converts.'

To some extent Manson's 'shock value' was diminished by the advent of Slipknot, whose grand guignol theatrics oustripped Manson's and then some. Younger and angrier pretenders like

Amen, Mudvayne and Disturbed mopped up some of the younger fans. Against the brutality of the masked men from Des Moines, Iowa, Manson looked effete. He had tried to make a dense, experimental album just at the time that the *Zeitgeist* was swinging back to loud, brutal and basic noise.

But the significance of Manson in the wake of Kurt Cobain's death is that he seemed to make rock and roll important again, even if that was in a negative way. Jaded veterans of the '60s were astonished to see battles they thought had long been won being refought. Southern Christians who had burned Beatles records after John Lennon said the band were 'bigger than Jesus' seemed at the time to be the last gasp of the Christian fundamentalists – who had tried a schoolteacher for teaching Darwin's theory of evolution in the classroom – rather than a wave of the future. Manson made the cover of *Newsweek* as well as *Rolling Stone*. He may have won a moral victory over the forces of reaction but not over Limp Bizkit.

Chalk that as one up to the illiterate apes and no points for the Beautiful People.

EMINEM AND KID ROCK

There are white rappers and there are white rappers. The difference between Eminem and Fred Durst is that black people, hardcore rap fans, will go to see Eminem and buy Eminem records and show respect for Eminem as a rapper, whereas the faces you see at a Limp Bizkit show are going to be mostly white. As (hed) pe frontman Jared told me, 'The only black people you're gonna see at one of those shows is the security guards and the folks working in the drinks concessions.'

The hip-hop press heaps respect on Eminem. *Vibe* magazine said of *The Marshall Mathers Album*, '[It] should forever erase the notion that Eminem is the Elvis Presley of hardcore hip-hop. If anything, he's rap's Eric Clapton: a white boy who can hang with the best black talent based on sheer skill – enhancing the art form instead of stealing from it.'

Black radio will play Eminem records. Interestingly, rock and roll radio will play Eminem records too, though not Method Man, DMX or Busta Rhymes, unless they are making a guest appearance with a (white) rock artist. Eminem won the 2001 Grammy Award for Best Rap Album. *The Real Slim Shady* (which ironically contains the line 'You think I give a damn about a Grammy?') won the 2001 Grammy Award for Best Rap Solo Performance. Yet the question arises: if Eminem were black would he get the same amount of coverage in the 'white' media?

The 'Jim Crow Line' in entertainment prevents black artists appearing on the covers of magazines unless they are aimed at a black readership. While music magazines are happy to put Eminem on the cover, a face whose controversy guarantees sales, they are more wary about using artist like Puff Daddy (currently known as P Diddy), who is also a controversial figure and whose forays into rock (such as his reworking of Led Zeppelin's 'Kashmir' and his rock remix of 'It's All About The Benjamins' with The Foo Fighters) have been landmarks. Kid Rock is closest in spirit and sound to the nu metal acts, creating a fusion of trailer-park rock – southern boogie like Lynyrd Skynyrd – with gangsta-style rapping and a superpimp image. Hailing from the American Midwest, Kid Rock moved to New York after years spent developing his rapping style at the Romeo, Michigan, housing projects. He was what was termed a wigga, whigger or whigga – a 'white nigger'.

As he told *Kronik* magazine, 'My parents used to ask me all the time, "Why the fuck you goin' down to DJ parties for them niggers?" Flat out! They'd say shit like, "You can go DJ a wedding and make $300 dollars, but you'd rather run down there with them niggers and play for $50 dollars and drink 40s all night." And they weren't that hardcore about us. I don't wanna make 'em out to be big Racial people. It wasn't that bad. It was more like I was truckin' outta there to go on some pipe-dream to do somethin' I loved and they couldn't understand. But truckin' I had to deal with a lotta that shit. Especially, even the whole whigger thing. There was a point in my like when I had a Troop suit. I had a little flat-top goin'. Shit like that. I thought I was doin' it! But I ain't no fuckin' front! Ninety per cent of the other white kids went thru that too, man! It's just somethin' we all just kinda went thru.'

In many ways the early '90s whigger scene was only an underground version of what would become a mass-market, though considerably watered-down, phenomenon a few years on. Apart from The Beastie Boys, the only white artists involved in rap were absurd novelty acts like Vanilla Ice. Kid Rock toured with Ice Cube, Too $hort, D-Nice, Yo-Yo and Poor Righteous Teachers. The young Kid Rock favoured a lascivious style similar to that which landed 2 Live Crew in court in 1990, charged with obscenity; the Kid himself landed himself a US$25,000 fine from the FCC over a track from his album *Grits Sandwiches For Breakfast* called 'Yo-Da-Lin' In The Valley' which was played on college radio much to the dismay of one dean who called it 'the most obscene song ever made'. The rap went thus: 'Yodel in the valley/And I'd do it at the drop of a dime/Sometimes goin' from behind/Slowly strokin', no jokin'/My tongue just keeps on pokin'/And the best type of oochie coochie/Is the kind that tastes like sushi/Eat it/Watch a girl get frisky/And then wash it down with a shot of whiskey.'

Oral sex – talking about it, rapping about it – was to loom large in his subsequent work. Signing to Atlantic in 1998, he and his band Twisted Brown Trucker released the breakthrough album *Devil Without A Cause*, which had him dubbed 'a moronic cross between Axl Rose and Vanilla Ice' by one critic.

The *New York Times*, inexplicably, compared and contrasted him with Beck: 'Harder than Beck's trippy pop raps, the Kid's tunes have some of the same charm that made Mr Hanson and his disc *Odelay* so popular. That charm, married to a surprising musical range, sets *Devil Without A Cause* apart from rap styles that have emerged from either the west coast or east coast schools of rhythm 'n' rhyme'.

Although he toured with Korn and Limp Bizkit in 2000, and his onstage DJ Uncle Kracker has collaborated with several other nu metal bands, Kid Rock can be said to be with them but not *of* them. His raps, occasionally puerile, are unremittingly positive in nature, loaded with bragging and bravado about sexual prowess (on the massive 'I Am the Bullgod'), oral sex and his attractiveness to women.

Kid Rock presented an image of a good-natured, cigar-chomping natural man, a red-blooded American patriot, watching Monday-night football, eating a bloody steak and drinking a beer in between a career as a full-time lady-pleaser that was way at odds with Fred Durst's angry, bitter white boy or Jonathan Davis's angst-ridden loner.

The music, too, was rock and roll of a more traditional kind, which sounded at best in the tradition of Run-DMC's collaboration with Aerosmith and at worst like *Frampton Comes Alive* self-indulgence. The other influence that fed into the work, and which was highlighted on his 2001 album, *Cocky*, was country and western – Kid Rock always named Johnny Cash and Hank Williams as his influences; Eminem, on the other hand, was like the missing link between Durst and Rock.

Kid Rock's notoriety in the gossip columns has recently been based on his relationship with Pamela Anderson, the is-she-isn't-she? pregnancy stories circulating and his refusal to talk about Tommy Lee.

There was nothing controversial about Kid Rock, or at least nothing apart from his attitude to women, that had not already been fired at Hugh Hefner, Norman Mailer and Larry Flynt over the preceding 40 years. But Eminem was different. Eminem had congressmen and churchmen expressing concern, TV pundits wringing their hands in despair about the culture of young white males in America and parents getting upset that junior had bleached his hair and was borrowing the chainsaw for the night instead of the car.

The life and troubled times of Marshall Bruce Mathers III have been so well documented in the press – both in front-page news crime stories and in the 'op ed' sections as well as the music reviews – that there is little point in contributing to the destruction of several acres of forest in order to add to it.

Sharing a label with Fred Durst – who is on the board of Interscope – hasn't stopped Eminem attacking him. On the D-12 album *Devil's Night*, on the track 'Girls', a track that parodies Limp Bizkit's 'Rollin'', Eminem raps, 'You fucking sissy/Up onstage screaming how people hate you/They don't hate you/They just think you're corny since Christina played you.'

What the success of Kid Rock and Eminem does prove is that rock-rap is now no longer the only route into hip-hop for young white wannabes. A new generation of rappers, like Bubba Sparxx are coming through in the wake of Eminem and Rock, at a time when the new wave of nu metal bands are veering back towards a more traditional rock sound. This has started a debate about the colonisation of hip-hop by white artists: while there is little actual hostility at present, there are those who feel that just as rock and roll was once a predominantly black music, which was wholly co-opted by whites, so hip-hop is in danger of going the same way.

Writer David Samuels, in his 1995 book *The Rap On Rap: The 'Black Music' That Isn't Either*, charged that 'gangsta' rappers like NWA, Ice-T and The Geto Boys '...appeal to whites rested in its evocation of an age-old image of blackness: a foreign, sexually charged and criminal underworld against which the norms of white society are defined'.

The white consumption of these artists resulted in the perpetuation of a harmful, negative stereotype of 'blackness'. Similarly, Eminem, Kid Rock and Bubba Sparxx all perpetuate a similar negative stereotype – the gun-totin' 'pimp-gangster' – in the way that early minstrel shows (where white performers in 'black' make-up sang 'negro' songs and performed comedy routines) perpetuated stereotypes of black Americans as being stupid, backward or criminal.

The facts don't necessarily bear out Samuels' thesis – there is undoubtedly a massive black audience for the same artists and a counter-thesis that sees the image of a black outlaw as empowering – and the biggest white crossover sales are for artists like The Fugees/Lauryn Hill, whose message is positive and non-violent.

Ultimately, the success of Kid Rock, Eminem, Crazy Town, Limp Bizkit et al may not signify so much a colonisation of hip-hop as much as the reverse: the impact of a confident and vibrant African-American music on a moribund white one, having more in common with the spread of hip-hop to the Caribbean, Asia, Africa and Europe.

AMEN

'We're not a nu metal band, we're a punk rock band,' proclaimed Amen's outspoken frontman Casey Chaos to London radio station XFM in the late summer of 2000.

Punk rock is a term as slippery and nebulous as nu metal. Do we mean a sound, a simplified rock and roll shorn of instrumental excess? Do we mean an anarchistic attitude, challenging the status quo? Do we mean pink mohican haircuts and studded leather biker jackets? Punk rock is the background noise of American rock, stripped of any meaning or dangerous content, reduced to a kind of keg-party soundtrack played by an increasingly anonymous and faceless clutch of bands like Blink-182, Everclear and Weezer. It is buzzsaw guitars, happy-clappy tunes and lame songs about sex with animals.

It's hardly the same music that rocked the British establishment during the Queen's Silver Jubilee week in 1977 or inspired a whole generation of American misfits to form bands in the 1980s or acted as a subterranean respite from the grim realities of life in the dying days of communism in eastern Europe and the former USSR, when having green hair could get you locked up as an anti-social element.

Yet the first time you set eyes on Amen onstage, it's as though the music has become threatening again; it has the power to cause mayhem and inspire revolt. Amen were formed in Los Angeles in 1994 by singer Casey Chaos and guitarist Paul Fig with former Ugly Kid Joe drummer Shannon Larkin and ex-Snot guitarist Sonny Mayo. Following the 1998 death of Snot frontman Lynn Strait, the group's bassist John 'Tumor' Fahnestock joined, linking Amen with the legendary, unpredictable and destructive punk act. Ross Robinson signed the band to his new label I AM, the first band he discovered, and produced their eponymous debut album. It was undoubtedly a great record but the best was to come.

'Amen goes beyond anything I've ever done. Amen taps into that sick, sexual, destructive bleeding with seething disease feeling. I get to feel it without having to suffer it,' the normally avuncular Robinson said during the sessions for the band's second album *We Have Come For Your Parents*.

Amen live shows descended into riots and fights, with songs like 'Whores Of Hollywood' and 'When A Man Dies A Woman' taking on an anthemic quality as the crowd erupted into a disaster area. It was, of course, all theatre, the way Marilyn Manson was theatre and Slipknot were theatre. But this did not make it in any way fake; it tied it in to a much older idea of theatre as ritual, like the Greek mystery plays or the notorious Parisienne 'theatre of blood', where people looked into the horrors that dwelt in themselves. Of course, maybe it was only the band who were actually aware that it was a performance.

Former Sex Pistol Steve Jones, now a resident of Los Angeles, stood at the back of the band's show at the Hollywood Dragonfly, nodding that he was impressed by the spectacle: 'They're more pissed off than we ever were.'

Rat Scabies of The Damned called them 'the punkest, heaviest thing out of America since The MC5'.

This was new metal, though not necessarily nu metal. It had the patented Ross Robinson sound – bass-heavy, forceful – and at times the same raw anger as Korn, but Amen were part of the masterplan to blast to pieces all that Robinson had created.

As Casey Chaos said of the second album, 'This is the most violent album in major-label history. With Ross being the king of Adidas rock and us getting this huge deal with Virgin, we could so easily have gone in and wrote a fucking "Nookie" or some three-dollar Adidas rock song, cashing in on the whole seven-string guitar movement. Instead, we went in an entirely different direction. Every single song is morally inept, every single song is completely violent. The guy who mastered the album asked us if we wanted "clean" versions made of any songs. We just looked at each other and laughed. If we made clean versions there wouldn't be anything left!'

UK music weekly *NME* leapt on the band and put them on the cover, overjoyed at having found a band who were like an antidote to everything that was anodyne and dull about modern rock. In her review of the album, Victoria Segal wrote, 'There isn't a single hint of pantomime, no self-parodic angst. You doubt they know what Napster is, let alone give a damn. Instead, they just flip the hinge in their heads and let the Amen breakdown begin. "The Waiting" and "Mayday" are sticky with The Stooges, fried on medication, and furious with the USA; "The Price Of Reality" is the last word in chant-a-long paranoia, all truth and lies and "human assembly lines", a DC Comics take on *The Matrix*, while "Ungrateful Dead" joins Ozzy Osbourne in a loose cannon salute.

'Disgusted, frustrated, paranoid; it's hard to imagine what could help them with their minds. But as psychotherapy, *We Have Come For Your Parents* is the pipe-bomb.'

The febrile writings of other critics matched the white heat of the music. They appeared on magazine covers, though it was mostly the British press that 'discovered' the band, with *Rolling Stone* failing even to review the record.

It looked like just another case of hype, of wishful thinking on the part of Ross Robinson and some journalists. It was a classic case of a band having to believe that they were the most important group who had ever picked up an electric guitar because there was as much chance that it would be true of them as of any other.

The problem with Amen is that they were and are essentially a critics' band, which doesn't usually mean a great deal in the world of the record-buying public. The Velvet Underground may have been every writer's dream band in the 1960s, but for their entire career they lived in poverty. There was not enough that was different about Amen to necessarily convince anyone outside of a small group of industry-watchers that this was something important; they had great rock and roll songs, great rock and roll attitude. Hell, Amen actually walked like a rock and roll band. They had smart lyrics and targets to rail against, like Calvin Klein on the opening track of the album, 'CK Killer'.

They also gave great interview.

Casey told the *LA Times*, 'I think that Calvin Klein's the biggest murderer probably America's ever had. When you go to school in America, you've got to fit these stereotypes. You've got to hit whatever scene you're in, and if you can't afford his clothes, or Hilfiger, or whoever might be the attraction at that moment – that's when you've got these people making fun of these kids who are wearing trench coats and listening to whatever music they like. I was that kid when I was growing up. I was that freak. The freak with the Mohawk.'

The only things they had missing that the nu metal bands had in spades were great, memorable pop songs. And as we have seen in previous chapters, it is precisely the ability of these bands to straddle rock and pop that endears them to the hearts of America's teens. And if Amen can't go one better than that, then their picture of the future is a three-stripe Adidas trainer stamping on a human face. Forever.

A PERFECT CIRCLE

It's hard to place A Perfect Circle in the middle of all this. For a start, Maynard James Keenan, their singer, is an established major artist with Tool. A Perfect Circle was almost like a side project that he and room-mate Billy Howerdel cooked up to fill the Tool hiatus between *Aenima* and their 2001 masterpiece *Lateralus*. But it was a side project that threatened to outshine Tool and actually caused some consternation in the ranks of America's premier progressive band, wondering if their singer would return after enjoying major success touring with Nine Inch Nails, headlining shows, having a hit album with *Mer De Noms* and being responsible for vital rock anthems like 'Judith'. A Perfect Circle reached the younger audience that were unlikely to find much appeal in Tool's dense, complicated, brilliant – if unapproachable – work.

Whether they were a nu metal band is a moot point; they did, however, reach the same crowd: Deftones, Coal Chamber and Korn fans. Keenan and Howerdel, whose credits included technical and session work with Tool, Nine Inch Nails and Guns N'Roses, looked at the current scene and saw the influence of all the bands they had worked with on groups like Coal Chamber, Orgy and even Slipknot, as well as more emotive bands like Ross Robinson protégés Glassjaw. Their slick, unashamedly commercial, modern rock was like a retort, proof that they understood it and could do it much better.

A Perfect Circle had a sense of aesthetics that many of the newer bands lacked; the band's collective experience and superior tradecraft – guitarist Troy Van Leeuwen and bassist/violinist Paz Lenchantin were members of various southern Californian punk outfits; drummer Josh Freese had played with everyone from The Vandals and Guns N'Roses to Dweezil Zappa – gave them the edge in writing, recording and performing. While nobody would ever question the ambition, enthusiasm and energy that fuel the new breed of bands, A Perfect Circle made it seem as if they were royalty slumming it. Even their choice of obligatory '80s cover versions – The Cure's 'Love Song' and Ozzy Osbourne's 'Diary Of A Madman' – was inspired rather than tired.

Rock press reviews seemed to concentrate on the band's connection with Tool and Nine Inch Nails, while mainstream reviewers used them as a stick with which to beat other nu metal bands. Typical was the *New York Daily News* review of their Roseland show in September 2000: 'A Perfect Circle is one of the few contemporary metal acts combining insightful lyrics with heavy music that occasionally dares to be beautiful. The Los Angeles-based band plays a variety of hard rock that has come to be known as emo-core, in which the battering, bombastic power chords of heavy metal are twined with sweeping melodies and plaintive, emotionally wrought lyrics... A Perfect Circle has capitalized on the slim percentage of metal fans who have not entirely given themselves over to the rap-rock ravings of Limp Bizkit and Korn.'

Nevertheless, there was an almost universally positive response to the band and the album from fans and critics alike. The band enjoyed a 'most favoured nations' status that most bands would envy. They enjoyed unprecedented press, a ready-made audience (Tool fans, mainly, though many were bemused by A Perfect Circle) and directors like David Fincher on hand to make the video for 'Judith', their big hit.

They were at odds with the concerns of the angst-rock generation; their songs continued Keenan's fascination with paganism and the occult, which he had already explored in Tool. This is an aspect that is entirely absent from nu metal: while Satanic rock bands exist, ranging from those who take the subject seriously to those who see it as an extension of horror comics, nu metal dumps all the baggage associated with previous generations of hard rock. No sci-fi lyrics or imagery (apart from Orgy's flirtation with future chic), no concept albums, no Dungeons And Dragons or *Lord Of The Rings*, no pentagrams or Goats of Mendes.

A Perfect Circle were most significant because they showed clearly a developing faultline within nu metal, never exactly a unified entity anyway. They seemed to tap into the extremes of emo-core while appealing to a small but significant neo-goth faction. They were less a continuation of Tool, Nine Inch Nails or any other metal bands and more a continuation of the numinous sound of bands like My Bloody Valentine. The original intention was that the band would have a female singer and sound like either The Cocteau Twins or Massive Attack. As they stood, A Perfect Circle saw way beyond the horizons of any genres in which other bands imprisoned themselves. They appealed to the kids who liked The Deftones – a band who were heavily influenced by Tool – but bewildered a lot of other fans.

As Billy recalled in a *Kerrang!* interview in July 2000, 'Recently, a fan came up to me after a show and said, "Hey dude, that was cool, but it just wasn't as heavy as Slipknot. What's up with that?" I just smiled – how else could I respond?'

They looked like no other band; they appeared live onstage lit only by what looked like candles, Billy with his polished bald head brooding in the background, Maynard sporting a waist-length wig and psychedelic flares, and female bass player Paz lurking in the background. They were everything that nu metal was not – mature rather than youthful, thoughtful rather than energetic, brooding rather than raging with anger. They were also sexually ambiguous and adventurous; they had an allure that was feminine, as opposed to the resolutely testosterone-fuelled bands of angry macho whiggaz and aggressive white rappers. For, as we have already discussed in the chapter on Kittie, nu metal is a party that is for boys only.

AT THE DRIVE-IN

El Paso band At The Drive-In seemed to be poised on the brink of major success in early 2001. They were exciting, action packed and had awesome songs. Their Ross Robinson-produced album *Relationship Of Command* was on every music critic's end-of-year pick-list in 2000, a dynamic and electrifying blend of early-MC5 radicalism and fresh speed-crazed attitude.

The *NME* said; 'Of the 11 tracks contained within, there is not a pedestrian moment. A lot is expected of At The Drive-In – thankfully they deliver in style. Absolutely storming.'

Rock website *Metal-Is* was equally enthusiastic: 'Through all the deliberately discordant riffing and primal bludgeon we actually have a band with good ideas and an ear for a clever arrangement. Take the superb and chilling spoken-word verses of "Invalid Litter Dept" – not only does it hook you in, but it's almost like listening to a poetic aural documentary. This is just one example of how *Relationship*...can affect on so many levels, and a risk that would only be taken by a band completely at home with their musical identity.'

Even the more staid and considered industry bible *Billboard* was moved to hyperbole: 'Devoid of sloganeering yet inherently political, *Relationship Of Command* challenges us to reassess the prevailing power structures, all the while reinvigorating a tired genre. While it may be a stretch to call At The Drive-In saviours, calling it anything less than revolutionary would be a crime.'

Robinson raved about them. Everyone who saw them did. They had played together since 1994, releasing a string of singles and albums (1997's *Acrobatic Tenement*, 1998's *In/Casino/Out*, 1999's *Vaya*) on independent labels before Beastie Boys-owned label Grand Royal signed them up and put them in the studio with Robinson.

According to At The Drive-In's guitarist Omar Rodriguez in an interview on Virgin Records website *The Raft*, 'Ross has got us to do a process of recording in a different way and open up and try things a little differently. Beforehand we had only had approximately four days to record a full record... It's always been really low budget and really quick in and out before, so we never really had the time to really find ourselves studio-wise, you know, to develop into the studio and figure out the art of recording. And with Ross, and the bigger budget with the label and everything, we were able to go in there and change songs around, and actually create songs in the studio and probably most importantly is, er, open up and approach recording in a different way. Because before it was like really stiff and contrived and, like, get the part right, we only have x amount of time to do it, and you know, with Ross he went and saw us for the first time in San Francisco and he wanted to capture what he saw, he wanted us to dance around...'

Yet in the opening salvos of touring to promote this beast of a record, the band just suddenly stopped. There was no high-profile fighting, no suicide attempts or other disasters. They just cancelled all their planned tour dates and issued a terse statement that read, 'After a non-stop six-year cycle of record/tour/record/tour, we are going on an indefinite hiatus. We need time to rest up and re-evaluate...just to be human beings again and to decide when we feel like playing music again.' There was no further comment. It was like they just opted out.

Ross Robinson had made no secret of the fact that he saw the band, along with Amen, as one of the forces that would destroy 'Adidas rock' and spark off an alternative to the bands he had created. He was not alone in this hope. Perhaps their abdication proved that there was just no alternative.

SOULFLY

From Sepultura, the world's greatest thrash band, to the more radical experimental work of Soulfly, Max Cavalera – dubbed 'the Bob Marley of metal' – has emerged as a champion of the indigenous tribes of his native Brazil as well as of the emerging and exciting cross-pollination of metal, rap, hardcore and even techno.

While Sepultura limp on as an increasingly retarded parody of their glory years, Soulfly – a project that allows Max to collaborate with lots of different musicians, bands and line-ups – are a growing and vital force and promise to be a second act in his career.

Hailing from the unlikely location of São Paulo, Brazil, Sepultura were at the forefront of metal in the late 1980s and early 1990s, particularly with their 1989 major-label debut *Beneath The Remains* on Roadrunner. On their 1993 album, *Chaos AD*, Sepultura started to experiment with Brazilian rainforest tribal rhythms on the track 'Kaiowas'.

When Sepultura released their Ross Robinson-produced 1996 record *Roots*, an album recorded with drummers from the Xavantes, an Amazonian tribe, it was a radical departure for the world's greatest thrash/speed metal band. It also marked the end of the road for guitarist Max Cavalera, who quit the band to work full time on his more experimental outfit Soulfly. Cavalera had been chafing within the confines of Sepultura for some time and had sought an outlet for his more progressive ideas in side projects like Nailbomb. For Soulfly Max recruited a former Sepultura roadie, Marcello D Rapp, to play bass, went into the studio and released the band's eponymous debut in 1998, an intense and angry record shot through with the very real pain that Max experienced with the split from Sepultura – his brother Igor is still a member and the break-up led to ill feeling – and the murder of his stepson, particularly on songs like 'Bleed' and 'First Commandment'.

For all the rage contained on that record, Soulfly's message was overwhelmingly positive, something reiterated on the more focused second album *Primitive*. The band's line-up had stabilised, adding Mikey Doling on guitar and Joe Nunez on drums, and guest artists included everyone from Chino Moreno of The Deftones, Grady from Will Haven and Corey (#8) Taylor of Slipknot to Sean Lennon, who co-wrote 'Son Song' about, respectively, the John Lennon assassination, the murder of Cavalera's son and the death of Max's father when he was young. What could have been horribly mawkish is actually genuinely affecting.

Soulfly is a great example of an old-school metal maven recognising the influence he has had on the nu breed and seeking to work with those people helping to push the music further. Cavalera has ruled out a Sepultura reunion and seems content to push the boundaries with Soulfly.

Epilogue

In the months following the 11 September 2001 attacks in the USA, on the World Trade Center and the Pentagon, we have seen Fred Durst, emotional and on the verge of tears, recalling that only a few days earlier, he had been at the top of the former, shooting a video. He urged people to hug their kids, hug their friends, hug each other.

At a candlelit show, Godsmack led the crowd in prayer: for a band fronted by a self-confessed witch, who have been targeted by Christian fundamentalists, there was not even a hint of irony. The outpourings of grief were heartfelt.

We had the strange sight of KROK shock-jock Howard Stern fronting a charity appeal for victims of the attack, and bands from Incubus to Ozzy Osbourne donating all proceeds from their shows to newly set up aid funds. Tattoo The Planet was postponed after US bands decided not to fly to Europe in the aftermath of the attacks and during the ensuing war in Afghanistan. Other tours, including Slipknot's Pledge Of Allegiance outing, were postponed or cancelled. A statement read, 'The Pledge Of Allegiance tour is dedicating the trek to the innocent victims and their families. Named in honor of the fans who have fiercely expressed their support and loyalty to uncompromising bands like Slipknot and System Of A Down, the tour and its name have taken on an expanded meaning for the bands in light of this week's horrific events.'

The reaction of most bands was different to that of bands during the Gulf War in 1990. At that time there was a lot of dissent

- many bands opposed America's involvement in Operation Desert Storm. The radicalisation of rock music began in the early 1960s when the protest movement, whose troubadours were Bob Dylan, Joan Baez and Phil Ochs, began to intersect with rock and roll. The war in Vietnam served to make Americans question what they were told by parents, politicians and members of 'the establishment'. Although *ipso facto* political radicalism as embodied by the rhetoric of The MC5, Jefferson Airplane on *Volunteers* and *Blows Against The Empire*, and by occasional angry outbursts such as Neil Young's 'Ohio' – written after the death of anti-war protesters at Kent State University, Ohio – was actually a short-lived phenomenon, a sense that rock and roll was in opposition never really went away. Even the most apolitical bands of the ensuing decades seemed to represent rebellion if not revolution. But the period after 11 September was different. There was a united front.

On the Limp Bizkit website, a statement from Wes Borland, posted shortly before his departure, read, 'In the aftermath of the recent attacks on the United States I have been hearing about numerous incidents of violence towards Muslims and other "Middle Eastern-looking" people. Not to say that all Muslims are "Middle Eastern-looking" but you get what I mean. I understand that everyone is angry about what happened, but taking your anger out on people who had nothing to do with these incidents is horribly wrong. These were not the people who attacked us. No matter what people around you are saying about someone, I urge you to think before you act. Remember that people by themselves are smart, but those same people put into a large group can become very stupid. Please try to understand that these are hate crimes against innocent people who are your neighbors. This needs to be a time for reaching out to others, not accusing them. Don't be a racist. Don't be a racist. Don't be a racist.'

As well as finding themselves the unlikely voice of reason, Limp Bizkit and a lot of other artists began to talk, privately and publicly, about changing the sort of music they produced. Celebrities toured Ground Zero, shedding tears for the camera and embracing the nearest New York cop or fireman until Mayor Giuliani told them to stay the hell away and let everyone get on with their jobs. After the emotional outpouring and the grief, people started to wonder where and how things would go on from here.

Overnight, guerrilla chic seemed to evaporate, to be replaced by a low-key American nationalism. As in the First and Second World Wars, popular entertainment seemed to take upon itself the duty of waving the flag, remaining resolutely upbeat, boosting morale and sending the boys off to war with a song on their lips.

Retailers reported a run on the likes of Celine Dion's 'My Heart Will Go On' and Elvis entered the charts with 'America The Beautiful'. There was a lot of talk about music being something to soothe rather than something to challenge. Incubus DJ Chris Killmore told *Billboard*, 'I think it gave us an all-new perspective on the power of music and how it does help people get through bad times. Music is a universal healing agent.'

'Healing' music usually means dippy women with acoustic guitars and slushy country songs; it rarely means abrasive hard rock. People wondered if there would be any market for adolescent angst once the dust settled.

There were other setbacks too: Wes Borland quit Limp Bizkit to form his own band Eat The Day, with Ross Robinson producing, still determined to knock down that whole house of cards he helped build. Wes was undoubtedly the major musical talent within Limp Bizkit and at the time of writing things did not bode well.

Korn's fifth album, recorded with producer Michael Beinhorn, was pushed back almost a year on the release schedules. With Coal Chamber, The Deftones and Linkin Park all scheduled to release new albums in 2002, there's an air of nervous anticipation.

Critics have always bemoaned the number of identikit rap metal and nu grunge acts who have sprung up in the early years of this new millennium, but there are some early indications that the seemingly insatiable desire for these on the public's part has now been sated. The big rock sellers at the end of 2001 were Alien Ant Farm with their dimwitted cover of Michael Jackson's 'Smooth Criminal'.

One senior independent record company executive told me, 'Even before September 11th we were looking beyond the next Limp Bizkit and Korn and Linkin Park records. We know that these things go in cycles and the smart money moves out before the cycle swings too far in one direction. We've had nothing but kids complaining about how down they are and how much they wanna slit their wrists and how their girlfriend hates them. This isn't forever. I think there are a lot of people out there who all of a sudden don't really care what Fred Durst is whining about.

'That doesn't mean that it's gonna be all happy songs. Heavy music is most definitely here to stay but I really think you're going to see a lot of those bands moving on. There are only so many groups who sound like Alice In Chains that the market can support. You're going to see a lot more bands like Deadsy, experimenting with image. You're going to see a lot more artists like Andrew WK who are going to have a much more robust and ongoing sound. You're gonna see a lot of these rap-metal groups try to make it as rappers in the hip-hop market. That's happening with Crazy Town. Don't know how successful that will be. It's funny but a lot of death metal seems to be coming back. I can envisage a sort of positive death metal doing good trade in the next two years.'

Quite what this means for the future of nu metal is hard to say at this stage. But whatever comes next is still going to be informed by the achievements of Slipknot, Korn, Limp Bizkit, The Deftones, Kittie, Staind, Linkin Park, Taproot, Ill Niño, Dry Kill Logic, Crazy Town, Disturbed, Vex Red, Cold, Deadsy, Adema, Glassjaw, Will Haven, Powerman 5000, Taproot, Sevendust, Coal Chamber, Boy Hits Car, Puddle Of Mudd, Godsmack, Godhead and (hed) pe in reshaping and retooling hard rock for the 21st century. These bands redefined rock and roll as American music and rebranded a post-Spiñal Tap joke musical form into the only game in town.

They won. Deal with it.

Tommy Udo
London, 2001

Essential Listening

This is in no way a definitive list of nu metal albums, merely a subjective selection of works that offer a good insight into the many forms to be found within the genre's boundaries.

KORN
Follow The Leader
(Immortal/Epic 1998)
Coming in the wake of the disappointing sophomore album *Life Is Peachy*, Korn were already being written off in some circles as having blown it. They were a band with something to prove and this was what they slapped down hard in front of a hungry public. *Follow The Leader* wasn't an album with answers, it wasn't there to comfort. It was a hard-driving smash-your-head-against-the-wall record, full of seething rage and red-eyed hatred.

The sound had moved on from the Ross Robinson-produced debut but the patented down-tuned instruments, the sheer weighty power of the seven-string guitars and the ferocious assault of Davis's voice were still intact. This was a work by a band who had honed their performances in the studio and onstage to a peak of excellence, a confident work, whereas the first two never quite meshed. On *Korn* the band had smeared their visceral negativity over the walls; on *Follow The Leader* the same ire was focused, refined and purified. While the debut had the emotional black sun of 'Daddy', the centrepiece of their third album was even more harrowing.

In 'Dead Bodies Everywhere' Jonathan Davis lets rip on a riff about trying to live up to the expectations of his parents, a path that led him to a career spent sticking his latex-gloved hands into the cooling necrotic flesh of the recently deceased in a California coroner's office. His experiences there also inspired the bleak and terrible 'Pretty', when he examined the body of a child who had been raped and murdered. It may sound trite, but Davis's howl of horror at the fate of the child and the world in which such evil can be perpetrated, shows some of the same creative urge that drove Picasso to paint 'Guernica' or Dostoyevsky to write *The Brothers Karamazov*. While Davis is less articulate an artist, the song he creates is the powerful and moving attempt of a man to live in the aftermath of a meeting with such evil. This is followed up with 'All In The Family', the verbal duel between Davis and Durst where such gems as 'Suck on my dick, kid, like your daddy did' are exchanged, just to show that they were capable of the dumb and the crass. And if you don't find it funny, pull that pickle out your ass!

Track list: 'It's On', 'Freak On A Leash', 'Got The Life', 'Dead Bodies Everywhere', 'Children Of The Korn', 'BBK', 'Pretty', 'All In The Family', 'Reclaim My Place', 'Justin', 'Seed', 'Cameltosis', 'My Gift to You'.

Also recommended: *Korn* (Immortal 1993), Ross Robinson-produced first album, a landmark cult record upon its release.

LINKIN PARK
Hybrid Theory
(Warner Brothers 2000)

This is proof that the Limp Bizkit formula scrubs up nicely as pop music. We have all the angst and anger, particularly on the searing opener 'Papercut', but it's all rather nicely packaged without the raw meatiness of Limp Bizkit. Linkin Park are a band aimed squarely at young kids, and criticisms levelled at them – that they are a safe, derivative and inoffensive version of metal, a Coke-lite hard rock – are unfair. They are in a much longer tradition of pop/rock acts such as Kiss, Depeche Mode and Bush who, like it or not, are very often the first bands teenagers discover when they get too old for toys. Sample-heavy with pristine breakbeats, a twin vocal attack and some slick harmonies, *Hybrid Theory* is an album that attempts to be all things to all people in the space of 40-odd minutes. There are straight-ahead hard rockers like 'Points Of Authority' and moodier oh-woe-is-me songs like 'Pushing Me Away'. Tracks like 'Cure For The Itch' suggest some rudimentary 'experimental' directions, which lead one to believe that there could be some life for the band after the initial excitement around this record has died down.

There's nothing really edgy or disturbing about any of the songs on *Hybrid Theory*. Criticism that they are sanitised is justified. Linkin Park do miss the potent, gut-punch of Korn or even the best Limp Bizkit. But they have solid, memorable tunes and whether the 'emotions' in the songs are ersatz or not, Chester Bennington's voice is the most powerful instrument they have, and if he sang the listings from a telephone directory it would still make for a great song.

Whether they actually release a second album is irrelevant. *Hybrid Theory* is a perfect pop album, a sound that is of the moment and unlikely to outstay its welcome.

Track list: 'Papercut', 'One Step Closer', 'With You', 'Points Of Authority', 'Crawling', 'Runaway', 'By Myself', 'In The End', 'A Place For My Head', 'Forgotten', 'Cure For The Itch', 'Pushing Me Away'.

LIMP BIZKIT
Chocolate Starfish And The Hotdog Flavored Water (Interscope 2000)

If there were any doubts at all about the sheer unstoppability of Limp Bizkit then this album blew them away. Although this isn't their best album overall – their debut album *Three Dollar Bill,*

Yall$ is – it is probably the most representative of everything that nu metal was/is/will be about, an album that captures perfectly the mood of the times, the voice of a generation, even if that voice is only insulting passers-by and reciting dirty limericks. 'My Generation', a stuttering rap that alludes to The Who's 1965 classic, an anthem for a previous generation, is particularly effective at getting up the backs of baby-boomers who now regard 'their' music and the sentiments contained therein to be sacrosanct. But if any of that generation just went beyond the surface they would find in tracks like 'My Way' and 'Take A Look Around' songs that match and better the acidic hard rock of the 1960s and 1970s. They have insight, even passion, and they have 'something' to say, even if that isn't necessarily anything profound.

The guitar work of Wes Borland is in many ways more important to the Limp Bizkit sound than the massive persona and whigger-whine of Fred Durst. Tracks like the ultra-funk of 'Getcha Groove On' show a greater breadth of musical taste and ability than most bands are actually capable of. When 'Rollin'' was adopted by WWF star The Undertaker as his theme song, it forged a perfect link between wrestling and rock. Fred Durst is, if anything, closer to Stone Cold Steve Austin and The Rock than to any other rock and roll or hip-hop performer of his generation. He's brash, he breathes fire, he picks fights; he's the bad guy that the fans hate but go and see. And while it may be 'all faked', he certainly makes it seem like it actually hurts when he falls down in the songs on this record.

Whether this represents the zenith of Fred Durst and the remaining band members only time will tell, but they are a band you write off at your peril.

Track list: 'Intro', 'Hot Dog', 'My Generation', 'Full Nelson', 'My Way', 'Rollin' (Air Raid Vehicle)', 'Livin' It Up', 'The One', 'Getcha Groove On', 'Take A Look Around', 'It'll Be OK', 'Boiler', 'Hold On', 'Rollin' (Urban Assault Vehicle)', 'Outro'.

Also recommended: *Three Dollar Bill, Yall$* (Interscope 1997), sparkling debut produced by Ross Robinson, which bagged up all the clichés into one mighty package and let rip. Poor Ross has spent the rest of his career trying to destroy what he helped create. *Significant Other* (Interscope 1999), Durst's album-long tirade against a former girlfriend had him tagged as a woman-hater, though it's more complicated than that.

PAPA ROACH
Infest
(Dreamworks 2000)

Apart from having the most toe-curlingly bad line in any opening track ever ('My name's Coby Dick/Mr Dick if you're nasty/Rock a mic/With a voice that's raspy/And I'm poetic in my operations/My God-given talent is to rock all the nations/We're going to infest'), *Infest* sets the tone for an album that is nasty, brutal and short, a Rage Against The Machine-like thrash where the guitars seem to be giving covering fire to Coby Dick's voice, which flies out of the speakers like grenades. Had this album been released in the late 1980s, it would almost certainly have been picked up by Dischord, the ultra-cool Washington DC label responsible for straight edge hardcore classics by Fugazi and Minor Threat. It's apolitical in comparison to Rage Against The Machine or those bands, though it may be political in a different way.

'Last Resort' is the Hamlet soliloquy if Hamlet had been a disaffected northern California punk-rock kid. 'Broken Home' is a raging rant for all the children of 'Generation X' while 'Binge' is 'The Lost Weekend' condensed into a short sharp shock of abrasive punk. Lyrically and musically, particularly the razors-for-plectrums guitar of Jerry Horton, Papa Roach stand head and shoulders above any would-be competitors.

Track list: 'Infest', 'Last Resort', 'Broken Home', 'Dead Cell', 'Between Angels And Insects', 'Blood Brothers', 'Revenge', 'Snakes', 'Never Enough', 'Binge', 'Thrown Away'.

THE DEFTONES
White Pony
(Warner Brothers 2000)

In many ways The Deftones fill the huge gap left in contemporary rock by the demise of Smashing Pumpkins. On *White Pony* they moved far away from the swaggering pimp-hop school of rock of which they were co-creators and towards a sound that had the same passionate intensity as classic Smashing Pumpkins, allying soaring melodies to diamond-hard icy guitar rock.

There's also something reminiscent of sorely missed alt.rock darlings The Pixies, perhaps in Chino's ability to go from a mellow singing-in-the-shower voice to a full-on death scream in the space of a few seconds.

Perhaps, though, it has more to do with their willingness to try new approaches to their own music, such as the effects-laden 'Digital Bath' and the single 'Change (In The House Of Flies)', both of which emerged from the fruitful addition of new member DJ Frank Delgado, who not only colours the songs but provides the foundation for an almost infinite number of new directions for The Deftones to go in.

White Pony as well as being an album that stands as a classic in the band's oeuvre, in the pantheon of nu metal, is also an album heavily pregnant with possibility for the future.

Track list: 'Feiticeira', 'Digital Bath', 'Elite', 'RX Queen', 'Street Carp', 'Teenager', 'Knife Party', 'Korea', 'Passenger', 'Change (In The House Of Flies)', 'Pink Maggit'.

Also recommended: *Around The Fur* (Warner Brothers 1997), a much more straightforward record than *White Pony*, which includes the radio-friendly 'My Own Summer' and the single 'Be Quiet and Drive (Far Away)'.

DRY KILL LOGIC
The Darker Side Of Nonsense
(Roadrunner 2001)

One of the best of the new names, New York's Dry Kill Logic – formerly Hinge – set themselves the task of becoming the world's most aggressive, intense and respected band ever. First and second albums, *Elemental Evil* and *Accidental Meeting Of Minds*, on their own Psychodrama label, didn't propel them too far along the road to this goal, but after a sabbatical, a change of guitarist and a new label, they should be taken very seriously at their word.

The Darker Side Of Nonsense is a high-impact album – no build-ups, no subtlety, no lulling you into a false sense of security. From opener 'Nightmare', Dry Kill Logic hit you with dum-dum power chords, heart-punch drums and Cliff Rigano's Rottweiler-on-crack vocals and keep hitting you until you're too punch-drunk to notice that they sound like they've been pilfering from Fear Factory's song box.

Dry Kill Logic aren't a band with an agenda. They are pissed off at everything. The exhilaration of pure aggro-rock can be exhausting, and the album closes with 'The Strength I Call My Own', which hints at future directions, a more slow-burning and spaced-out approach, but still imbued with the same spite and guts that permeate the rest of the album.

Track list: 'Nightmare', 'Feel The Break', 'Pain', 'Nothing', 'Assfalt', 'Weight', 'A Better Man Than Me', 'Rot', 'Track 13', 'Give Up, Give In, Lie Down', 'The Strength I Call My Own, 'Goodnight/Sab'.

SLIPKNOT
Slipknot
(Roadrunner 1999)

In retrospect, when this album was released nobody really had much of a clue as to the sort of impact these Midwest masked maniacs were going to have on rock and roll. Comparisons with Marilyn Manson and a few feeble shock-rockers from the past, like GG Allin or GWAR, failed to do any justice to what Slipknot actually represented. This was not an adjunct to something, this was a phenomenon in its own right. If you do the math, it's obvious that a nine-man band can make double the amount of noise of a conventional four- or five-piece. Slipknot's percussion section alone is enough to drown out the sounds of wimpier bands.

Capturing that on record is perhaps Ross Robinson's greatest achievement: this sounds louder than every other record in your collection, even with the volume down. In comparison with its bigger, bolder and better follow-up, *Slipknot* seems almost dated, though tracks like 'Wait And Bleed' and the terrifying 'Scissors' still sound as fresh as ever.

Track list: '7426100027', '[sic]', 'Eyeless', 'Wait And Bleed', 'Surfacing', 'Spit It Out', 'Tattered And Torn', 'Frail Limb Nursery', 'Purity', 'Liberate', 'Prosthetics', 'No Life', 'Diluted', 'Only One', 'Scissors'.

SLIPKNOT
Iowa
(I AM/Roadrunner 2001)

From '515' – one minute of Satanic noises and a subsonic pulsebeat – to the spectacular 15-minute title track, *Iowa* drives 100 per cent pure primal rock and roll into our skulls with the fanatical efficiency of a maniac with a nail gun and a grudge. There are no stand-out tracks because there are no weak links; there are some pyrotechnic death metal killers like 'The Heretic Anthem' and some ruthless commercial ventures like 'My Plague' and some chilling moments of pure horror like 'Gently' (an old song from *Mate. Feed. Kill. Repeat* days, brought bang up to date with some bad-acid noises and an ever-building riff). But, like Ted Bundy picking up a hitch-hiker, it all inevitably leads to the terrible and awesome title track.

There are those who have dismissed Slipknot as some tawdry update of Alice Cooper/Kiss, a *Rocky Horror Show* for malcontent brats. 'It's all just theatre!' they sneer. But theatre, from Oedipus fucking his mother, killing his father and gouging out his own eyes onwards, has always revealed something sickening and ugly and dreadful inside all of us. Slipknot is musical theatre all right, but we're not really talking Andrew Lloyd Webber here.

'Iowa' is a staggering piece of drama using the sound of screaming, machinery and the juxtaposition of lines like 'You'll live forever' with manic giggling to suggest the inner world of a sicko killer at work. Like 'Scissors', taking up a quarter of the album, it is repelling and compelling simultaneously.

Musical comparisons – maybe The Stooges' 'Dirt' from *Fun House* or 'Sister Ray' by The Velvet Underground – are inadequate; *Iowa* is closer to the last minute of *The Blair Witch Project* or *Se7en* or *The Exorcist*. Only in this case you can't cover your eyes because all the ugly images are inside your own skull.

It's a fantastic record, an album that will be a benchmark that everyone else will be measured against for years to come. Most, of course, will fail to come close.

Track list: '(515)', 'People=Shit', 'Disasterpiece', 'My Plague', 'Everything Ends', 'The Heretic Anthem', 'Gently', 'Left Behind', 'The Shape', 'I Am Hated', 'Skin Ticket', 'New Abortion', 'Metabolic', 'Iowa'.

STATIC-X
Machine
(Warner Brothers 2001)

Skinny Puppy, Front 242, Nine Inch Nails, Marilyn Manson, System Of A Down, Fear Factory – all have applied the Ministry blueprint to their own particular sounds and done very well, thanks. Static-X, based in Chicago, hometown of the Ministry/Wax Trax scene, have also absorbed the lessons of their forebears well.

Wisconsin Death Trip, their debut album, created a sound they dubbed 'rhythmic trancecore', taking its inspiration from techno as well as our scary goth/industrial pals.

For no discernible reason, *Machine* kicks off with what sounds like a live recording of a Mexican Mariachi band before blasting straight into 'Get To The Gone', a nasty, brutish and short steroid-fuelled barrage that pretty much sets the tone for the whole album.

While Ministry built a tight but limited cult of true believers, Static-X have no intention of staying in the ghetto; 'Black And White' is an unashamed radio-friendly pop song; 'This Is Not' and the mighty 'Shit In A Bag' sound like they have been written with no other purpose than to sucker-punch stadium crowds into happy submission.

Closing track 'A Dios Alma Perdida' is a partly successful experiment in claustrophobic grind, reminiscent of some unholy genetic fusion of early Public Image Ltd and early Sabbath, while the comparatively mellow title track 'Machine' and the sample-laden 'Otsego Undead' both suggest future directions Static-X may explore.

Static-X are a band who are still finding their voice. Recorded with new guitarist Tripp (ex-Dope, replacing Koichi Fukada) and producer Ulrich Wild (Deftones, Pantera), *Machine* is a respectable album, not a truly awesome one. That's OK, because it's only album number two and they're here for the long haul.

It's part of the marketing smarts of the new generation of American bands like Static-X that they can dip into genres that were previously thought to be profoundly underground, bland them out ever so slightly, and sell shedloads of records and merchandise to the planet's suburban malcontent teens. You can call it sell-out or you can call it shrewd business sense, the fact remains that more people will probably hear Static-X's live cover of Ministry's 'Burning Inside' than ever heard Ministry play it. And while Fear Factory have cornered the market in paranoia-drenched cyberpunk metal, Static-X are more likely to be on MTV because in that particular beauty contest they win hands down. Sad, but welcome to the real world. Still, Fear Factory-lite or a clean-and-sober Ministry, these aren't such bad things to be.

Track list: 'Bien Venidos', 'Get To The Gone', 'Permanence', 'Black And White', 'This Is Not', 'Otsego Undead', 'Cold', 'Structural Defect', 'Shit In A Bag', 'Burn To Burn', 'Machine', 'A Dios Alma Perdida'.

Also recommended: *Wisconsin Death Trip* (Warner Brothers 1999), a less formed though still interesting debut, much lighter and more 'techno' in some ways than its successor.

VARIOUS
Strait Up
(Immortal/Virgin 2000)

A tribute album to Lynn Strait, former singer of California punks Snot, who died in a car crash in 1998 aged 30. The line-up on the record is a who's who of nu metal. The album has contributions from Limp Bizkit, Korn, Incubus, Slipknot, System Of A Down and Sugar Ray, and a eulogy from Ozzy Osbourne. Snot were a band who could have been a potentially huge nu metal/hardcore crossover band, as Jonathan Davis's heartfelt raging vocals on 'Take It Back' prove.

Track list: 'Starlit Eyes', 'Take It Back', 'I Know Where You're At', 'Catch A Spirit', 'Until Next Time', 'Divided (An Argument For The Soul)', 'Ozzy Speaks', 'Angel's Son', 'Forever', 'Funeral Flights', 'Requiem', 'Reaching Out', 'Absent', 'Sad Air'.

STAIND
Break The Cycle
(Flip/Interscope 2000)

Staind's third album is already becoming this generation's essential collection for the angst-torn bedroom existentialist, just as *Pornography* by The Cure and *Songs Of Leonard Cohen* supplied the soundtrack for a previous generation of sorrowful teens.

Staind are the band most likely to succeed in stepping beyond any categories and into the mainstream of American music alongside the likes of REM; already the songwriting partnership of Mike Mushok and Aaron Lewis has set its stamp on the charts with the mournful, almost folky, 'It's Been A While' and the harder 'Can't Believe'.

Although there's some justification in seeing them as grunge grave-robbers, stealing the still-warm licks from Soundgarden, Alice In Chains and Nirvana, Staind at least try to do something new with those influences, unlike compatriots Cold and Puddle Of Mudd who are content to recycle them. The progress that the band made between *Dysfunction and Break The Cycle* is quite staggering, and the quality of the songwriting promises great things from Staind in the coming years and even decades.

Break The Cycle does more than set complaint lyrics to cranked-up rock; songs like 'Epiphany' actually sound introspective and searching while their own version of 'Outside' – the duet Lewis recorded with Fred Durst, which first brought Staind to the attention of a lot of Limp Bizkit fans – is a warm and uplifting power ballad, a style thought played out with the demise of Heart and Poison. But Staind carry it off with style and make it sound fresh and relevant.

Track list: 'Open Your Eyes', 'Pressure', 'Fade', 'It's Been A While', 'Change', 'Can't Believe', 'Epiphany', 'Suffer', 'Warm Safe Place', 'For You', 'Outside', 'Waste', 'Take It'.

ALSO RECOMMENDED

COAL CHAMBER *Chamber Music* (Roadrunner 1999)
Brilliant second album from LA originators, a dark and sensual blend of goth, punk, metal and hip-hop.

SYSTEM OF A DOWN *Toxicity* (Columbia 2001)
Adventurous and febrile album, with overtones of Middle Eastern and east European music underneath the piledriver riffs.

KITTIE *Oracle* (Artemis 2001)
Second release from Canadian female trio, an unholy collision of death metal growling, glam-goth and even a Pink Floyd cover.

ILL NIÑO *Revolution Revolucion* (Roadrunner 2001)

Debut album from the New Jersey-based band whose Latin influences map out a whole new continent's worth of directions for heavy music to go in.

(hed) pe *Broke* (Jive 2000)
A good album of hard rap and hard rock. Captures some of the excitement of the live show, though doesn't quite do it justice.

INCUBUS *Morning View* (Sony 2001)
Best yet from Incubus, a more atmospheric and introspective album than funk rocker *Science*.

WILL HAVEN *WHVN* (Revelation 1999)
Potent, vicious and loud art metal.

DISLOCATED STYLES *Pin The Tail On The Honkey* (Roadrunner 2001)
Second album from this Phoenix-based band. A mix of styles and influences. Very funky, very hard – as the name suggests...

ROOTS OF NU METAL

A very random selection of some of the titles whose influence is most pronounced. (It's a given that we include Nirvana's *Nevermind* (Geffen 1991) Often imitated, seldom bettered, even by Nirvana themselves.)

SEPULTURA *Roots* (Roadrunner 1997)
Seminal transitional album as Brazilian thrash kings begin to mutate, no longer a band known only for piling as many heavy riffs into as short a space as possible. *Roots* saw them adding rap, tribal drums and an open-minded attitude that ultimately took Max Cavalera away from the thrash confines of these giants to the more experimental Soulfly. Sepultura have never really come close to this form again.

RAGE AGAINST THE MACHINE *Rage Against The Machine* (Epic 1992)

Brilliant debut from LA politico-rap-rockers whose sound probably had more influence on the course of nu metal than any other band except Nirvana. This was one of the most explosive albums of the 1990s, bringing angry anti-government messages to a mass market, their brilliant sound ensuring that they never only preached to the already converted.

BIOHAZARD *State Of The World Address* (Warner Brothers 1994)

First major-label album from New York thrash-rappers, already riding high after their collaboration with rappers Onyx on 'Slam', a key track. Biohazard's old-school thrash/hardcore looked to the rappers with whom they had grown up for inspiration. This and 1999's *New World Disorder* are their finest works.

THE BEASTIE BOYS *Licensed to Ill* (Def Jam 1986)

Still as loud, dumb and full of cum today as ever, 'Fight For Your Right To Party' and 'No Sleep Til Brooklyn' have had enormous influence on nu metal but also on neo-punk bands like Blink-182.

Although *Paul's Boutique*, their second album, is an altogether finer work, *Licensed To Ill* still sounds like it was made last week, a testament to their staying power.

INFECTIOUS GROOVE *The Plague That Makes Your Booty Move...It's The Infectious Grooves* (Columbia 1991)

Obscure but important funk-punk offshoot band formed by Mike Muir of Suicidal Tendencies to explore the proto rap-rock sound.

RUN-DMC *King Of Rock* (Def Jam 1985)

The classic '80s rap album from whence the version of 'Walk This Way' was taken. A major influence on the development of gangsta rap as well as nu metal/rap-rock.

FAITH NO MORE *The Real Thing* (Slash 1989)

Their huge hit, 'Epic', paved the way for a generation of soundalikes. Chugging guitar and drums, rapped verse and sung chorus with monstrous guitar licks set the pattern for so many bands. If they had a nickel for every song that follows the 'Epic' blueprint they'd all be farting through silk today.

Mike Patton seems to shun the genre with a vengeance but this is still a genuine classic rock album.

RED HOT CHILI PEPPERS *BloodSugarSexMagik* (Warner Brothers 1991)

Rick Rubin-produced funk-rock extravaganza loaded with sex and high-energy slap bass. It includes two classics in 'Under The Bridge' and 'Give It Away', the latter particularly sounding like an early whining rap from Fred Durst. *Mother's Milk* (Warner Brothers 1989) is also highly recommended as a stop on the road to nu metal.

BOO-YAA TRIBE *New Funky Nation* (Polygram 1990)

Hard-assed Samoan gangstas, a rap crew who wedded the high-bodycount hip-hop of NWA with tasteless high-energy guitars. Miles better than their 2000 comeback *Mafia Life*.

PUBLIC ENEMY *It Takes A Nation Of Millions To Hold Us Back* (Def Jam 1988)

Still the classic Public Enemy album, notable for the hard-edged DJing of The Bomb Squad and the track 'Bring The Noise', which provided the common ground for Public Enemy and Anthrax.

ALICE IN CHAINS *Dirt* (Sony 1992)

A massive influence on everyone from Staind to Cold; nu metal abounds with vocalists who sound as though they went to Layne Staley School to get that detox baritone blues voice just right. This album contains the track 'God Smack', which, despite their protestations of its occult origin, must have influenced the name of the band of the same name, particularly since Alice In Chains are a definite influence on their sound.

PRIMUS *Sailing The Seas Of Cheese* (Interscope 1991)

Surreal funk-rock, Primus are one of the great exceptions of American music. Like a more experimental and atonal version of The Red Hot Chili Peppers, Primus play a curious mixture of metal, punk and George Clinton-like experimental funk, playing the bass high on the neck, using every instrument, including the voice, as percussion. Still unjustly obscure, they are the indirect link between Fred Durst, Captain Beefheart and Tom Waits. This is a neglected classic.

Index